SIR HENRY DOULTON

The Man of Business as a Man of Imagination

HUTCHINSON & CO *(Publishers)* LTD
178–202 Great Portland Street, London W1

London Melbourne Sydney
Auckland Johannesburg Cape Town
and agencies throughout the world

First published 1970

*This book has been set in Bembo type, printed in Great Britain
on antique wove paper by Anchor Press, and
bound by Wm. Brendon, both of Tiptree, Essex*

ISBN 0 09 103590 2

SIR HENRY DOULTON

*The Man of Business as
a Man of Imagination*

Edmund Gosse

EDITED BY DESMOND EYLES

HUTCHINSON OF LONDON

Sir Henry Doulton (*circa* 1864)
From a drawing by Frederick Sandys

CONTENTS

FOREWORD

by Desmond Eyles

To the general reader Sir Edmund Gosse is perhaps best known for his remarkable book *Father and Son,* a relentlessly candid and yet surprisingly affectionate account of the clash of two temperaments and outlooks during his strange upbringing by a father who contrived to be a Fellow of the Royal Society and yet remain a strict Plymouth Brother.

Students of literature are indebted to Gosse for his critical studies of Swinburne, Gray, Congreve, Patmore, Ibsen and other authors, his *History of Modern English Literature* and many similar works.

It is not generally known that between 1899 and 1900 Gosse wrote also a biography of his friend Sir Henry Doulton, the great Victorian potter.

It was while I was collecting material for my history of the Royal Doulton Potteries (*Royal Doulton: 1815–1965,* Hutchinson, 1965) that the late Mr. Eric Hooper, the then chairman of Doulton & Co. Limited, asked me one day if I was aware that a *Life of Sir Henry Doulton* (his maternal grandfather) had been written by Gosse. On my saying that I had never heard of this, he replied in his typically quizzical way: 'That is hardly surprising, for my mother would not allow it to be published.'

Some time later, Eric Hooper gave me a faded brown-paper parcel, tied with pink tape. 'This is the biography I mentioned,' he said. 'I had a fair amount to do with Gosse while he was writing it and I did not care over-much for either him or his work. An obstinate, cantankerous, self-opinionated fellow! Anyhow, you may have this if you think you can make any use of it.'

Needless to say, I read the various manuscripts and typescripts, after I had sorted them into order, with intense interest. Gosse had obviously drawn upon many of the same sources which I was using for the earlier chapters of my own book—especially Sir Henry's *Random Recollections of a Lifetime,* his other lectures and addresses, the recollections of friends and employees, and various Doulton publications of the nineteenth century. My own particular concern, which was to occupy me off and on for several years, was to write a general history of the rise and expansion of the Doulton enterprise over a century and a half. In those chapters relating to Sir Henry I was therefore concentrating on his work and influence as a master potter rather than attempting a detailed study of the man himself and his many other interests. I was none the less very grateful indeed to be able to make use of several of Gosse's personal recollections to amplify what I had already discovered.

The thing that mystified me greatly was why this unusual example of Gosse's authorship, so different from the main trend of his creative and critical work, had never been published. It seemed to me that this interesting portrayal of Sir Henry Doulton's vivid personality and unusual character, by one who had known him for almost twenty years, should be made generally available. Whenever I tried to discuss this seriously with Eric Hooper he adroitly changed the subject and I could never persuade him to go through the biography with me and tell me what, if anything, he particularly objected to in it. The fact was that he had disliked Gosse for some reason and he was not going to change his views. I think too that because it was his mother who was partly responsible for vetoing publication he did not want to reverse her decision. Eventually, however, he relented so far as to say: 'Well, you may publish it *if* an opportune moment arises after my death—and you think that people would still be interested.'

From my conversations with Sir Henry's grandson and from a study of the letters and notes which had passed between Gosse and the Doulton family I discovered why things had gone awry.

The hundreds of laudatory articles, obituaries and letters which appeared in the world's press after Sir Henry Doulton's death show that he was regarded as the greatest potter of the Victorian era and one of the great potters of all time. When it was suggested to his only son, Lewis Doulton, that a full-length biography ought to be published he had no hesitation in deciding that Gosse was the right man to approach.

He had known Sir Henry for many years and had already written in 1883, at his request, a study of the life and works of George Tinworth, one of the most famous of the Doulton artists. Sir Henry had been delighted with the book about Tinworth and was always singing Gosse's praises.

Lewis Doulton discussed the project with Gosse on the 30th of June 1898 and on the evening of that day Gosse wrote to him from 29, Delamere Terrace:

> It is very touching and gratifying to me that you and your sisters should have formed the wish that I prepare the biography of your Father. I feel it an honour and a privilege, and if the task is entrusted to me I shall do my best to make it a work of art as well as of love.
>
> I think his character had a quality of unique charm which it ought not to be difficult to reproduce. My key-note, as I said this afternoon, would be *The Man of Business as a Man of Imagination.*

It was agreed that Gosse should receive £400 for all rights in the work and this was paid in four instalments as the work proceeded. Gosse was unable to begin the Doulton biography until early 1899 after he had seen his *Life and Letters of John Donne* through the press— a work which was 'received with a chorus of praise'.

While Gosse was writing the biography the Doulton business was going through a difficult period and Lewis Doulton was pre-occupied with many pressing commercial and manufacturing problems. The responsibility for reading Gosse's drafts and suggesting revisions was therefore unfortunately left to Lewis's two sisters. It was only after they had had their say—and they evidently had much to say—that Lewis Doulton eventually saw the final complete draft.

The unruffled relationship which had prevailed between Gosse and Sir Henry while the former was writing his study of Tinworth was not destined to be repeated. By 1899 Gosse was far more famous than in 1883 and apparently much more difficult to handle. Bernard Shaw described him later as 'at times morbidly touchy . . . far too ready to fancy slights, "cut up rusty" and mobilise his forces of resentment'. There is no doubt that Gosse found writing the commissioned biography of his friend Doulton a very different proposition from his critical studies of famous authors. Every paragraph, every sentence, almost every word, was closely scrutinised and often criticised by Sir Henry's daughters. Gosse's fairness and objectivity, so evident in his other works, demanded that he should present as true a portrait as he possibly could, including 'the roughnesses, pimples, warts and everything', as Cromwell is said to have instructed Lely. On the other hand, he was also anxious to meet all the Doulton family's reasonable wishes.

His dilemma is reflected in the following extract from a letter he wrote to Lewis Doulton on 17th December 1899:

> I am to see Miss Doulton this week and to learn what changes she wishes to make in the last two chapters.
>
> All the preceding chapters I have now carefully revised, carrying out the suggestions which Mrs. Hooper and Miss Doulton made. I have, at their wish, greatly shortened the first two chapters and melted them into one. I very much hope that the book is now, in the main, what the ladies and yourself like.
>
> I need not repeat, what you so kindly suggested, that my portrait of your father cannot possibly be what you, and *particularly what the ladies* have formed in your minds as an ideal.

Two days later Lewis Doulton wrote asking to see the complete revised draft so that he could carefully read it through. 'I feel,' he said, 'I have a rather disjointed idea of the book as a whole.'

Unfortunately it was not only Lewis Doulton's idea that was disjointed. The book itself had become disjointed and lacking in incident. From the alterations—especially the deletions—which Gosse had rather reluctantly made in his original drafts it is clear that what the two ladies, all unwittingly, had been doing was to emasculate the biography and frustrate the author's efforts to make it 'a work of art as well as one of love'. Typical of the deletions were references to the humble origin of the firm, the early struggles of the founder and his son as working potters, the days young Henry went to school hungry, his youthful vanity, his occasional misjudgments, and so forth.

Sir Evan Charteris, K.C., has said of Gosse that 'he brushed aside the tradition of Victorian biography with its richly furnished monuments and lapidary inscriptions, and took a notable step in the direction of modern methods . . . presenting a portrait which satisfied the reader that he has been shown the truth'. But what Sir Henry Doulton's children wanted, with the ideal picture they had formed in their minds, was probably something more in the earlier tradition.

I gathered from Eric Hooper's description of Gosse as 'obstinate, cantankerous and self-opinionated' that there were limits beyond which he could not conscientiously go in attempting to reconcile his own views with those of the family. This is, I think, confirmed in a letter he wrote to Lewis Doulton on 18th May 1890 in which he said he could not 'with advantage' do more to it, adding that the text was ready to go to press 'as it stands'.

In the meantime Lewis Doulton had already written to Gosse to say that he and his sisters had 'decided not to publish the Life, at all events for the present'. Although this decision probably did not come as a complete surprise it must none the less have been a bitter disappointment to Gosse after all the time and effort he had spent on the biography.

This work is the only long contemporary account of Sir Henry Doulton that we shall ever have. One could wish that more details of his early life and activities had been available, but Gosse made the most of the material at his disposal and comparatively little additional information has since come to light. This year, 1970, will see the 150th anniversary of Sir Henry's birth and there could surely be no more opportune time for the long-deferred publication of Gosse's biography to take place.

In editing the work for publication I have 'unmelted' the first two chapters which Gosse had been obliged to merge into one and have restored most of the deleted passages in those and the other chapters where my own researches into the early Doulton history gave me no grounds to doubt their accuracy. Gosse's own changes of style (as distinct from content) between the earlier and final drafts were fortunately easy to distinguish; these, indeed, were few, but where they occurred I have adhered to the final typed version. A few very minor errors have been corrected in the text and some others, more important, in the footnotes.

There is one really extraordinary omission in the biography for which Gosse is clearly not to blame. There is no account at all of one of Sir Henry's most interesting and important ventures—his entry into the field of fine earthenware and bone-china manufacture in Burslem, Stoke-on-Trent. It is evident from the references to Burslem on pages 122 and 169 that Gosse had in fact described this. One can only surmise that the way he dealt with this episode may have so displeased the family that they had the whole section removed. Be this as it may, no account of Sir Henry Doulton's life and work could possibly be considered complete without some information about the origin and development of the Nile Street, Burslem, Pottery. I have therefore added in smaller type at the end of Chapter 7 some extracts from the section dealing with this matter in my book *Royal Doulton 1815–1965*.

I have also added as Appendices the complete text of an address given by Sir Henry Doulton on *The Culture of the Imagination* and extracts from other addresses on a variety of subjects. These, I feel, amplify Gosse's portrait.

It only remains for me to thank Mr. J. G. Beevor, o.b.e., chairman, and Mr. Peter Medd, group managing director of Doulton & Co. Limited, for encouraging me in the task of editing Sir Edmund Gosse's work for publication; Miss Frances Lovering and Miss Olive Manders for their great help with typing and proof-reading; and the Brotherton Library, University of Leeds, for permission to quote from letters in its archives.

PREFACE

The task of writing a biography of Sir Henry Doulton has not proved to be an easy one, since the materials from which a biographer builds up his narrative were largely absent. There was no correspondence preserved to guide the narrator, for Sir Henry Doulton had been impatient of letter-writing at all stages of his career. He would never write a letter if he could write a note, nor a note if a personal interview would serve his purpose. The consequence is that none but the most meagre specimens of his correspondence have survived, and even these contain scarcely a trace of autobiography. Nor did he at any time keep a journal or a diary, so that the precise elements of biography are during large spaces of his life absolutely wanting.

The writer of the following pages, therefore, has been largely thrown back upon oral tradition and the memory of survivors. He has to express his warm thanks to all those to whom he applied for information; without exception, and in proportion to their powers, they responded with the utmost kindness to his appeal. Unfortunately, in dealing with the early stages of a career which began more than eighty years ago, the sources of unwritten information rapidly grow less and less. It is unavoidable, in the conditions, that a detailed account of the early years of the subject of this memoir should now be unattainable.

In dealing with the character of Sir Henry Doulton—of whom I have attempted to draw a portrait as I saw him, or believed I saw him, during a friendship of many years—I have endeavoured to keep the elements of his duplicate nature constantly before me. Unless I have read him wrongly, it was his distinguishing feature to be a shrewd man of business who was at the same time an idealist and a man of enthusiastic imagination. The two cords run through the whole texture of his mind, marking with their double colours, his tastes, his actions and his convictions; and their combination is what made this particular manufacturer a peculiarly interesting subject for biographical study. Such at least is the conviction of his biographer.

I

Childhood and youth
1820 to 1835

Almost the whole life of Henry Doulton was spent in the parish of
Lambeth, and the other names identified with the early part of his
highly concentrated life—Vauxhall, Kennington, Nine Elms,
Stockwell, Wandsworth—are those of places clustered closely
together on one side of the Thames, directly south or south-west of
Westminster. He was accustomed to say that the Globe Theatre and
Lambeth Palace were on the Surrey side and that he would pluck
up heart to stick by Shakespeare and the Archbishop of Canterbury.
He was even known, with much less conviction, to compare
Kennington Common with Hyde Park. In any case, for better or
for worse, he was a convinced South Londoner, and what had
originally been forced upon him by circumstances became in
process of time a whimsical sort of patriotism, and nothing would
induce him to take up any other allegiance. All through his long life
he was proud to be a citizen of Lambeth, to be identified with the
interests of Lambeth and to share the local enterprises and entertainments. It would be a mistake to approach the biography of Sir
Henry Doulton without making this concession at once, that what
value the study of it has must depend upon its intensity and individuality, and not upon its extension. He was not a cosmopolitan, he
was hardly a Londoner; but he was an Englishman in sentiment and
a Lambeth man in fact.

Henry Doulton was the second son of John Doulton, potter, of
Vauxhall Walk, where he was born on the 25th of July 1820. John
Doulton, who was born at Fulham on the 17th of November 1793,
had been apprenticed as a lad to a potter in that parish. He was soon

enjoying the reputation of being one of the best large-ware throwers in London, and he and Charles White, afterwards a rival in the trade at Fulham, used to compete as to who could work the quicker.[1] During his apprenticeship John Doulton had but one holiday in each year: that in 1806 he spent in the City, witnessing the burial of Nelson in St. Paul's Cathedral.

When he had served his time he and his life-long friend John Watts started a pottery of their own on a very small scale in Vauxhall Walk.[2] About this time, Mrs. Duneau, a widow with several children, came from Bridgenorth in Shropshire, and settled in Vauxhall. She offered a distinct addition to the social life of the place, for she and her family were accomplished and agreeable, while her three daughters had been known as 'the Belles of Bridgenorth'. Mrs. Duneau took a large house, at a low rent, since the death of her husband had left her in reduced circumstances; it seemed both convenient and natural that she should accept a lodger, and young John Doulton, who was looking about for rooms contiguous to his new pottery, became her boarder. Jane Duneau, not the least attractive of the beauties, was at this time about twenty-one. John Doulton fell deeply in love with her, and they were

[1] The Fulham Pottery at which John Doulton was apprenticed had been founded about 1671 by the famous John Dwight—sometimes described as 'the father of English pottery'. Charles White was a descendant of Dwight's granddaughter, Lydia, whose second husband, William White, re-established the business after it had gone bankrupt in 1746.

Throwing is the traditional art of shaping hollow pottery by hand from a mass of prepared clay after centring this on a revolving wheel. Although the clay is often flung on to the wheel this is not, as sometimes stated, the origin of the term 'throwing' which originally meant 'turning' or 'twisting'.

The smaller wheels in John Doulton's time were foot-propelled by a treadle. The wheels for making 'large ware' such as filter cases and chemical vessels were turned for the potter by a boy assistant.

[2] This is not correct. The Vauxhall pot-works was owned in 1812 by Martha Jones, the widow of a Lambeth stoneware potter. Doulton worked for her for three years after coming out of his apprenticeship. In 1815 she took John Doulton and John Watts into partnership and the firm became Jones, Watts and Doulton. Martha Jones retired in 1820 and Doulton and Watts then took over the business [see *Royal Doulton: 1815–1965,* Desmond Eyles (Hutchinson 1965), pages 12 to 19]. Gosse is not to blame for the error. He took the information from an official Doulton publication issued in connection with the Chicago Exhibition of 1893 by which time Martha Jones' part in the origins of the firm had seemingly been forgotten.

married in 1817, the bridegroom having reached the not very advanced maturity of his twenty-fourth year.

From the first, however, and in spite of being afterwards hampered by a long chain of children, success of a kind was assured to John Doulton by his activity, probity and endurance. He was himself the most persistent of workers and he expected the people about him to work. I am told of a quaint remark an old man now surviving recollects having been made to him, when he was a boy, by John Doulton. 'Are you working, boy?' 'Yes, sir.' 'Well, I don't see any sweat on your nose.' The nose of John Doulton himself was usually shining.

There were born to John and Jane Doulton no fewer than eight children. The eldest was John, born on the 27th of September 1818. The second was also a son, Henry, the subject of this memoir, born, as I have said, on the 25th of July 1820. The others may be recorded here; Frederick, 1822; Jane, 1824; Alfred, 1827; Marian, 1829; Josiah, 1832; James Duneau, 1835. All of these lived to maturity, and the one who died first, Alfred, reached his twenty-seventh year. There was unquestionably a great physical vigour about the whole race, but it took in Henry alone the features which stamped themselves vividly upon the imagination of contemporaries.

The house in Vauxhall Walk, at which Henry Doulton was born in 1820, had no particular attractions, and his childish memories were most agreeably associated with the picturesque and delightful abode at Lambeth into which the family removed in 1826. He was rather a precocious child and of his infancy there are retained some pleasant anecdotes. For a long time he was accustomed to describe, as the report of an eyewitness, and as an instance of extremely early memory, a certain picturesque incident. He used to say that he saw some oxen stray through the yard into the wash-house at Vauxhall Walk and pierce the roof with their horns. His mother had to explain at last that he could not possibly have seen this, as it happened two months before he was born. The truth was he had been shown the holes made by the horns, and had heard the scene so vividly described, that in after years he was convinced that he had seen the occurrence.

He used to describe with more certainty of original observation the aspect of Vauxhall in his early childhood. Vauxhall Cross early in the 1820's was as rural a spot as can now be found within ten miles

B

of the vague rim of London. Where Vauxhall station now stands, Sir Henry recollected orchards and woodland lanes. The river Effra was then a pretty stream running through South Lambeth on which a boat might occasionally be seen, and where, as a youthful sportsman, the future potter occasionally tried to angle.

His uncle, Charles Duneau, who lived not far off, upon the waterside, was a merry, cheerful man. His nephew reported of him long afterwards that he 'was very clever at everything except keeping money'. In 1824, at all events, he won a small sum through speculation in his youthful nephew's wits. Walking along Vauxhall Walk with little Henry, not yet four years old, at his side, Charles Duneau was met by two friends; he stopped to converse with them. At that time, bets were the rage, and Mr. Duneau laid a wager with these gentlemen that young Henry could read any chapter in the Bible. The company withdrew to Mr. Duneau's house, and, by some clever juggling, the fourteenth chapter of St. John's Gospel, which Henry knew pretty well by heart, was selected. He half read, half recited the chapter glibly enough, and the amount of the wager was transferred to Mr. Duneau's pocket.

Close to the house where Henry was born stood Vauxhall Gardens, even then greatly shorn of the glory which had made them so illustrious from 1750 to 1790, and with far less brilliant supper-parties collected in the umbrageous arched pavilions; they were, nevertheless, still high in local favour as a place of amusement. From the Doultons' window, the child could see the celebrated 'Vauxhall Lights', elaborate and doubtless rather gaudy arrangements in coloured lamps. He used, from this same window, on great occasions, to be permitted to watch the fireworks and the set piece which always closed the grand display. He was excessively anxious to be allowed to enter this voluptuous and enchanted paradise, all lamps and actresses, where the nightingales were heard above the popping of the beer bottles; but he longed in vain. At last, in response to his pathetic entreaties, he was taken inside, but with a refinement of cruelty, *by broad daylight,* so that the Arabian palace of his dreams was smashed to atoms of tinsel, and he never wanted to visit Vauxhall Gardens again.

In the early Vauxhall days, Henry was sent to a dame's school, in the corner house of Vauxhall Walk, kept by an old lady of the name of Huntley. He did not consider that he gained much instruction

from this dame, but he spoke of her in after years with more toleration than of a later local schoolmaster, whose vagaries will presently
be described. It is very probable that Henry Doulton's quick and
nervous brain was best served in his early childhood by this incom-
petent kind of teaching, but he was accustomed to wax wroth, to
the last, at the recollection of the stupid people who taught him at
Vauxhall and Lambeth.

He gave, at the end of his life, the following account of Vauxhall,
as he remembered it up to 1828:

> To show the change that has taken place in the neighbourhood
> let me instance Vauxhall Terrace, which you doubtless know.
> The houses were then tenanted by families in good position.
> Successful business men, who could afford to keep several ser-
> vants, lived there—such people as those now [1899] living in the
> better parts of Brixton and Clapham. The end house of the row
> was occupied by a potter named David Hill. He was particularly
> fond of me, and would walk by the side of his large Newfound-
> land dog, while I was riding on its back. I remember how pleased
> I was, and I made up my mind that as soon as I could afford it I
> would buy a horse to ride.

People were excessively military in those days, and Henry
Doulton recollected with great distinctness the impression caused
by the final defeat of Napoleon so few years before. The exile of
St. Helena was still a legendary bogey of the first class, and nurses
had not ceased to frighten naughty children by saying, 'Look out,
here's Boney coming.'

Towards the close of 1826 the Doultons moved to High Street,
Lambeth. Young as the boy was he recollected in after-life the
anxiety which this step caused. 'The matter was debated most
earnestly in our family circle, and the pros and cons thoroughly
weighed.' The elder Doulton had, by the exercise of great industry
and thrift, managed, in spite of his numerous family, to economise,
and had saved a comfortable sum of money. It would have been
disastrous to have lost this in what then seemed rather a bold speculation. As it turned out, John Doulton began to thrive, though in a
modest way, directly he moved to Lambeth. The property he took
consisted of an excellent house, a small factory with but one kiln,
and attached to it the best and largest garden in Lambeth, better

even than that of the Archbishop's Palace. The little estate had borne the name of The Vineyard, and as if to support this idea, on the street side, where a narrow garden divided the house from the pavement, there flourished a luxuriant vine bearing excellent grapes.

To Mr. R. T. Parsons, who was connected with the firm for upwards of seventy-four years, I am indebted for some interesting particulars. Mr. Parsons entered the service of the Doultons in February 1825. He has a personal recollection of the energy and persistency of Sir Henry's father. He went to work on his wheel at 7 a.m. and was closely occupied until 5 p.m. every week-day in making two-gallon and four-gallon bottles. This was more or less the scope of the ambition of the Lambeth potters in those days. In order to enlarge his business John Doulton had entered into partnership with John Watts.[3] At Vauxhall Walk they had had two kilns, and they were therefore at first less favourably situated at Lambeth where they had but one. Mr. Watts used to wheel the barrow of coal to the kiln, test all the ware, and supervise the packing; Mr. Doulton's part of the business was the pottery-making. It is explained to me that 'they always broke the clay with a hammer and then put it in a large tub; for many years the men used to tread it with their naked feet'. Later Mr. Doulton bought a small piece of back garden in order to enable them to set up a small pug-mill which was worked with exemplary patience by one blind horse.[4]

Such were the small beginnings of so great a business. Mr. Parsons remembers overhearing a conversation between the partners and a local potter, Mr. Hill, in 1827. Struck by the enterprise of his humbler rivals, Hill said, patronisingly, 'Do you mean to cut us all out?' Watts laughed and said, 'We will try to do so.' The inconvenience of the one small kiln at Lambeth was acutely felt at first, and as business increased became intolerable, but in 1829 there was built a kiln capable of manufacturing glazed red ware and garden pots, a great advance.

We have brought the narrative, however, to Henry Doulton's

---

[3] See Note 2.

[4] This must have been before the move to Lambeth where there was a large garden.

A pug-mill is a form of closed cylindrical mixer, containing revolving blades which mix and compress the clay and other ingredients into a compact mass for the potter to use.

twelfth year, and we must return to his recollections. Some of the earliest of these were connected with the waterside life, and the gaiety of the ever-shifting flotilla of small craft calling at the wharf at Ferry Street. One of the recurring scenes which imprinted itself on his childish recollection was that caused by the ringing of a bell, the cry of 'Oyez, oyez, a boat-load of sprats has just arrived off Lambeth stairs, a penny a plateful', and the commotion resulting from the response of the population to this appeal. Lambeth was not destitute of gentry in those days, and in Paradise Street there existed a house with a large forecourt, with a riding-stone attached. One of little Henry Doulton's pleasures was to watch, at a certain hour every afternoon, for the advent of the old gentleman who lived in this house. Followed by his groom he would come out with clockwork regularity, get on the stone, mount his cob and ride away, to the child's deep admiration and envy. To this repeated incident, Henry Doulton attributed the fondness for horses, which began in his childhood and amounted in later life to a passion. He used to say, at the end of his career, 'I don't think I am "horsy", but all my life I have been passionately fond of horses.'

For a romantic and contemplative child, the house in High Street, Lambeth, was an ideal one. In the immense garden at the back there was everything to make one happy. There was an old fish-pond, with a little grove of willows round it; there were apple-trees and pear-trees; and against the inner walls quite a profusion of peach-trees, beautiful both in blossom-time and in fruitage. At the end of the garden in the middle of the pottery-ground stood a windmill, such as were formerly not infrequent in that part of London. This windmill, for a reason to be presently explained, was often mentioned in the Doulton family in tones of mingled annoyance and respect. To Henry it became a sort of fetish. It was particularly large, and when it revolved it was awe-inspiring. There were few buildings around it to break the force of the wind as it swept over the Thames and in a storm the arms of the windmill would rush round with a terrific clatter heard high above the noise of the elements. But if this windmill was an object of terror to Henry it was a source of intense annoyance to his parents. When they took the property it was understood that the miller who had the tenancy of the mill would leave immediately, as the place had ceased to be advantageous for his trade; but when once they were installed, the miller perceived that it was his policy to stay as long, and to make himself as much of a nuisance, as possible, both of which schemes he carried out; until at length the law had to be resorted to, and the miller ejected at the expense of an enormous fine.

When the move was made to Lambeth, Mr. Watts and his family lived in the same house with Mr. Doulton and his, until their growing broods of children made the pressure uncomfortable. Mr. Watts then bought the house next door, the ground floor of which had previously been used as a milk-shop, fitted it up as a residence, and opened a doorway.

The work in those days was severe. John Doulton would often make two hundred or so two-gallon bottles early in the day, and when he had been driving round afterwards in the business-chaise, canvassing for orders and collecting money, would often turn to in the evening and make a quantity of five-gallon cans—which he looked on as a sort of relaxation.

Doulton was a man of much determination of character. He seems to have resembled his son Henry in some of his qualities. He was a very quickly moving, bright and somewhat impatient man. In physical appearance he had less regular features and less luminous eyes than his second son, but in other respects he was much like him in face. He was a man of liberal and spirited views, a great reader, a warm politician, and a man of original religious views. Early in life he had deliberately left the Church of England, and had joined the Congregationalists, because of the coldness and latitudinarian dullness of the national Church towards the close of the eighteenth century. John Doulton was one of those who conceived an enthusiastic admiration for Robert Hall, the celebrated Baptist orator; and in those days the Doultons might have been more exactly termed Baptists than Congregationalists.

John Doulton enjoyed the personal friendship of Robert Hall, and attributed to Hall's brilliant conversation much of his own interest in literature. Henry Doulton told me that he himself heard Robert Hall preach, and that his impression was that this was in Bristol. Nothing is more likely, for Robert Hall's congregation was in that city, but the event must have taken place in Henry Doulton's early childhood, since Hall preached for the last time in February 1831, and died a little later in the same year. Henry Doulton, therefore, must have heard him before he was eleven.

The memory of Robert Hall, who had long been in feeble health, and who died at the age of sixty-seven, was particularly venerated at High Street, Lambeth, and Henry Doulton preserved through the whole of his life what may now be thought a somewhat exaggerated appreciation of the oratory of the famous Baptist minister. A little while before he died, Sir Henry expressed the opinion that Robert Hall's address to the volunteers at Bristol—in which he said that 'England was the last asylum of liberty'—was the grandest sermon in the English language. He was wont to compare him with Chalmers, greatly to the advantage of Hall.

It was perhaps the family enthusiasm for the oratory of Robert Hall which turned the youthful Henry into a preacher. He used to organise a regular performance at home, rigging up a three-decker, with one brother below as leader, and another in the middle as clerk, he himself thumping the sofa-cushion as parson at the top of all. The rest of the family, including the servants, were induced to form the congregation, and the youthful minister was exceedingly strict in insisting upon discipline being maintained. The homily was usually read—for at ten years of age Henry was scarcely prepared for extempore exhortation—out of Alexander Fletcher's *Sermons to the Young,* but sometimes the preacher defied criticism by reading from some secular book which was interesting him at the moment. The elaborateness and success of these amusing performances are evidences of the predominance which the second brother had, at this early age, already gained in his family. Indeed, there seems to have never been a time at which the intense vitality of Henry Doulton was not perceived and acknowledged.

He was always ardently fond of reading, and did all he could to become the possessor of good books. When he was ten years old he attended a sale of books held at a chemist's shop at the corner of Paradise Street and Lambeth Walk. After he had unsuccessfully bid for several books, his pocket-money being but small, he offered eighteenpence for some book. A man in the crowd who had been watching him called out good-naturedly, 'Let the little chap have one', and it was knocked down to him. Henry Doulton was proud of securing that volume, and bore away in triumph the nucleus of what was to become a valuable library. Unhappily, in later life, he could not remember what the particular book had been. He would have liked to be able to think that it was Mr. Wordsworth's *The*

Excursion, but on pressure he was obliged to confess that he was quite sure it was not. The love of poetry and of Wordsworth, which were like a religion to him in later years, had not begun at the age of ten.

Towards the end of his life, Sir Henry Doulton described the aspect of the neighbourhood, as he recollected it from 1828 onwards in the following terms:

The walk to Clapham is one of the most delightful recollections of my youth. Passing Brunswick House and Nine Elms, one came to Springwell, so called because of a bubbling spring of water which was reputed to possess certain medicinal properties. Here I would occasionally turn aside for a cup of cooling water. Continuing our walk, we would eventually come to St. Paul's Church, Clapham. Today, when the sun is shining, and I am sitting quietly in my country retreat, listening to the hum of the bees, and smelling the sweet scents of the flowers, wafted on the breeze, I am often transported in thought to those happy times when, holding my father's hand, I walked with him along the Wandsworth Road to Clapham, looking over fields reaching to the river.

Although I do not remember the particular elm trees that gave the Nine Elms Lane its title, yet it was quite a country lane when first I knew it.

Battersea Fields consisted of extensive market gardens and fields. These fields were sufficiently far from London to be considered a locality for duels. One of the last that took place there caused considerable notoriety. It was fought between the Duke of Wellington and the Earl of Winchelsea, and was over some dispute arising out of the Catholic Emancipation Bill of 1829. Wellington fired first and missed his opponent, the Earl returned by firing into the air, and then proferred the apology he should have made before.

Lambeth Walk and Gray's Walk—now Regent Street—were pleasant country spots in those days where people strolled when work was over.

What memories cluster, too, about the river! Westminster Bridge was the centre of much interest to me. Searle, the boat-builder, had his workshops on the banks, and groups of boats

were to be seen drawn up on the shore. The boys from Westminster School used to come over to hire boats, and their presence
lent interest and animation to the scene. All boat races were then
rowed over the course from Westminster to Putney, instead of
from Putney to Mortlake, as at present. The river was used much
more than it is now for pageants, and some of these were well
worth witnessing. There was the Lord Mayor's procession, in
which the city barges with their fourteen rowers, all resplendent
with badges, and the barges with colour and gilding, took part.
It seems a great pity that the Watermen's Companies do not now
encourage river shows and passenger traffic. It is positively a
disgrace that Londoners allow such a grand highway as the
Thames to go almost unused, not only for pageants, but even for
passenger traffic. The river lends itself so admirably to such usage.
Rowing was one of the special pastimes of this neighbourhood in
my young days. Charlie Campbell of Lambeth was the champion;
and Paddy Knoulton of Lambeth and Phelps of Fulham, were in
the first rank as rowers.

With his uncle, Charles Duneau, Henry went to see old London
Bridge, then already doomed to be pulled down. Later on, he once
adventured rowing down the river, and 'shooting the rapids' at
London Bridge, an exciting though hardly a dangerous exercise for
a skilful oarsman. An early event which made an impression on
Henry Doulton was the opening of new London Bridge by King
William IV on the 1st of August 1831. The entire Doulton and
Watts establishment went in a large boat or barge from Lambeth
to witness this ceremony.

Politics always had a certain interest for Henry Doulton, and he
was accustomed to say that this interest dated back to the Reform
Bill of 1832. He perfectly well remembered the discussion of that
Bill in June, and the excited speculation of the people as to whether
it would pass or not. Lord Brougham was his boyish hero, and he
recollected the thrill that went round the family circle at Lambeth
when they were told that at six o'clock on the morning of the
eventful day, while the first gleams of sunshine were stealing through
the windows, Brougham had dropped on his knees as he ended his
speech, saying, 'My Lords, on my bended knees I beseech you reject
not this Bill.' Almost every house in London was decorated the

night after the result was known, and the little politician, having
seen to the proper decoration of the house in Lambeth High Street,
was taken by his father to admire the illuminations in Vauxhall and
Kennington and down Newington Butts.

The first members of Parliament elected under the new Act were
Charles Tennyson (afterwards D'Eyncourt and the uncle of the
Laureate) and Benjamin Hawes (afterwards Sir Benjamin and a
Minister); these gentlemen were returned for Lambeth amid
unparalleled rejoicings on the 12th of December 1832 and little
Henry Doulton was one of their enthusiastic supporters. He said, in
an address in 1896 referring to this long-past incident:

> We made a large number of the stoneware 'Reform Bottles'
> which some of you may perhaps have seen in museums. They
> were flat bottles, with necks representing the head of the King,
> Grey, Russell and Brougham. We had as many as fifteen or twenty
> men employed making these bottles, and although some thou-
> sands must have been sold, it is now most difficult to procure a
> specimen. My father went to Birmingham and Manchester with
> samples of these bottles. He started on his journey at six o'clock
> one cold wintry morning, and I went with him to The Swan
> with Two Necks, in Lad Lane, to see the coach off. While saying
> good-bye he told me, as though it were something extremely
> wonderful, that he would be eating his supper in Birmingham that
> same night. I have lived to have tea in Birmingham and to reach
> London in good time for my supper.
>
> One of our local public characters was an eccentric cow-keeper,
> named Hoskins, who lived in High Street, adjoining the Wind-
> mill public house. He would lead down to the river as many as
> thirty or forty cows to water, passing to the shore by the free
> White Hart Dock. He kept a goose he had trained to follow him.
> On election days it was his custom to decorate the goose with his
> party colours, and then to walk to Kennington Common, the
> goose waddling behind. I need hardly say that an ovation awaited
> both the goose and its master when they reached the hustings.
>
> I remember Joe Hume, the member of parliament who excelled
> at figures and delighted in criticising the Budget of the Chancellor
> of the Exchequer. He used to speak of 'tottling up' the accounts.
> At one Lambeth election I saw him on the Brighton coach at

The Horns, Kennington. The crowd cheered him and enquired how he got on with his 'tottling up'.

Elections were always times of much excitement. Before the Reform Bill county elections lasted fourteen days, and there was no such thing as the secrecy of the ballot. With all the abuses of these elections, which of course I heartily deprecate, voters had the courage of their convictions and were not ashamed openly to acknowledge the principles they professed and to bear with courage what this involved. The sacrifices were not frequent and rarely serious.

Joseph Hume, whose popularity Sir Henry thus recalls, was at the height of his vogue in 1834, when he was the unquestioned leader of the Radical Party and in consequence was called upon to move the repeal of the Corn Laws. Sir Henry Doulton was slightly acquainted in later years with Hume, who lived to be nearly eighty and did not pass away until 1855.

There were only very indifferent schools in most of the outlying parts of London in the early thirties. Henry Doulton, on leaving the excellent but illiterate Dame Huntley, fell into no better hands. He was sent to what was called a commercial school in the neighbourhood, where the education purveyed was of the most meagre kind. The schoolmaster was a man whose only qualification for the post lay in the fact that he was a parson, for it was then an accepted axiom that a man who could preach on Sundays must be fit to teach on week-days. Henry Doulton was 'grounded', as it was called, in Greek and Latin, but the value of this basis may be gathered from the fact that the master himself was entirely ignorant of the grammar of those languages. He had one favourite sentence—'Salt beef well boiled pleaseth me'—and at any moment which threatened to be critical he used to crush inquiry by ordering the boys to translate it into Greek or Latin. All this preposterous fellow did, by way of carrying out his duties, was to give out the classical words from one column of his textbook and ask for the English equivalents printed before his eyes on the opposite column.

Henry Doulton had a great desire to learn the elements of drawing, but there was no one in Lambeth in those days capable of teaching them to him. The only artist they knew was young Samuel Nixon, the sculptor, who executed a bust of the elder John Doulton, and had a studio near by, at Kennington. He was born in 1803, and therefore seventeen years senior to Henry Doulton, who regarded him with curiosity and respect, as the representative of that mysterious fine art, which was already beginning to whisper its fascination to him. Nixon was a sculptor of some promise, but his talent dwindled for want of appreciation. He died in 1854, and is remembered, if at all, for his statue of King William IV in King William Street, on the site of the Boar's Head at Eastcheap.

In 1833, to his very great satisfaction, Henry Doulton was permitted to go to University College School, in Gower Street, and this formed a great epoch in his life.[5] Although he was only thirteen, his active and ambitious mind rebelled against the incompetence of his local teachers at Lambeth, and lamented the fact of his imperfect training. He was quick to find how much he had lost by delay, and he worked with extreme diligence. It was a long distance from Lambeth to Gower Street, and in wet weather it was a serious fatigue for a little boy to perform the journey twice. There were no omnibuses, no trams, no Underground or electric railways in those days, and it was a weary double trudge. Even to be ferried over from Lambeth to Westminster cost fourpence, and was an extravagance to be avoided if by any means it was possible to do so. In those days the best and most thoughtful of parents seemed to think that the outsides and insides of children were cut out of sheet-iron, and no provision was made for Henry to eat a proper midday meal. He lunched, as a rule, on penny buns, and suffered—as so many sons of well-to-do parents needlessly suffered around him—from positive hunger and exhaustion. All this was thought, then, to be part of the wholesome discipline of life, and perhaps the excessive care we now take of the physical comfort of children errs in the opposite extreme. But there would be wailing and weeping if we went back today to the Spartan methods of 1833.

Little is recorded about Henry Doulton's two years at University

[5] Referring to University College School, Sir Henry Doulton said on 8th May 1895: 'The principles which animated the founders were broad, liberal and comprehensive, and indicated an important advance in education. The establishment of the school supplied a want and set an example. It was founded not on the doctrine of toleration but on one far more fruitful—*comprehension*. It offered the educational advantages of a public school to children of parents of all denominations.'

College School. He worked with zest, already conscious of responsibility, and anxious to gain as much knowledge as possible in what he knew would be a short spell of education. He had been too long neglected to blossom out into a good scholar at once, but he gained two prizes in the first year, and he did reputably all through. What was perhaps most important was that at University College School he gained the solid basis on which he could build up an afterstructure of *self-education*. He had always loved reading; at University College he learned what to read, and where to find it, and he gained that respect for authority in the abstract, mingled with a shrewd eye for the imperfections of individual authorities, which is as fine a quality as a youth in his position can acquire. In after life it was often very noticeable that Henry Doulton, with no technical knowlege to convince himself of intellectual excellence, by a wonderful instinct or flair, would almost always manage to perceive the best and cling to it. No doubt the two years at University College School were of immediate service in warning him away from the charlatans of literature and art.

He was fortunate in some of his school friendships. A boy of his own age, but of far higher accomplishments and more classical training, was James Baldwin Brown, afterwards highly distinguished as a nonconformist divine, who became in 1870 President of the Congregational Union, an archbishop among dissenters. This was a very happy intimacy formed by Henry Doulton, and though, when he left in 1835, James Baldwin Brown continued to mature his studies at University College School, *his* name will often recur in this narrative. He became a Congregationalist minister in 1843, and in 1846 was appointed to Claylands Chapel, Clapham Road, thus becoming a near neighbour of the Doultons. He lived on until 1884, and Henry Doulton enjoyed his friendship unbroken to the end.

Another friend, no less excellent and no less durable, but of a totally different class, was James Anderson Rose. He was 'ever a fighter', fierce and bellicose to a quite laughable degree, and he early took the somewhat fragile Henry Doulton under his protection. It was Rose's ambition to institute in the dreamy purlieus of Gower Street something of the 'town and gown' spirit which adorned our older universities. He punched the heads of so many messengers and cads 'of sorts' that his admiring schoolfellows called him 'Tiger Rose'. To conquer this stalwart champion, the vulgar residents brought out of Soho a certain famous butcher-boy, known far and wide as a first-class fighting man. There was a stand-up encounter in the course of which Tiger Rose was licked, but he was a Briton of the sort which had so lately endured many things at Waterloo, and he challenged the butcher-boy again. It is pleasant to record—it is particularly pleasant for those who recollect in later years the still fierce, but exquisitely courteous and genial old gentleman, to be assured—that on this second occasion it was the butcher-boy who fell. He retired to Soho, his native heath, and the ascendancy of Tiger Rose was unquestioned on either side of Gower Street.

Other school friends were C. P. Mason and Birkbeck, a son of the founder of Birkbeck Bank and Educational Institute. A delicate boy, considerably his junior, who attracted Henry Doulton's sympathy was a son of the then so eminent politician and dramatist, Richard Lalor Shiel. Doulton recollected the tender and anxious assiduity with which the father looked after this motherless boy, and when the latter's health broke down altogether the great orator threw up all his engagements and went out to Madeira where, in spite of all his care, the child presently died.

2

The young potter
1835 to 1845

There are some men who are marked by their circumstances and their qualities for celebrity from the very outset of their careers, and there are others also who by dint of character and merit lift themselves slowly out of obscurity. Henry Doulton was one of the latter class. In his youth, although his influence was felt by those around him, they formed but a small circle. No one seems to have foreseen that he would become a very prominent man and for many years, although estimable and ingenious, he was not prominent. For many years, that is to say, he was obliged to build the foundations of his future reputation in silence, working diligently and persistently, slowly advancing on ground which he had to conquer and to guard step by step. Hence, it is not to be wondered at that not much material remains to guide the biographer in these early years. Henry Doulton was an indifferent letter-writer then, as later, and no one seems to have preserved his correspondence. The nature of his work precluded any public notice being taken of it in what we may call its experimental and unornamented stages, and of those who associated with him there were not many who cultivated the habit of personal observation.

The present writer has therefore had, in the main, to depend for this portion of his narrative on the memories of survivors, and the number of these grows rapidly and pathetically smaller. Of the earliest generation of Henry Doulton's intimate friends, Mr. John Hardcastle alone survives, and the picture which we shall now endeavour to present of Henry Doulton as a young man owes much to his help.

When the time came, in 1835, for Henry Doulton, after the fashion of those years, to choose a profession, his intellectual aptitudes were taken into consideration in the family councils. Of all the children of John Doulton, he was the one who showed bookish tastes, the one who might easily be turned into a scholar. His elder brother was already in the business; Frederick was destined for it; and Mr. Doulton was quite prepared to spend on Henry's education the necessary expense. His friend, Baldwin Brown, was going to stay on at University College, that he might fit himself for the ministry, and this would have pleased John Doulton for his son. 'You may be a parson or a lawyer, whichever you like,' he said. To his astonishment, his son Henry, the bookworm of the family, expressed his wish above all things to be a practical potter. He said that neither pulpit nor bar had anything like the same attraction for him as his father's factory at Lambeth. Accordingly, since, in the face of such a vocation, it would have been madness to interfere, at the age of fifteen he entered the business.

John Doulton the younger was already acting as accountant, and afterwards, to help his father, as traveller. This was not the work that Henry wished for; he desired, from the very first, to master every detail of the practical manipulation of the goods turned out by the firm. These goods, it must be understood, had none of the romance and beauty afterwards identified with the name of Doulton Ware. They were prosy in the extreme; they mainly consisted of beer and ginger-beer bottles, and of blacking bottles for the great firm of Warren.[6] The boy had anything but an easy time of it. His father was still capable of as much labour as any three of his workmen, and had no idea of encouraging idleness. Nor had Henry, although his strength was often considerably taxed by the duration and severity of his work, the slightest wish to shirk. At 6 a.m. he had to be up to ring the bell which summoned the hands together. Then he took his place amongst them, learning—with extraordinary and native facility —every practical detail. It was understood that he was to be informally apprenticed to his father for a few years, but, so quick was he

[6] Charles Dickens as a boy worked at Warren's warehouse near the Hungerford Stairs in the Strand. When he visited the Lambeth pottery many years later he recalled that during this distressing period of his childhood he had pasted labels and tied covers of oil paper on thousands of Doulton & Watts blacking bottles.

and so ardent, at the end of eighteen months it was found that nothing was left for him to be taught.

He had to kick his own foot-wheel, for there were neither string nor steam wheels at that time. This persistent exercise, before his physical frame was thoroughly set, induced that curious shamble or catch in his walk which was noticeable to the close of his life. Not less curious was the mode in which, if at all excited or interested, he protruded his thumbs—the result of years of habit in 'trueing the ball' or slapping the clay on to the wheel, and then with the thumbs driving the air out.

When he was seventeen he succeeded in making a twenty-gallon stoneware receiver. The large-ware thrower of the firm died about this time, and to Henry was forthwith entrusted the whole of the making of the large chemical vessels. He was fond of telling the potters of a later generation that he remembered having made fifteen three-gallon filters on a foot-wheel before he touched his breakfast. This was earlier than the maturity of his strength, for he recollected also that—to his annoyance—he had to call a boy to help him get his wheel back over the centres.

To a slightly later period, no doubt, must be attributed the following fragment of autobiography:

I constructed [he said in 1896] the first steam potter's wheel that was ever made, with the assistance of a man named Berry. It was ten years later before there was another steam-wheel in either London or Staffordshire. When my wheel needed repairing, there was no engineer's shop on the premises to which I could take it. I had either to mend it myself, or carry the defective part to a rough engineer in Prince's Street, and take very important work all the way to Holborn.

It was about 1837 that Messrs. Doulton and Watts turned their thoughts more closely to that useful and interesting branch of their industry, the manufacture of chemical vessels.[7] These had not been

---

[7] In a lecture given to the Royal Institution on 17th February 1888 Sir Henry said: 'The increasing demand for chemical vessels of stoneware capable of resisting acids may be regarded as giving the first impulse of importance to the Lambeth Potteries.' In 1841 Doulton celebrated his coming-of-age by making a 300-gallon chemical transport jar which his father proudly exhibited in the yard outside the offices with a notice bearing the words 'The largest stoneware vessel in the world'.

C

easy to procure, and this brought to Lambeth a new and important class of clients. In 1839 the firm was much interested in a young customer of the name of Lawes, who had lately taken up practical and scientific farming, and who was making some of the earliest experiments in the manufacture of artificial manures. This young man, who was some six years Henry's senior, greatly interested him by his enthusiasm, and he himself made the vessels to suit Mr. Lawes' requirements. The scientific farmer used frequently to come to Lambeth to give his instructions, and Mr. John Doulton would shout out, 'Here, Henry! Here's little Mr. Lawes; just see what he wants.' The two men did not meet again for fifty-five years, when, in 1894, as a vice-president of the Society of Arts, Sir Henry Doulton went to Marlborough House to see the Prince of Wales present to Sir John Bennet Lawes the Albert Medal. They renewed their acquaintance, with stories of the old time at the Lambeth Pottery, and Sir John invited Sir Henry to inspect his scientific wonders at Rothamsted, an invitation which the latter was no longer able without undue fatigue to accept.

It is necessary, in order to form a conception of the position of Messrs. Doulton and Watts at the time of which we are speaking, to recollect that their firm was but one amongst many. We must disabuse our minds of the vision of minarets which now strikes the eye of a country visitor entering London from the south.[8] In 1840 Lambeth was given up to small pottery establishments, with each and all of which Doulton and Watts had to compete. But for the genius of Henry it is more than probable that they would never have risen out of this respectable mediocrity. But from boyhood he was determined to be the first in the field, to be the Lambeth Pottery, to be Lambeth itself, and all the little events of these years quietly worked together towards the slow realisation of his dream. From 1838 to 1868, for thirty years, Henry Doulton was gently and persistently striving towards this goal.

He achieved it not by intrigue, not by capital, but by sheer intensity of imagination. He saw what was wanted before anyone else. When he came into the business there was a very serious declension in one most important branch of trade. The Bristol

[8] Gosse is referring to the two large brick and terracotta buildings described later in Chapter 6. Badly damaged during World War II, they were demolished in 1951-2.

potters had invented an opaque cream coating or 'slip'[9] which made their pots even and uniform in colour and texture; this they kept as a close secret, and in consequence the Lambeth potters, who could still supply only the brown salt-glaze ware, found themselves hopelessly cut out by their rivals. The Bristol ware proved particularly acceptable to chemists and to spirit merchants. This was the first great crisis which Henry Doulton had to face, and he found neither his father nor Mr. Watts prepared to suggest anything but that they should go on as long as possible in the old groove. Henry devoted his days and nights to the problem, and he discovered either the 'slip' itself or an excellent substitute. The traders soon found that they could get at Lambeth stoneware as handsome in appearance as they could at Bristol. But not from all the Lambeth potters—only from the firm of Messrs. Doulton and Watts, so that already the house took a step in front of the line of its local competitors.

Henry Doulton made several efforts of this kind in his early days and not always, nor at once, with success. For instance, in the first years of the century a great deal of delftware was still being made at Lambeth, but by 1840 the earthenware trade in Staffordshire had snuffed it out. This Henry tried for a time to revive but was not able to achieve much success. Yet the business gradually, almost noiselessly, spread.

In 1840 the Jolly Potter public house, near the pottery, was bought, and turned into a factory for fireclay, with a new front. A few months later, since Henry Doulton was hankering after the manufacture of terracotta, a small factory and kiln were built at the end of the garden and dedicated to this purpose. An enthusiastic and talented potter, Blashfield, whose name deserves to be remembered, had created a demand for decorative vases of terracotta, and this attracted Henry Doulton. In 1841, at the age of twenty-one, he was making attempts at decorative sculpture under the advice of Samuel Nixon. The coat of arms for the Kennington Lane School was the first commission, and a little later the terracotta manufacture was applied to a much more ambitious work, the monument to Sir John Crosby in Bishopsgate.

In 1840, too—for this was a critical year in the chronicle of the

[9] 'Slip' is the potter's term for a suspension of fine particles of clay and other materials in water, usually of a cream-like consistency.

business—John Doulton got rid at last of the mill which had been such a costly nuisance at the back of the garden. In 1844 Messrs. Doulton and Watts joined with Mr. Green, a potter in the neighbourhood, to buy a kiln in Keen Place, which a disappearing firm wished to abandon.[10] This they pulled down, and divided the materials; presently four small houses, with a garden in front, shared the same fate, and their site was annexed to the growing Doulton potteries. In all these changes, and others which it would be too tedious to enumerate, Henry Doulton took a leading part; his was the general's eye, his the ingenious forethought; and only too often was he momentarily depressed to find a bold suggestion lost owing to the vacillation or want of faith of his more timid elders.

In consequence of the long hours' work at the pottery, Henry Doulton had scant leisure for the cultivation of his tastes. It may be said at once that at no time of his life had he much love for games, nor interest in athletics of any kind. The active practical work at the potter's wheel was sufficient bodily exercise, and the only sport Henry ever cared for was riding. When he was a little child he had hung, enviously, about the stable, and it was a very proud day when, about his eleventh year, he was trusted to drive his mother in the business-chaise along the Wandsworth Road out into the country and back. He teased his parents for a steed of his own, and when he left school his father told him that as soon as he was man enough to make a three-gallon filter he would buy him a horse. This was an incentive indeed, and before very long he had made a filter very much larger than what had been agreed upon. The horse was bought, and it is still remembered that on his first ride he became so stiff that the water stood in his eyes with pain; but he would not give in, and persisted until he had made what he considered a proper and dignified round on horseback.

To riding was occasionally added a little perfunctory cricket on Kennington Green, then a market garden, but Henry's heart was not in the game. By this time he had become an insatiable reader,

[10] Stephen Green was the owner of the Imperial Pottery in Princes Street, Lambeth. He manufactured, among other things, drainpipes, general stoneware and chemical ware, relief-figured 'Bacchanalian jugs' and pistol-shaped spirit flasks. He and Henry Doulton were two of the founder members of the London Potters Association in 1853.

chiefly, though far from entirely, of poetry. There was a considerable difficulty in those days in procuring cheap editions of the poets
of the romantic age just passed, the writers who by their genius had
broken up the dry tradition of the eighteenth century and let the
imagination out of prison. Most of them had passed away, but not
all; Rogers was still alive, and Southey, and Campbell, and Moore,
and Leigh Hunt; above all, in the recesses of the Cumbrian Moun-
tains, Wordsworth lived, clothed about in glory as with a mantle.
All these, and the more fuliginous Byron, and the safe poets of the
eighteenth century, and Milton (whom Robert Hall had recited
with oracular mouthings), and of course Shakespeare, all became in
process of time the familiar companions of the young Doulton, who
used to chant their numbers to the whirring of the potter's wheel.
But the full intensity of admiration was called out early by Wordsworth. Curiously enough, this dweller in Lambeth, this youth who
had never seen a mountain and for whom the walk along the
Wandsworth Road was the most rural of excursions, took Wordsworth to his very heart. No writer, perhaps no human being, impressed the nature of Henry Doulton so deeply as Wordsworth did.

In order to facilitate the reading of expensive books, Henry
Doulton actively encouraged the formation of a book club at
Lambeth, and actually carried it out at a very early age. This was
the first of many such local efforts for the cultivation of intellectual
and social interests which he created in his life. Not one other
member of the club, however, cared for verse, and therefore a good
deal of intrigue and a good deal of disappointment had to follow
Henry's efforts to lead the book club in the way it should go. He
told me that he read Sara Coleridge's beautiful romance of *Phantas-
mion,* which had appeared in 1837, by jockeying the unwilling club
into buying it, and a little later, with a rapture of delight, he secured
the two-volume Tennyson of 1842.

But although, like Damon, his time with the Muses he happily
spent, he was set all the while on more practical forms of self-
improvement. He had, as I have said, greatly regretted his lack of
training in draughtsmanship, and as soon as he left school he
looked about for means of obtaining a knowledge of design. Mr.
Hardcastle and he were among the earliest students who attended
the evening lectures on perspective drawing given in Exeter Change
under the Privy Council, about 1837, and the instruction Henry

Doulton gained was of direct value to him at the works. His eye became still more exactly trained than it had before been in realising the form of vessels and machinery, and therefore more skilful in the suggestion of improvements.

It must be said, however, that he developed no talent for design. He became appreciative of art, but he was never able to draw well. And in this connection, as we shall have so much to say of his extreme cleverness in reference to machinery, it is advisable to explain at once that at no period of his life had he any real talent for mechanical handicraft. Where his genius lay, where he was able to be of such supreme service, was in his quickness of mind, his perception, his positive clairvoyance. The great thing was to know what ought to be done; he could always find men able to execute the work under his orders, when it was once conceived. I claim for Henry Doulton that his gifts were those of the imagination. Where other men saw only what was before them, his mind travelled with amazing swiftness on to what would be the results of such and such composite alterations. In short, he rose to be the greatest potter of the age, simply because he had the incommunicable gift of seeing further and deeper than others.

All sorts of difficulties occupied his mind in these early years. He observed practices in the potter's trade which were obviously incorrect. Enormous weights had to be borne on the backs of men. A labourer would be required to lift, in the course of one day, twenty-five or even thirty tons of stuff from depths of eight to ten feet, and carry this weight fifty or sixty yards before he deposited it. Henry Doulton noted, moreover—for his thoughts were keenly alive, even in early youth, to the welfare of those who worked for him—that as a rule the lives of such labourers were short, and their lot less endurable than that of beasts of burden. He did not rest until he had secured a mechanical arrangement by which these vast loads should be hoisted and arranged for distribution by hydraulic apparatus managed by the adjustment of a lever which a child could move.

He was accustomed to say that the applications of science are fewer in the potter's trade than in most others. This is perhaps true, but he was eager to secure all that presented themselves to him. He had long deplored the hard and trying work involved by the preparation of clay under the old system, and the exhausting toil connected with slip-making. It was therefore with particular pleasure that he accepted the beautiful process invented by Needham and Kite by which the superfluous water is pressed out of the slip by hydraulic power.

In his own early days he had been obliged, as a practical thrower, to turn his own potter's wheel by a treadle fixed to a crank, and to manipulate at the same time from a quarter to a half a hundred-weight of clay. Often a kiln was blazing immediately in front of where he stood. In work of this exhausting kind, with very little relaxation, and practically no holidays, the years from 1835 to 1846 were spent. At this time his experience was growing, his ambition and his imagination were vividly at work, and he was building up for his father a strongly based business. But his own part in the growth was as yet invisible to the outside. And how modest was as yet the output of the business may be gathered from the fact that all this time the distribution of products was all done by a con-tractor. The Doultons had no van of their own until 1849.

Of the family life in these quiet years some recollections have been preserved. The mother, whose long succession of children only came to a close with the birth of James, on the 22nd of May 1835, was completely absorbed by her household duties, and very seldom left home. Her health gradually gave way, and on the 9th April 1841 she died at the age of forty-six. During these six years, from Henry's leaving school to his mother's death, although Mrs. Doulton rarely visited, she encouraged the young people to bring in their friends and the evenings were often very gay. It is difficult to form an exact idea of Henry's behaviour at these gatherings. On the one hand I am told that he was the life and soul of them, on the other that he was gauche and shy. Both accounts may be true, for he had his violent ups and downs of temperament, like other eager, ardent people. But evidence is unanimous on certain points; among others, that his restlessness was phenomenal, and sometimes embarrassing, and that he was one of those irrepressible youths for whom no furnished room seems large enough for the safety of its contents.

He was very good-looking in those early days, and a great favourite with the ladies, young and old. The social centre of the little group of families living close together was Regent Street Chapel, Lambeth, the pastor of which had been since 1834 the Rev. Eliel Davis, a prominent Baptist minister in his day. It may be said at once that Henry Doulton, though a pious was never a pietistic man, and that the profession of religion never took a prominent part in his life. His father, on the contrary, had his periods of enthusiasm, and in one of these started a service of his own over a gateway close to Lambeth Chapel. These meetings were attended by John and Henry, who helped with the hymns, and this led the young gentleman's attention to music. Early in the forties, a friend, Joseph Pewtress, started musical parties in his house in Gracechurch Street, and both Mr. Hardcastle and Henry Doulton joined.

Unwilling that such a light of melody should be kept under a bushel, Henry and his friend offered their services as vocalists to the Regent Street Chapel, and were duly admitted into the choir, which sat in the great table-pew under the pulpit. At this time Henry Doulton had developed a considerable dressiness, and he created no small scandal by appearing in the choir, on the first occasion, not in the sober black, which was *de rigueur* in sacred places, but in a bright cinnamon-coloured cut-away coat, a crimson waistcoat, and a splendidly voluminous satin stock, covered with embroidered flowers. It was all in vain to appeal against this parade. His only answer was to appear next Sunday in the same attire, but with one unspeakably worldly addition to it—the curling of his hair by a hairdresser.

In some curious way he seems to have held his own among his relations and friends, exceedingly little affected by criticism. He recited his poetry, and tootled on his flute, and changed his waistcoats, and curled the wonders of his hair, without receiving any severer reprimand than the jests of his brother John, who was a practical joker, given to doing irritating things with lumps of wet clay. But, jester though John was, Henry could outwit him in any matter involving mental ingenuity, and, besides, the younger brother was far the better workman. This is, indeed, the keynote of Henry's independent position and freedom to pursue his own whims and eccentricities; he was before the age of twenty-one the mainstay of the business and its most active and ambitious member. If a youth of the greatest gaiety and good temper, who is at the same time the principal bread-winner of a large group of mouths, insists on wearing a goat-skin tied around him with a string, there will be a good deal said in the family for letting him have his way.

A story connected with these independent notions of dress—in which, indeed, he was only importing into Lambeth some of the smartnesses of his age—gives, I think, a good impression of Henry Doulton in his earliest manhood. A French lady, who met him for the first time, was asked what she thought of him. She gazed at the lapel of his coat, then at his waistcoat, then at his great dark-brown eyes, and she exclaimed in a whisper, 'But, my dear, he is *beautiful*; he is *all velvet!*'

The social occasions at which Henry Doulton polished his wit against his contemporaries were of a simple kind. He was seen at the Rev. Eliel Davis' 'short-coating parties', occasions of a kind so drolly out of date that some account of them may be given. The Rev. and Mrs. Davis were a very young couple, and the quiver of their happiness was being steadily filled, one arrow once a year. When each new baby arrived at its first change of costume, a 'short-coating party' was instituted, to which the parents were invited (though in their own house) by the members of their congregation. Having discreetly betaken themselves elsewhere the day before, they returned—with the babe, of course, short-coated for the occasion—to find their house full of their friends, and welcome, practical gifts in every room. In fact, these parties were what in America used to be called 'bees', a sensible sort of reversed hospitality. At such occasions Mrs. Doulton would make an effort to put in an appearance with a son on either arm; a small, pretty lady, she is described to me, with handsome eyes and ebon ringlets pressed to each side of the smiling face by a rather voluminous lace cap, a quiet, devout, motherly little woman, not strong in health, nor high in spirits.

Another set of social occasions was connected with the Book Society, by this time brought under the cognisance and immediate protection of Regent Street Chapel. Once a month the members, with their families, met in the sacred precincts, and from those meetings nothing short of a miracle prevented Henry's presence. He was the life and soul of these affairs. After the discussion of business, which was mainly the selection of new books for purchase, a supper of bread and cheese, biscuits, ale and porter was consumed, and the rest of the evening was devoted to music and conversation. It was at these entertainments that Henry Doulton, who had been spending some of his pocket money upon lessons on the flute, displayed his talent before an admiring audience.

Once a year the members of the Book Society indulged in a

summer outing to Box Hill, dining at the famous inn below. By the young ladies of the company Henry Doulton was considered a little serious and one occasion is remembered when a group of girls suddenly flung a gay knitted quilt over his shoulders and danced him round and round entangled in it. But this could only be an exaggeration of his usual movement, for all agree that he was never still, rushing from chair to chair, retreating and advancing, gesticulating, nodding, wagging his bright and handsome head, and—alas! —in some of these movements sweeping a figure off the mantelpiece or upsetting a vase upon the table.

In these days Henry Doulton's affections were entirely untouched. He used to say—as boys have done since the world began—that he would never marry, but would devote himself entirely to the kindred arts of pottery and poetry. His little room at Lambeth was a sanctum full of his own treasures, full in particular of books to overflowing. His favourite sister, Marian, who was nine years his junior, had the sole privilege of entering this abode, and of dusting it. For this the young occupant offered no remuneration, but he did propose to pay her a small sum a week if she would stay and read some of his favourite poets with him. This is rather a pathetic circumstance as showing the isolation in which he lived in this respect. Marian was so deeply bored by verse that she seldom earned her pittance, preferring poverty to the slow death of song. Indeed, it appears that all through his youth Henry Doulton had not a single ally among his family in the favourite relaxation of his mind. The family thought this preoccupation with the poets madder than his embroidered waistcoats or his curled locks. Although, however, Marian refused to sacrifice to the Muses, Henry was deeply attached to her, and in schemes of the future, when wealth came, they were to share a smart little house, and drive out together every afternoon in a cabriolet with a diminutive 'tiger' behind.

Towards the year 1844, Henry began to take his father's place in travelling for the firm, first in London, then in the counties of Kent and Surrey, then through many parts of England. He told me that he suffered much at first from the very rough and uncongenial company he met with at inns, at the commercial travellers' ordinary, where more drinking and swearing, more bragging and more coarse story-telling went on than was in any degree palatable to the sensitive young potter from Lambeth. To the disgust which these

meetings produced—they were the first occasions, it must be
recollected, in a very sheltered life, in which he was brought face to
face with the crudity of existence—he attributed a horror of in-
delicacy and excess of any kind which continued throughout his
career to be a marked feature of his character. He was perhaps
inclined, all his life, to be a little timid and prudish, a little unwilling
to face subjects which (after all) not everybody is called upon to
face. He cultivated an adroit little way of changing the subject,
when it was no longer necessary, as it had been in those inn-parlours
in the forties, to sit out the unsavoury anecdotage. As soon as he
could, he told me, he used to steal away, and he liked summer best,
for the reason that in the long evenings there was generally a bridge
to lean over or a brook to saunter along by, with Wordsworth or
Shelley in his breast pocket.

His first lengthy journey, indeed his earliest sight of the world at
full length, was made when he went to Scotland in the autumn of
1844. From this period a letter, written to John Hardcastle from
Inverness on 1st October 1844, may be selected giving some taste
of the young man's quality.

I should have written to you before, but my time has been fully
occupied. I have now done business for a few days, and if the
weather is fine, I expect to enjoy myself in the Highlands. My
intention is to start from here on Thursday morning and travel
down the Caledonian Canal to Glasgow.

For the first time in my life I have just caught a glimpse of
something worthy of the name of a mountain. Hitherto I have
not been so interested with the scenery of Scotland as with its
inhabitants. I have met with some very agreeable and interesting
people of both sexes in the course of my travels, and in future I
shall contend in spite of all *Punch* may insinuate to the contrary
that the Scotch are remarkable for hospitality and intelligence.

I find from your letter that you have been made acquainted
with my movements in Glasgow, I shall call my brother John to
account for this. Last Sunday week I spent in Edinboro'. It is a
splendid city, romantically situated and well-built; the architecture
mostly of a very superior character. I was particularly pleased with
a monument to Sir Walter Scott which is now nearly completed.
It was the first design of a young man and was the means of

bringing him into notice. Unfortunately he died a few months ago.

From Mary's friends I obtained letters of introduction to families in towns where I was likely to stop and thus fell in with some very agreeable society. I had a letter from a friend in Edinboro' to a gentleman in Aberdeen. The family I found to consist of his mother and two charming sisters, and in their company I spent some very pleasant hours. I stayed there from Thursday to yesterday morning. The ladies particularly pleased me and notwithstanding I assure you my heart is still my own. I have since been able to counterbalance these impressions by the easy, pleasant, lightly-come, lightly-go style of living of two or three bachelor friends.

As I have quite decided upon a certain course of life (for some years to come at all events), I begin to think I shall be left alone in my glory, and that all my friends will *settle*. . . .

I am happy to say the Queen has not come in my way. Had she done so, I fear her influence over my customers would have prevented them from giving me orders. Of course you saw the very interesting picture in the *Illustrated London News* of her Majesty and the Prince witnessing Highland sheep-shearing! The Scotch laugh at the gullibility of the Cockneys. Sheep-shearing at this season in the Highlands is absurd. The reporter heard of sheep-*smearing,* which is done to keep them warm, and told the artist, who for the information of such loyal subjects as yourself gave an accurate representation of a scene which no one ever saw.

You must excuse this rambling letter, there are twelve 'commercials' in this room talking away as fast as they usually do after dinner.

Remember me very kindly to all your family and

Believe me,
Yours very truly,
Henry Doulton

Henry Doulton's practical experience in 'travelling' was of great service to him in later years, when he began to employ a large number of men in this branch of the business. He knew what such men ought to do, and he knew, also, what their difficulties were. He had battled against an obstacle, however, which did not interfere with the comfort of his successors. When, in the forties, he was traversing the country, he seldom found a likely customer who had heard of the name of Doulton, or with whom business could be conducted without a tiresome preamble. Not many years were to pass before a card, or the mere mention of the firm, was enough to ensure a courteous and intelligent reception.

He was particularly fond of recalling the visit he paid, in these earlier years, to the Messrs. Berger, then already famous as colour and dye manufacturers in Homerton. After taking an order from them, Henry Doulton would sometimes make the articles, deliver them and receive the money himself. The heads of the firm were like the Brothers Cheeryble; they were two kindly, smiling old gentlemen, always seen together, and so exactly alike that you could never distinguish one from the other. Although very wealthy men, they could be found any day, at their factory, overlooking and directing its working, in white aprons and paper caps. Away from the works, however, they were always smartly dressed and carefully in the fashion. On one occasion they were taking Henry Doulton round their garden, and he exclaimed at the beauty of certain tiny bantams. No remark was made at the time, but a day or two afterwards a groom in livery rode up to the works at Lambeth, and, asking for Mr. Henry Doulton, left in a little basket, with the Messrs. Berger's compliments, a little bantam cock and two diminutive hens. These were the occasional rewards of a very trying and unsympathetic branch of his training, which Henry Doulton resigned into other hands as soon as he possibly could.

In 1846 Henry Doulton took an independent step which was to prove the turning point of his career. It had for some time past appeared to him that stoneware ought to take a prominent place in sanitary work, and he resolved that he would inaugurate this new branch of business. Lambeth was at this time in a deplorably insanitary condition. Even High Street was paved with large boulders which caused horses and carts to make an awful clatter as they moved along. Now one of the healthiest districts in London, it was then one of the most dangerous. The courts and small streets, down which Henry Doulton's avocation constantly took him, such as Straddle Alley, Naked Boy Lane, Black Boy Alley and Frying Pan Alley, were hot-beds of disease, in which virulent fevers were for ever being hatched for distribution throughout the parish. Sir

Henry once told me that it was in hurrying along Naked Boy Alley one day, with his handkerchief pressed over his nostrils, that it was suddenly borne in upon him that there were few bigger tasks for a plain man to accomplish than the resolute and efficient drainage of such sinks of pollution as this.[11]

It is hardly needful to point out today, when the work is done, that only half a century ago it seemed as though the drainage of London was an absolute impossibility. Not only were there no instruments and no plans for carrying it out, but public prejudice was intensely against any drainage system. Doulton used to say that when he first proposed that Lambeth should be drained, and attempted to argue that the awful state of things then existing was the result of human laziness and the lack of proper sanitary pre-cautions, he was met with great opposition, and told, even by people high in authority, that epidemics were visitations of God, which it would be impious to try to restrain. Lambeth was at that time a perfect congeries of evil odours; it presented a richer and more varied nosegay of stinks than any other part of the metropolis. This was due, not merely to the open drains, but to the fact that the industries of bone-boiling, bone-crushing and manure-concoction were specially carried on at Lambeth, making it like Cologne in Coleridge's epigram, a 'body-and-soul-stinking town'. All evil odour was remarkably offensive to Henry Doulton, and it was a great vexation to him that passers-by were apt loosely to attribute these stenches to the potteries. As a matter of fact it was the Doultons who gradually put a stop to them by buying up these works one after another and so getting rid of one insupportable stink after another.

In 1846 Henry Doulton separated himself from his father, while remaining close beside him. He took 63 High Street, a few hundred

[11] This and the next paragraph might tend to imply that it was Henry Doulton who first suggested the use of stoneware pipes for drainage and sewerage. This was not so. In an address which he delivered to representatives of the firm on 25th March 1892 he said: 'It was not until 1845 that any suggestion was made to employ pipes of pottery for sewerage purposes. The proposal emanated from the late Mr. Edwin Chadwick who before he died earned the title "Father of Sanitary Science". . . . Foreseeing the magnitude of the demand likely to arise, I did not think it advisable to graft the business to the existing factory but commenced special works in High Street, Lambeth, devoted entirely to the production of pipes for house and town drainage.'

yards off, and commenced the manufacture of stoneware pipes for the sewerage of towns and the drainage of houses. Sanitary science was then in its infancy, and the difficulties which met him in the outset were almost insuperable. Many influential engineers refused to listen to a plan for the use of stoneware pipes at all. 'There was a hard fight,' as Sir Henry said fifty years later, 'with the public outside, while inside we suffered from a lack of suitable machinery. At first we had either to throw the pipes on the wheel, or else to turn them on drums.' Henry Doulton had been living, as we have seen, the quietest life possible, and he had contrived by strict economy to save £800. It was on this small fortune that he started independently in 1846, and in a very short time all this money was gone. He was forced to make an appeal to his father, who read him a lesson on his extravagant ambition, and advised him to give up the unequal struggle with the engineers, and return to his employment. This was more than Henry Doulton could endure, and he pleaded passionately with his father to make an examination with him of the condition of his business. He explained that the money had not been wasted but sunken; that the business was moving; that the experiments were beginning to succeed; and finally the old gentleman, partly carried away by his son's enthusiasm, partly anxious to indulge him, consented, with many shakings of the head, to advance £400. This made the elder John Doulton a partner in Henry's concerns, although he took no further part in their development.[12] In after years Sir Henry Doulton used to say that he should never forget the agony of entreaty and argument which was required to persuade his father to be made a very rich man. After this, however, everything began to improve; the experiments were carried on and were entirely successful, and several active young engineers were brought over to the adoption of stoneware pipes. Among them was prominent Robert Rawlinson, who in 1849 became chief engineering inspector of the Local Government Board, a post which he occupied

[12] Frederick Doulton, one of Henry's younger brothers, invested £200 and also became a partner in the new firm, Henry Doulton & Company. In later years, after he had left the business, Frederick gave his family a good deal of worry by unwise speculation but Henry never forgot his support in the early days and did all he could to help him and his family. See page 76.

John Doulton, Senior, in fact continued to help from time to time with loans until the business became firmly established.

for forty years. He was convinced of the value of the stoneware
pipes, and very notably encouraged their adoption. This eminent
engineer, who although ten years Sir Henry Doulton's senior, out-
lived him until 1898, was a life-long friend, and was identified with
many of the successes of the Lambeth Potteries. Sir Robert Rawlinson had reached the great age of eighty-eight when he died.

The following account of the impulse given to the pottery trade
by the introduction of stoneware pipes for drainage purposes is
founded upon notes drawn up by Sir Henry himself. He was
persuaded in 1845 that the cleanly and imperishable nature of the
material rendered the stoneware pipes obviously superior to the old
brick drains, and he created a demand which has been increasing
until at the present time, and indeed for fifteen years past, the industry has spread over the whole world.

Glazed stoneware pipes [wrote Sir Henry] were first used by
Mr. John Roe, of the Holborn and Finsbury Vestry, and by
Mr. J. Phillips, of the Westminster Commission of Sewers.
Previous to this time stoneware pipes of small bore had been used
for down pipes for rain water and were made by preparing a
thin slab of plastic clay which was afterwards rolled round a
cylinder by hand. The first great impulse to sewer and drain pipe
making was given by the Public Health Act in 1848, when works
of town sewering were commenced in various parts of England,
and to meet the demand I commenced a special factory devoted
entirely to the production of pipes for house and town drainage.
These were first made by hand upon the potter's wheel, but within
a year of their introduction machinery was employed for their
manufacture, the use of which ensured greater regularity of form
than could be attained by the manual process. By these machines
the plastic clay is expressed by steam-power through metal dies.
Some time previous to this the same method had been employed
for the manufacture of agricultural pipes of small diameter up to
four inches. The production of larger pipes, however, involved
the use of a different material, and very extensive modifications
of the process.[13]

[13] At first the sockets were made separately and stuck on to the tubes by hand.
Many unsuccessful attempts were made to design presses which would extrude
pipes and sockets in one piece. Henry Doulton, though no engineer, evolved a

In the year 1847 Henry Doulton was encouraged by success to enlarge the scope of his engines. He erected a factory at St. Helens for the supply of Liverpool and its neighbourhood, followed by another at Rowley Regis, near Dudley, for the supply of Birmingham.[14] These latter are now the largest works of the kind in the world. In all these cases, the success of Henry Doulton was eminent and direct, but he often found himself baffled from a want of imagination on the part of those with whom he dealt. For instance, in 1846, he was identified with Robert Rawlinson in a proposal to supply the city of Liverpool with water from Bala Lake in Wales, and an estimate was formed for the necessary work. But the young men were met with incredulity, and no one would believe that water to feed a great town could possibly be brought from a lake at such a prodigious distance.

The Public Health Act of 1848 greatly aided the development of Henry Doulton's sanitary business. It brought him into closer relations with Edwin Chadwick, who was on the first Board of Health, in company with Lord Morpeth, Lord Ashley and Dr. Southwood Smith. Of the first four engineering inspectors appointed, two, Robert Rawlinson and Edward Cresy, were life-long friends of Henry Doulton, and as warmly convinced as he of the utility of stoneware drain pipes.

If we turn from the commercial aspects of this part of Henry Doulton's life to the intellectual and spiritual, we find the central interests of his mind to have moved around a little local union of friends, of which he was the founder and the main supporter, and which continued for very many years to occupy the most serious part of his leisure. His position was a unique one for a young man of

press which solved the problem to some extent but when Thomas Spencer of Prescot patented in 1848 a much more satisfactory press Doulton immediately recognised its superiority and ordered several to be installed in his works, paying royalties to Spencer for several years. It was a long time before Spencer's patent was extensively adopted elsewhere, and even as late as 1896 sockets were still being applied by hand in some of the smaller pipe-works. This willingness to recognise the superior ability of others in spheres where he was but an amateur was another secret of Doulton's success.

[14] This is incorrect. The Dudley factory was established by Henry but the one at St. Helens was set up independently by his elder brother, John Doulton, Junior, who although at first very dubious about the prospects for stoneware pipes, was now encouraged by the growing demand to embark on their production.

D

his ardent intelligence. Circumstances—that intensity of local concentration which we have already noted in him as so marked an
external characteristic—separated him from association with other
young men in London. The Thames, odd as it sounds, was really a
practical barrier against society in general, and the cultivation of
societies in particular. His work began too early in the morning
and lasted until too late at night for it to be possible for him to
cultivate friendships outside of Lambeth, and Lambeth, in those
days, was a perfect Abdera of art and letters. There was every chance,
there was every likelihood, that a young fellow situated as Henry
Doulton was, should give way to this density of his surroundings,
and acquiesce in intellectual mediocrity by the sheer force of inertia.

But this was not his nature; and I remember his quoting to me, at
least forty years later, as expressing his own conditions at this time,
those lines of Matthew Arnold's:

> An impulse, from the distance,
> Of his deepest, best existence,
> To the words 'Hope, Light, Persistence,'
> Strongly sets, and truly burns.

Nor was it sufficient for so gregarious a soul as Henry Doulton's
to feed this flame merely by the use of books. His nature was
restless and expansive, he demanded the attention of others, the
stimulus of discussion and debate. Even into the old boyish meetings
of the Book Society he had introduced something of this element,
but he needed to have it cultivated and emphasised. About this
time the popular anger of Hood, expressed in those last poems of
his which ran through London sympathy like wildfire, and then the
pathetic career of Hood himself, and his premature death, produced
a great impression on Henry Doulton. He gained from Hood a
certain sympathetic fervour, a certain indignation which made an
indelible impression on his character. I do not know that it was the
wit, so much as the generous effusion, of Hood that particularly
affected him, but the latter must be recorded among influences
which tended to make Henry Doulton what he became.

While he was full of these feelings, this political anger and this
craving for the excitement of a dialectic, he gathered together on the
7th of October 1843 a little meeting of his friends at the house of
the elder Mr. Hardcastle, at Vauxhall.

There were present besides himself, his friends John Hardcastle, R. W. Laing and John Turner, and these four youths formed themselves into the Lambeth Friendly Debating Society. They drew up rules; Henry Doulton was appointed treasurer and Mr. Turner secretary. They met again on the 31st of October, when the older Mr. Hardcastle led off with an address—much needed by the inexperience of the members—on 'The Nature and Advantage of a Debating Society'. It was determined that they should meet in the school-room of the chapel, and they did so during the year 1844. Members, however, continued to join, and in the autumn the place of meeting was changed and certain alterations, which experience had shown to be desirable, were made in the rules. Mr. Turner having resigned the secretaryship, Mr. John Hardcastle was appointed his successor; and the reorganised Society began a fresh lease of existence. Among many early members whose names it is perhaps not needful to recall, occur those of certain life-long friends of Henry Doulton. In particular, on the 17th of October 1845, Mr. J. W. Pewtress and Mr. James Anderson Rose were elected.

It is feared that the record of the early meetings has been lost, and perhaps in the general fullness of the world's documents this is not extremely to be regretted. But the subjects are in many cases preserved. An early theme was 'The Benefit to us of our Colonies', on which Henry Doulton's views were, even at that date, what they remained, essentially imperialist. On an evening devoted to 'Prose and Poetry' he held the fortress of verse alone against a combined force of members who thought that prose sufficed for all practical purposes of life. In its first year the Lambeth Debating Society discussed 'Cromwell' and 'Tithes', 'Napoleon' and 'The Slave Trade', 'American Institutions' and 'Military Enterprise'. It is not to be doubted that the views of the very young orators on these miscellaneous matters were crude and their knowledge insufficiently based, but there was vitality in them; they were fired with 'hope, light, persistence'. Persistence, least of all, could be denied to the Society, for in one form or another, it lasted without a breach of continuity for more than forty years, and during the whole of that time Henry Doulton was the moving spirit of the adventure.

3

Early married life
1849 to 1860

It was indicative of a marked increase in Henry Doulton's settled sense of business success that in 1849 he seriously contemplated the step of marriage. He met a charming lady, Miss Sarah Kennaby, at the house of the Rev. Baldwin Brown in the early spring of that year, and almost immediately determined to ask her to be his wife. She was cultivated, gentle, enthusiastic, and she was in close sympathy with his views on the conduct of life. The only drawback was a certain delicacy of constitution, which it was hoped she would outlive, but which, in fact, grew more and more accentuated. In 1849, however, a certain fragility was all that seemed to be threatened in the health of Miss Kennaby.

A letter written from Lambeth, on the 9th of April 1894, to Mr. John Hardcastle, who was then travelling in Ireland, gives a warm impression of Henry Doulton's sentiments at this crisis in his life:

I hardly know whether I should take this opportunity to assure you of, what I hope you have never doubted, my unabated friendship for you. I excessively dislike telling in words the esteem in which I hold your character and the value I set upon your friendship. Actions speak louder than words, yet I find so many of my friends think I forget them, that upon the principle that 'what everyone says must be true' I suppose some blame must attach to me; till, then, I can testify by *action*, you must take the words with my assurance that they are heartfelt and sincere. Some day when you know by experience the all absorbing influence of the master-passion of the human soul you will freely and fully acquit me.

If, however, I am blameworthy, allow me to offer a word or two in extenuation. To run the even tenor of our way when a crisis of such moment happens in our history would be unnatural —a fig for such love. The whole current of our being is turned in a new direction, the mind is absorbed in thought, the soul in feeling. A new sphere of action is opened to us with new joys and duties and an altered destiny. Is it then to be wondered at that with so much to engage our thought and feeling, we should be a little bewildered by the tumultuous passions which have us in possession? How much is there to engross us, when our perceptions are quickened and the whole realm of truth, beauty and purity is to us an open sesame. Hope kindles hope, and, in spite of the prognostications of some old men and disappointed old women, joy seems to rise behind joy in endless perspective. How much also is there for study, the best opportunity for which is then afforded and perhaps for the first time in one's life. Not only the charms of beauty and the grace of manners, but something beneath the surface, the deep affection, the self-sacrificing spirit, the devotion and purity of a noble woman's love. Then the joy in knowing all this is yours—ah! talk of wealth—the noble, generous and gentle spirit I have sought and won I would not barter for universes of Californias.

Such knowledge is high; that you may speedily attain to it is the earnest wish of

Yours very truly
Henry Doulton

They were married at Baldwin Brown's Chapel by the Rev. Caleb Morris on the 16th of August 1849, and Henry Doulton started, with his bride, for the Cumberland and Westmorland lakes. It may be said at once that this was a union of perfect affection upon both sides. Henry Doulton was most tenderly attached to his wife, and when the romance of marriage wore off it was only to be merged in a touching and self-sacrificing devotion to one who came to need more and more a soothing and protecting hand. No marriage was ever more completely one of love than this, nor any less troubled in the smoothness of its course by any accidents of temper. Husband

and wife, to the very last, were absolutely wrapped up in one
another's interests and thoughts. They settled at 7 Stockwell Villas,
South Lambeth Road, in a small, but comfortable house, opening to
the road in front with a shrubbery garden behind. In this house they
lived for some eight years, and here their three children were born.

The honeymoon was marked by one incident of peculiar interest
to Henry Doulton. He was driving his wife in an open trap from
Ambleside to Grasmere on the 26th of August when they met an
elderly couple leisurely stepping along the road. In a moment
Doulton saw who they were, and bowed, whereupon the old
gentleman with equal courtesy took off his hat, and revealed the
snowy hair, and tall, bare forehead of the Poet Laureate. It was an
intoxication to Henry Doulton to have seen the object of his
highest veneration, the man then living in the whole world whom
he most admired.

The young couple spent the night at Grasmere, and next day
Henry Doulton took his bride up to the outside of Rydal Mount,
where, with the ardour of a convinced Wordsworthian, he was
explaining the lie of the land to his wife when Mr. Wordsworth
himself appeared at the gate. He recognised his young friends of the
preceding afternoon, and paused to greet them. Henry Doulton, in
a high degree of rapture (for those were enthusiastic days), murmured
that there was no one to whom he owed so much pleasure and
instruction as the great poet to whom he spoke.

Mr. Wordsworth was extremely pleased. He regretted that he was
starting to keep an appointment at Ambleside, but nevertheless
insisted on their entering with him the garden at Rydal Mount.
Henry Doulton had struck the right chord in using the word
'instruction'. Mr. Wordsworth remarked that it was a poor thing
for a poet to write merely to amuse or please; that at the outset of
life he had set before himself a higher aim, and that the frequent
testimony he received in his old age, proving his efforts not to have
been fruitless, was a great satisfaction to him. Descending from
these ethical heights, he plucked Henry Doulton by the sleeve, and
complimented him on his bride's sweet face. 'She is an amiable,
kind creature, I am sure!' he added.

At this moment, his famous sister, Dorothy Wordsworth,
appeared, drawn in a chaise, Mrs. Wordsworth and Miss Cookson
walking at the side, and to these ladies the poet presented his young

visitors. Wordsworth then took them round the garden, pointing out his favourite views, and bidding them read his well-known inscription:

> In these fair vales hath many a tree
> At *Wordsworth's* suit been spared.

He spied a volume of his own poetry under Mrs. Doulton's cloak, and rather quaintly recommended the young couple to procure a later edition, the volumes of which were more portable. He was forced, then, to hurry away, but not until he had recommended Mr. and Mrs. Doulton to the care of the gardener, who was 'to show them everything'. At that time, although Wordsworth was to die six months later (April 23, 1850), there were no signs of speedy decay, and his courteous and dignified affability were extreme. No doubt the incense burned by the worshipper was not stinted in quality or quantity. This interview with Wordsworth made a profound impression on Henry Doulton. There is no exaggeration in saying that it formed a landmark in his life. To the end of his own career he remained the most unflinching Wordsworthian that I have ever known. He saw something to praise in 'Julia and Vaudracour', and was pained if one laughed at the Spade of Mr. Wilkinson.

In the Stockwell life in the early fifties, all seems to have been quiet and uneventful. The prosperity of the business was assured, but the young people played no tricks with fortune and were slow to believe that they were on the high road to a great position. Henry Doulton was closely occupied with affairs, and gave his personal attention to every section of the work. Early in his career as a manufacturer, an accident occurred which made a great impression upon his habits. He had not been, up to that time, particularly careful about punctuality, but he had a chance of a very large order from Mr. Thomas Brassey, and had an appointment to present himself, with his competitors, at the office of that eminent contractor, whose business was just then widely advancing. The appointment was for 10.15, but Henry Doulton, nervously anxious, was on the spot ten minutes before the appointed time. There was nobody there, and he waited in the outer office. At 10.15 he heard Mr. Brassey enter briskly, and say to his clerks, 'Have those gentlemen come?' 'Only young Mr. Doulton, sir,' was the reply. 'Well, show him in, then, I have no time to waste.' Ten minutes afterwards, as Henry Doulton was leaving the office with the signed order buttoned up in his breast pocket, he met his two belated rivals hurrying in. He registered a vow on the spot that he would never be late for an appointment, and as far as accidents would permit, he kept that vow through life. To those who knew the order of Sir Henry Doulton's movements, he was an absolutely perfect time-piece.

About this time he cultivated music with much assiduity. His favourite sister, Marian (later Mrs. Buckland), developed a very beautiful voice and her brothers clubbed together to give her a simple musical education. The house of the Doultons at Stockwell became the centre of an enthusiastic little glee and madrigal society, in which Henry Doulton sang bass. Among the friends which these musical meetings confirmed in their place in Henry Doulton's group of intimates were William Blades, afterwards the famous printer, his brother Rowland Blades, and, above all, Mr. Joseph Pewtress, who had joined the Lambeth Debating Society in 1845. Mr. Pewtress, an unambitious man, was possessed of very unusual accomplishments in many directions and his companionship was of rare value to Henry Doulton for many years. About this time, too, the Addison Book Club, which Henry Doulton had instituted in 1845, a friendly association for the purchase of new publications, took a fresh lease of life.

The spread of the business was marked during this period by the extension of the Lambeth premises, which grew like a living object. Soon after his marriage, Henry Doulton bought three properties in Need Alley, and then three more at the back of the King's Head yard. It was a little later on in March 1857 that a fire broke out under an archway at the back of the Red Lion. This spread into the Lambeth Potteries and burned down a great portion of the back premises. This was, however, a blessing in disguise, since it made it imperative to improve the place. Once started on bricks and mortar it was not easy to stop, and Henry Doulton absorbed the premises of Buckridge, the barge builder, who found there was no longer a demand for barges to be built in Lambeth. Then followed the acquisition of properties in Ferry Street and Brothers' Row. The existing office was then found quite insufficient, and a new one was built. All these extensions and developments had been completed by March 1861 and they indicate the growth of the business during the critical years of which the present chapter is a record.

Between 1848 and 1856 an extraordinary change came over the underground economy of London. Glazed vitrified stoneware pipes were gradually being adopted for town and house drainage. Henry Doulton, as already described, was at the forefront of this movement, and made it his business to supply the rapidly developing demand. To the argument that cheaper porous earthenware pipes, even when they absorbed as much as one-sixth of their weight, were not objectionable, Henry Doulton opposed a more and more strenuous contradiction, and in this he was supported by all the leading sanitary engineers. He grew to be certain that impermeability is an indispensable and primary requirement in pipes used for drainage, and his own stoneware, which was close and highly vitrified, 'impervious', as was noted in 1851, 'to the action of acids, and of peculiar strength, differed from all kinds of glazed earthenware in this important respect, that the glazing is actually incorporated with the material itself'. This made it the ideal substance for use in the new and grandiose adventure of re-draining London.

About the year 1856 some of the vestries determined to use cheaper earthenware in the place of the vitrified stoneware pipes in the draining of the respective parishes. This was a somewhat critical moment for the Doultons; Henry met it with his usual decisiveness. On the 14th of June 1856 he addressed a brief circular note to all the leading engineers, begging them to give an opinion as to the relative merits of the two classes of pipe. 'We manufacture both kinds,' he wrote, 'but have always considered it important to recommend and supply only stoneware glazed vitrified pipes for sewage, and have only recommended our earthenware pipes, which are slightly porous, for park and land drainage.' The replies of the engineers, which he printed in a pamphlet, left no room for question that he had expert opinion wholly with him. It was acknowledged in the profession that whatever might be the qualities of the other pipes they would not bear comparison with those of the Doulton stoneware. The crisis was thus met, and a public calamity probably averted by the general introduction of stoneware pipes for drains and sewers. This was not the last occasion on which Henry Doulton's admirable firmness and promptitude benefited the public while singularly advancing his own fortune.

The first prominent public appearance made by Messrs. Doulton was at the Great Exhibition of 1851. The Doulton objects consisted of brown stoneware bottles, jugs, jars, and the like, exhibited in the name of Doulton and Watts. Among them were a few 'fancy articles', as they were called, such as Nelson jugs, jugs with relief decoration depicting a boar-hunt and the old Toby jug.[15] The parent firm, moreover, showed samples of chemical apparatus, filters and a few terracotta vases, together with a terracotta figure of Father Time, with hour-glass and scythe, the whole as little suggestive of the later art work as it would be possible to conceive. Henry Doulton and Co. exhibited sewer pipes, but the entire space allotted to English potters was too small to allow any one firm to make a really effective display. This was the day of small things, and the two affiliated firms were very well pleased to have a silver medal allotted to each of them. The Commissioners, with Prince Albert at their head, were not profuse in bestowing distinctions.

About this time another pipe factory was started at Smethwick, in Staffordshire, then an obscure village in the parish of Harborne, but now a large town almost united to Birmingham, which lies to the south-east of it. Long afterwards, when a saloon carriage took Sir Henry Doulton with rapidity to his works there, he used to reflect with amusement on the changes of the years. In 1891, when speaking at Smethwick, he said:

> I think of my journeys to Dudley by the only conveyance of the time, the canal boat; or by omnibus to Smethwick, and the frequent 'refreshers' of the driver at the wayside inn, which made the journey so tedious; of the notices on the road between Birmingham and Smethwick, warning any traveller who might be tempted to leave the dusty road that man-traps and spring-guns were set on the grounds. When I contrast with all these memories,

[15] The so-called 'Toby jugs' were of a traditional type which had been made by Fulham and Lambeth potters since the eighteenth century. Unlike the Ralph Wood and other Staffordshire earthenware Toby jugs modelled in the form of a seated or standing toper, the Fulham and Lambeth stoneware jugs were of conventional shape but decorated with applied reliefs (made separately in small moulds) depicting topers with foaming tankards, cottages, windmills, horsemen, stags, foxes, dogs and other designs. John Doulton, who had learned to make jugs of this kind at Fulham, continued to produce them at Lambeth and the tradition was carried on there right up to the time the Lambeth factory closed in 1956.

your present railroad conveniences, and your public parks for recreation, I realise in some poor degree the marvellous changes of the past forty years.

On the 31st of December 1853 Mr. Watts retired from the business, and the firms of Messrs. Doulton and Watts, and Messrs. Henry Doulton and Co. were amalgamated. From the 1st of January 1854 the business was carried on as one concern.[16]

Henry Doulton's first attempt to extend his business abroad was made in 1854, when he went to Paris to endeavour to obtain orders for pipes to be used in the projected drainage works there. Later on his merchandise became greatly appreciated in France, and the firm sent very large quantities of pipes and kitchen sinks to Paris.

This was Henry Doulton's earliest expedition abroad. He was probably in a hurry, and absorbed in business anxieties, for no one seems to recall having heard him expatiate upon his first impression of Paris. His intense devotion to natural scenery developed later on. Even in the Lakes he had been much more excited at seeing Wordsworth than at seeing Helvellyn. With poetry and music there competed in those early days a great interest in politics. We have already mentioned in these pages the early appearance of Mr. Charles Tennyson D'Eyncourt on the platform of radicalism in South London. From 1831 to 1852 Mr. Tennyson D'Eyncourt was M.P. for Lambeth, and at the close of that period Henry Doulton was his active henchman. He was prominent among those who on the 22nd of June 1853 presented a testimonial to the late member. This same summer Henry Doulton went down for a few days to stay at Bayons Manor, Mr. D'Eyncourt's place in Lincolnshire. It

---

[16] John Watts had been in failing health for several years and for a long time had confined his activities to office administration. He is said to have been of a modest and retiring disposition and is a rather obscure figure in the Doulton story.

The business of John Doulton, Junior (see Note 14), was also included in the amalgamation. The proceeds of the three liquidations were: Doulton & Watts £14,009; Henry Doulton & Co. £33,972; John Doulton, Junior, £9,276. These figures reveal that the pipe business founded by Henry Doulton only seven years previously had already far outstripped the original Doulton & Watts concern.

The new firm, Doulton & Co., was established with a capital of £51,682 in the following shares: John Doulton, Senior 42/125ths; John Doulton, Junior 23/125ths; Henry Doulton 47/125ths; Frederick Doulton 12/125ths; and Alfred Doulton (a younger son of John, Senior) 1/125th. Although Henry did not hold a majority, his shares now exceeded in number those of his father or any of his brothers.

was the first time that he had ever visited at a large country house.
He could not be induced, however, to take any interest in sport, and
usually slipped away as soon as he could to the library. Mr. D'Eyncourt was the uncle of the late Poet Laureate, but, although he had
written verse himself, he did not appreciate his nephew's. Unfortunately the subject of *In Memoriam* (then a comparatively recent
publication) was raised one day at Bayons Manor. Mr. D'Eyncourt,
in his lordly way, said that he could see neither sense nor beauty in
it. This inflamed Henry Doulton, who had become a great admirer
of Tennyson, and in order to convert Mr. D'Eyncourt he began to
recite specially admirable stanzas of *In Memoriam,* with such profusion and emphasis that his host, who had probably never heard so
many verses of his nephew's in the whole of his previous existence,
was fairly put to flight.

Of Henry Doulton's family life during these years comparatively
little is recollected with any exactitude as to detail. His three children
were born during the residence at Stockwell, and the birth of each
of them left their mother more fragile than before. This weakness,
and the constant solicitude which it involved, created almost the
only drawback in the life of Henry Doulton, in other respects full
of serenity and happiness in its gradual flow of prosperity. He bore
the burden of his wife's inability to share his active interests with
inimitable patience and good humour. He was never betrayed into
an expression of petulance. The only sign he gave was of redoubled
attentiveness, a more constant solicitude to be beforehand in gratifying Mrs. Doulton's smallest wish. She, on her part, was marvellously docile and long-suffering under the hand of affliction, and bore
her weakness with a resolute quietness. There are those living still
who remember the young husband tenderly and skilfully carrying
his wife up and down the house and who recall her smile of responive
cheerfulness. But, of course, this condition of things tied Henry
Doulton very closely to his home. He was one who did not find
much pleasure away from those whom he loved, and the difficulty
his wife had in moving from place to place made him also stationary.

Even when the pressures of the business grew less heavy, and his
brain only worked where his hands had once been busy, Henry
Doulton seldom travelled far from his own hearth, curbing, no
doubt, a restlessness which made him at times long for a livelier and
more variegated existence. But he stayed at home. He was fated

never to be, for any length of time, far from the Lambeth where he was born.

His friends occupied, as ever, a large part of his thoughts. He was one of those of whom Edward Fitzgerald speaks, whose 'friendships are more like loves'. He collected around him, or kept close to him, a little group into whose interests and pursuits he entered with passion, and who possessed in full degree his confidence also. We have mentioned Mr. John Hardcastle, to whom on the 19th of November 1849 we find him writing:

> The friendship of boyhood has survived the vicissitudes incident to opening life with all its new connections and engrossing claims, and now it has survived a trial fatal to many only to convince me of its genuineness and strength. I have now no fears for its strength and permanence.

He is speaking, of course, of his own marriage, and in the summer of 1850 Mr. Hardcastle, by his union with a lady whom the Henry Doultons greatly esteemed and admired, merely soldered the link between the friends, which remained unbroken until death snapped it in 1897.

The Lambeth Debating Society continued to be the centre of his intellectual interests. In 1849 Henry Doulton was elected permanent Chairman, and the prosperity of the Society, in many respects a unique one, was from this period secured. Somewhat later than this Mr. Edward Cresy was elected a member, and proved to be a most valuable acquisition. It was at Cresy's house that Henry Doulton formed Charles Darwin's acquaintance about this time. His powers as a philosopher not yet manifested, nor his great theory evolved, Darwin was now no object of theological suspicion or resentment, but only a working naturalist, ardent and obscure.

In 1851 Henry Doulton had become a member of the Society of Arts. It was doubtless in connection with the Great Exhibition that he took that step, for the Society was a principal guarantor of the World's Show. As time went on, this connection was of increasing importance to him, and he owed considerably to it. The advantage, however, was strictly mutual, for Henry Doulton was able on many occasions and in various ways to further the interests of the Society of Arts.

Early in this time of enterprise and experiment, he had a little manufacturing adventure which produced a strong effect upon his mind. He gave the following account of it:

> In connection with the use of lucifer matches which superseded the old sulphur match and tinder box, I remember receiving a visit from a young man named Crampton, who afterwards became a noted engineer. His mother was the proprietress of the bathing machines at Margate. At the request of two gentlemen he had designed a box, to be made of pottery, with a separate compartment for each match, as it was thought by them that it would be dangerous for matches to lie together. After seeing our method of working with clay, he planned and delivered, without a hitch, as perfect a machine as I have ever had to do with. Having put some lumps of clay on a projecting shelf and set the machine in motion, the boxes were rapidly delivered, finished and perfect. I need hardly say such boxes were not needed.[17]

It ought to be explained, perhaps, that each box was a cube of pottery, pierced with holes, each perforation containing one match. As the match was drawn out, by friction against the pottery, it lighted, and came forth spluttering and flaming. The ingenuity of Doulton's mind was exercised and pleased by the difficulty of making such a thing; it had, of course, to be squeezed out of a die. It was a great success as a feat of manufacture but the public would have none of it. Although a great many were made, they totally disappeared. In 1896 Sir Henry Doulton gave out publicly that he would give a good sum of money for one of these match-boxes, but none was forthcoming.

We have already spoken of his schoolboy friendship with James Anderson Rose, the 'tiger'. This relation had at no time ceased, but it was drawn much closer immediately after Henry Doulton's marriage. James Rose was now a solicitor and was cultivating a great interest in the fine arts. At his house on Wandsworth Common, Doulton was first brought into touch with aesthetic interests.

[17] Although Crampton's stoneware match-boxes were not a success, the method used for pressing them out from a die made a great impression on Henry Doulton who later adapted the process successfully for insulators and other products.

Thousands of these boxes were made but they were expensive and few were sold. The remaining stock was eventually carted off in 1850 or thereabouts to be used as hard core for new roads in Brixton and Tulse Hill.

William, the brother of James—afterwards Sir William and Lord Mayor of London—was another associate of these years. James was a cultivated man, and he was, to an unusual degree, an exhilarating and stimulating companion. There was no better company, to the last, than James Anderson Rose. At his home Henry Doulton met Mr. Frederick Sandys, the now-celebrated artist, then quite unknown, and recently arrived from Norwich, bent on distinguishing himself in the manner of Holbein. In 1863 he had painted the portrait of old Mrs. Susanna Rose, which remains not merely one of Mr. Sandys' masterpieces, but one of the notable productions of English art in that generation. It is as exact and as radiant as a Mabuse. Fired with the idea of encouraging such very brilliant talent as this, Henry Doulton sat to Mr. Sandys for the exquisite portrait reproduced in this volume.

Edward Cresy too was not unconnected with art. He had, indeed, been educated in Paris as an architect, and had then contracted a friendship for an artist a little older than himself, afterwards famous throughout Europe as Eugène Viollet-le-Duc. This acquaintance was kept up until Cresy's untimely death in 1871. Cresy was one of the founders of the old Board of Works, and his father before him had been professionally engaged in engineering. At the very beginning of his independent career as a maker of pipes, Henry Doulton had been brought into relation with the elder Cresy, who lived at Dartford in Kent. Thus he met Edward, and immediately recognised in him a zealous and imaginative spirit, closely akin to his own. It was through Edward Cresy that Doulton became acquainted with Calderon, Marks, Storey and other young painters who were just coming forward as the St. John's Wood school.

His social interests, however, throughout the Stockwell period, largely centred in the house of James Baldwin Brown. This refined and enlightened man, by only three or four weeks Henry Doulton's junior, had been one of the ornaments of the University College School when Doulton also was a student there. He began his clerical career, as an Independent minister, under the influence of Carlyle, and from the first he had attracted attention by his teaching, catholic at once and spiritual. The elder John Doulton was one of the most prominent of those who persuaded Baldwin Brown to come over into South London in 1846 and accept the ministry of Claylands Chapel, Clapham Road, which he held until, in 1870, his congregation overflowed and carried him upon their tide to the much larger Congregational church in the Brixton Road.

At the Baldwin Brown's it was, as we have seen, that Henry Doulton met Sarah Kennaby early in 1849. Mrs. Baldwin Brown still remembers his invasions of the house—'such a bright creature, always ablaze and flaring with some new idea'. Her husband exactly appreciated his friend. To someone, who in these early years complained that Henry Doulton was 'erratic', Baldwin Brown replied, 'Oh! no, not erratic, but enthusiastic; his spirit is off with a start and a leap, but, believe me, it always knows exactly where it is going!' Baldwin Brown, without question, gained a great deal himself from Doulton's enthusiasm and freshness. They made it a practice to discuss together the burning questions of that revolutionary period. Religion, education, politics, poetry—all were hammered out by the brilliant pair of talkers.

In those days the cry of 'heresy' was in the air. Anyone who was anxious for an unconventional aspect of truth was branded as a 'heretic'. Baldwin Brown, the most spiritually minded of men, did not escape the accusation; he was looked upon by some as a dangerous man. In these conditions he was not unwilling to have a champion; he had, in fact, many, but none more ardent than Henry Doulton.

Two distinguished men whose acquaintance Doulton formed about this time were Maurice and Lynch. Frederick Denison Maurice was drawn to Baldwin Brown by similarity of views. He was at this time greatly impressed with the prospects of the so-called Christian Socialists. More interesting to Henry Doulton than F. D. Maurice's religious views were his schemes for pushing forward the principle of co-operation. On this subject Doulton had several conversations with him about 1855, but to his own strictly business-like and somewhat positive habit of mind, the sentimental vagueness of Maurice was rather annoying. He, nevertheless, offered his help when Maurice proposed to arrange some lectures on those and kindred subjects in Lambeth, but I do not find any record of their coming to anything definite.

Another accomplished and charming heretic was Thomas Toke Lynch. Between 1856, when on account of ill-health he resigned his church in Grafton Street, and 1860, when he resumed a charge in Gower Street, Lynch was a very frequent visitor at Stockwell. He had published in 1855 a small volume of hymns called *The Rivulet* the theology in which was considered unsound; Lynch carried the Wordsworthian worship of Nature to the very edge of pantheism. He was violently attacked in several quarters, and the once-famous 'Rivulet Controversy' shook the world of Congregationalism and waked echoes far beyond those limits. Lynch was a good and gentle man, in poor health, with a touch, perhaps, of hysteria. He was scandalously attacked, but his replies lacked dignity; he published an answer in a volume of *Songs Controversial,* which answered nothing. He was defended with great warmth, and the protest which really settled the 'Rivulet Controversy' in Lynch's favour was signed by the fifteen leading ministers of the Union, of whom Baldwin Brown was one. Lynch's visits to the Doultons' at this time were long remembered, and how he used to sit and sing at the piano, throwing so much energy into the melody that first one of his slippers and then the other would fly from the music-stool. Lynch died in 1871, at the age of fifty-three.

A painful incident interrupted the even tenor of family life in 1857. Mr. and Mrs. Henry Doulton were driving one afternoon in a mail-phaeton along the Clapham Road, with their little son, Lewis, ensconced between them, when the horse bolted, and presently came into violent collision with a coal-waggon. The carriage was smashed to pieces, and its occupants flung into the street. Henry Doulton himself escaped with some bad bruises, and little Lewis was absolutely untouched, but unhappily Mrs. Doulton received internal injuries from which she never recovered, although she lived on for more than twenty years. By a curious coincidence, the accident happened exactly opposite the house of the family physician, and Mrs. Doulton had the immediate advantage of the most careful attention. What was very unfortunate was that, although she did not appear to be severely hurt, the accident greatly exaggerated the delicacy of her nervous system, and tended to make her henceforward a confirmed invalid. Her children have no memory of ever having seen her walk after this distressing occurrence.

The doctor, who has just been mentioned as attending the Doultons in their Stockwell days, was an interesting man. This was Dr. Ward, to whose remarkable invention of the Wardian Case botany owes so much. He had observed the difficulty, nay, the impossibility, of bringing living specimens of tropical plants safe to

E

England, and he had, after a long series of experiments, constructed a case so sealed that it contained an atmosphere which would condense and evaporate in rotation without commerce with the outer air. In these Wardian cases the chemical circulation was perfect; each was a living world in miniature. Since that day, botanists have brought almost all their delicate treasures home in this way. Dr. Ward had a very curious botanical garden round his house, called The Roses, opposite the Union Road, at the Stockwell end of the Clapham Road, and this was a favourite haunt of Henry Doulton. Mrs. Doulton's constant ill-health made the ardent and intelligent botanist-physician a frequent visitor and in time a familiar friend at 7, Stockwell Villas.

From time to time, with the growth of sanitary science, Henry Doulton introduced many special inventions. It is difficult in a work of this kind, which is not intended for scientific readers, to dwell on technical matters. However, it is worth recording that he patented stoneware junction blocks in 1854 and invert blocks in 1858. About the latter year, stoneware street-gullies were first made, and this was an innovation attended with considerable difficulty; however, in the course of time, their use gradually became universal. Domestic arrangements in stoneware, as improvements were made in town drainage, came by degrees into extensive use in the humbler class of dwellings, and were supplied by the firm to all parts of the kingdom, but especially to those towns which were sewered and drained under some of the engineers of the 1848 Board of Health.[18] It would hardly be possible to exaggerate the public benefit which accrued from this adaptation of stoneware to the requirements of the modern systems of drainage. During this early period, Doulton and Co. were very extensively manufacturing an oval species of pipes of large diameter which they had patented about 1848. These were largely adopted in the drainage of several important towns of the North of England, notably Manchester. But, as Henry Doulton early admitted, 'the insertion of junctions was always a difficulty as the form of the oval pipe does not admit of adjustment of the angle at which the branch enters'. Hence, although the oval pipe held its ground until about 1863, and though at first many advantages were claimed for it, yet it gradually died out, and now has for a long time been practically obsolete.

[18] By 'domestic arrangements' Gosse meant water closets.

It was in 1859 that Henry Doulton began to make stoneware sinks, which rank among his important sanitary innovations. That his mind turned to this neglected matter is an instance of the quickness of his observation. When he took the house at Tooting which will presently be described, he noticed an old stone sink, which had been taken out of the kitchen. The smell from it was offensive, and it suddenly occurred to Henry Doulton that sinks would be much more cleanly if they could be made in pottery and so be no longer liable to have grease driven into the pores. To invent a process, however, proved to be singularly difficult. In order to be practicable, the sinks must be flat, with a rim. Whatever he could do, they would insist on warping. For the advantage of the non-technical readers, it may be explained that in all pottery there is a double drying process. First of all, the free water evaporates and the clay seems dry to the touch. But it is really still full of water, chemically combined, inappreciable to the senses, and this has to be driven out in the fire. The difficulty of driving off this without loss of form is one of the potter's great solicitudes. In the case of sinks, for a long time, do what Henry Doulton would, they insisted upon curling up like so many cocked hats.

When this initial drawback was at length removed by the exercise of patience and ingenuity it was a considerable time before the public would appreciate these articles. Henry Doulton was in the habit of saying that had it not been for the warm support of Sir Robert Rawlinson he would have been obliged to discontinue their manufacture. For the first few years these sinks were chiefly used in Paris, and very few in our own country. In time, however, their excellence became universally acknowledged, and for many years past scarcely a stone sink has been found in even the most humble dwelling in England.

It was somewhat earlier than this, in 1852, that screw stoppers for bottles were first made in stoneware. Henry Doulton's power of absorption of ideas was extraordinary. Almost all his most valuable results were led up to by some trifling observation. He was not always looking at objects; in fact he had a curious way of falling for a few moments into a sort of dreamy concentration in which he did not seem to see anything at all; but out of this absorbed condition he would suddenly wake up in a mood of preternatural alertness, and when he did notice a thing he took it in with extreme exactitude.

As an old friend of his says to me, 'his soul had hungry fibres'. Thus the important invention of these stoneware screw stoppers arose from so trifling a circumstance as Henry Doulton watching a man cut a rough screw in a piece of wood to keep the air out of a bottle. 'If in wood,' he said to himself, with his quick intuition, 'why not in stoneware?' and at once began his experiments. Immense difficulty was experienced in devising a suitable machine for the manufacture of this invention, but when this was surmounted, the importance of the appliance was proved by the eagerness with which the public welcomed the stoneware screws which were later turned out in myriads from Lambeth.

In 1861 the earliest record is made of one of those visits to the pottery by eminent persons which later on became so striking a feature of the life at Lambeth. Archbishop Sumner, who had held the Primacy since the death of Howley in 1848, had had several pleasant relations with his active and growing neighbours at Doulton and Co.'s. The Archbishop—although now both aged and in bad health, for he was over eighty, and in May 1861 had been weakened by a serious illness—was greatly interested in all the new developments of the industry. He sent a message to Henry Doulton that he should like to see 'so many men and boys busy making blacking-bottles under his very windows', and accordingly he made a lengthy visit to the works. Sumner was the third of seven Archbishops of Canterbury of whom Henry Doulton had personal recollection at the time of his death.

During these last years at Stockwell, Henry Doulton found the necessity of more frequent changes than he had felt before. He was prosperous, and he could afford to remit occasionally, for a few weeks, the vigilance of his watch over the Lambeth Works. He went in the summer with his little children to the seaside, but in these years his great passion for scenery was not yet developed. He spent the great part of his leisure not in sightseeing but in reading. His eldest daughter recollects spending a morning with him on the beach at Weymouth. The sea gradually rose and cut them off from the shore, while Henry Doulton, absolutely absorbed in a book of poetry, remained oblivious of the fact. The little girl, on the contrary, was wide awake to it, but so absolute was her confidence in her father that she did not think it necessary to draw his attention to the rising tide. At last the water touched the dreamer, as it had touched

King Canute, and it became needful to wade back to the shore as promptly as might be.

Another small incident illustrates Henry Doulton's absorption in literature. About 1853 he took, for the summer, for his family, a house at Datchet, coming up to Lambeth every day by train. He immediately reflected that the daily double journey offered a chance not to be allowed to escape. He determined to dedicate it to Gibbon, and by persistently working away morning and evening, he contrived, before the family returned to Stockwell, to have read in the train *The Decline and Fall* from beginning to end. He was, indeed, at once a rapid and a solid reader, of a type becoming more and more rare in this age of patches and snippets.

4

A tentative period
1860 to 1868

A change of residence from Stockwell to then almost rural Upper Tooting was indicative of Henry Doulton's advancement in prosperity. Woodlands, as the house to which he moved was called, was a double-fronted house of no architectural pretensions, standing pleasantly secluded in a largish garden. There was a huge cedar-tree at the back of it, which, to the disappointment of some of his friends, Henry Doulton was eventually led to sacrifice to a system of meandering paths. He greatly enlarged and improved Woodlands before he left it. At first it was commodious enough to take in his little family of five persons, and the situation attracted him. He was tired of the 'towniness' of Stockwell, which was too near to Lambeth to offer him either the certainty of rest or an inducement for exercise. He wanted to keep a horse for riding, that being then, as always, his favourite and indeed almost unique active amusement.

At Woodlands he touched the country, and the earliest thing he did was to go over to Cresy, and to insist on his joining in horse exercise. The very first time the friends went out they made a round of thirty miles. Henceforth, his horse was a main element in Henry Doulton's existence; he rode every morning to Lambeth and back to Tooting at night. Whenever he could he used to tempt Cresy away for excursions. They scoured Kent and Surrey together, and Cresy's knowledge of antiquities and of geology were a constant source of delight to his companion. 'Cresy,' Henry Doulton used to say, 'is sensitive to any change in the surface of the land, and keeps me all agog for a crisis in stratification.'

Cresy possessed to an extreme degree a genius for trespassing, in the exercise of which he was followed somewhat timidly by the more law-abiding Doulton. Cresy would read a notice-board, warning trespassers off, and would say: 'That fellow must have something good in there to be so anxious to keep it to himself. Let's go in!' And Henry Doulton, quaking a little inwardly, and mildly deprecating, would enter into the frolic, and trespass too.

It is said that the first introduction to one of their intimate friends was brought about by a freak of the uncontrollable Cresy, who insisted on entering some attractive property, and held the keeper and a policeman spellbound with bewildering Socratic conversation until the owner also arrived, to be drawn into the same web, and kept there for the remainder of his existence. Henry Doulton was accustomed in later years to tell those and similar stories with a little shudder and shrug of the shoulders, for, when not led away by the frivolity of Edward Cresy, he was a very great respecter of other people's property.

About 1861, Henry Doulton began a systematic study of the writings of Mr. Ruskin, which then included not merely *The Seven Lamps* and *The Stones of Venice,* but the full series of *Modern Painters,* then recently concluded. These books he read greedily, to the neglect, for the time being, of every other species of literature. His devotion to Wordsworth had prepared him for subjugation to Ruskin's religion of beauty, and he fell before it without a struggle. He was accustomed to declare in after years—when some of Mr. Ruskin's economic irregularities had sorely tested the disciple's constancy— 'but I ought not to say a word that is ungrateful, for no one can tell what Ruskin has been to me'. The interest which Henry Doulton presently began to take in the art-product of his pottery, and his newly born enthusiasm for natural scenery, were both due in large measure to the teaching of Ruskin. He began to feel ashamed that at the age of forty he had never seen an Alpine mountain.

Accordingly in August 1862 Henry Doulton, in company with three friends, started on the first important visit which he made to the Continent. A journal of this tour is preserved. Through Paris and Geneva, they passed directly to Martigny, and over the Tête Noire to Chamonix. The weather was brilliantly fine, and Henry Doulton's earliest impression of the colour of Swiss scenery, and especially of its various blues and whites, was rapturous. They descended by Aosta to Milan, and passed on to Baveno; by

Domodossola and over the Simplon they returned to Switzerland. They rode on horseback up to Zermatt, where the unwavering note of ecstasy which has hitherto pervaded the journal changes— 'Zermatt neither clean nor picturesque—rained heavily all day.'

They went up to the Riffel and wandered over the Gemmi to Kandersteg, but, at whatever point they tarried, the weather was now hopelessly bad, and the friends hastened in torrents of rain to Interlaken. They ascended the Righi and sailed on the Lake of Lucerne; and then, by Zürich and Baden, loitering as they went, they reached Germany, and so returned to England on the 12th of September after an absence of five weeks. It would be impossible to describe a journey more commonplace in its outlines, but its effect on Henry Doulton was considerable. His observation was now at its quickest, and was entirely unspoiled; at the age of forty-two, with the eyes which Ruskin had brightened for him, he was seeing snow-mountains and the Alpine sublimity for the first time. This journey vastly increased his susceptibility to natural beauty.

The 1862 International Exhibition in London was a triumph for the Doultons. The arrangement of the Lambeth wares was made with great pains by Henry Doulton himself. It became obvious now that he was ahead of any of his English competitors in his particular fields of activity and they were the first to acknowledge it. On the opening day one of the leading country potters came up to him and said, 'Mr. Doulton, you are supreme for the next ten years.' Another, after a careful inspection of the goods sent in from Lambeth, turned and generously expressed the universal opinion, 'Your exhibition is superb!' It must not be forgotten, of course, that it was almost entirely of the sanitary and general wares of which these admiring rivals spoke. Utilitarian stoneware was the Lambeth staple, and it mainly consisted of pipes, chemical vessels and house-hold requisites, with stoneware bottles and figure jugs.

In all this there was little connection with the later so-called 'art-pottery'. Practically the limit of colour-decoration applicable at this time to the Doulton salt-glaze stoneware was that set by the beha-viour during firing of red ochre, in which the tops of bottles and jugs were dipped to give them a rich brown colour in contrast to the lighter brown or buff below. Decoration with runners or relief-moulding was the only ornament, pretty enough in its limited extent. When, therefore, the idea of attempting to produce really artistic work was first suggested to Henry Doulton he was indifferent and even adverse. His mind was fully occupied with the useful manufactures. The great thing was that the stoneware, and above all the sanitary stoneware, should be correct and cheap. That its fittings should be exact and its surface smooth, that it should properly fulfil its practical purpose, was all that he cared about. Anything beyond this struck him as chimerical, as a matter of a fantastic nature which it would only waste his time to entertain. It must be clearly borne in mind that this was Henry Doulton's attitude up to 1860, and even later, and that it needed pressure from outside, and a combination of favourable circumstances, to turn his mind, so remarkable for its unity of purpose, to that new order of thoughts which was soon to become its special occupation and chief delight.

The history of the revival of the old *grès de Flandres* pottery at Lambeth naturally occupies so large a place in any record of the life of Henry Doulton that no apology is needed for a somewhat detailed description of the events which led up to it. It was closely connected with the Lambeth School of Art, which had been founded by Dr. Gregory soon after he first came to Lambeth as curate in 1851. This gentleman, afterwards greatly distinguished in the Church—he became Dean of St. Paul's in 1891—had felt the requirement of some centre of artistic influence in his vast and laborious parish, and the year after he became incumbent of St. Mary the Less, Lambeth, in 1853, he set up, under the aegis of South Kensington, an elementary class for art study, in the Boys' School which was attached to his church.

This was an inconvenient place; the classes could only be held at night, and everything had to be cleared away each time, in preparation for the school next morning. In 1857, however, the classes had become so far encouraging, that it was determined to loose this connection with South Kensington, and Mr. John Sparkes, then an ardent and successful young teacher, having his choice of several new centres at a distance, refused them all as less practically hopeful than the population of 700,000 souls in South London, whose darkness was illuminated by nothing whatever artistic except this little trembling rush-light in the Boys' School-room.

In 1857 Mr. Sparkes took sole charge of the Lambeth School of Art, and set it on an independent basis. He had not long been settled at his work when it occurred to him that a school situated in the heart of a settlement of potters ought to do something to advance the beauty as well as the utility of pottery. He consulted Dr. Gregory, afterwards so warm a friend of Henry Doulton, as to the advisability of taking the great potter into his confidence. He was not encouraged to do so. The name of Doulton, in those days, seemed little associated with the idea of art, and the incumbent of St. Mary the Less, moreover, with his High Church and High Tory views, was at this time extremely out of sympathy with Henry Doulton, whom he identified, correctly, with dissent and the heresies of Baldwin Brown, and, less correctly, with a radicalism from which the potter was already swerving towards what came to be called the Liberal-Conservative Party. In any case, Dr. Gregory offered no introduction and no encouragement.

Mr. Sparkes was not to be daunted. He presented himself at the potteries, and called upon the master. Henry Doulton was polite but indifferent. He told the artist that his ideas were unpractical; that what they had to do at Lambeth was to provide a utilitarian class of goods for the general public, and to see that they were the best of their kind for practical purposes. He told Mr. Sparkes that the heat and salt necessary for the manufacture of stoneware were fatal to colours, and that it was no use to talk about it.

Even as he spoke his eye wandered; he was evidently taking no heed of what his visitor urged, but was impatient for him to go, and leave him to his practical affairs. Mr. Sparkes was disappointed but he could urge his scheme no more for the moment. At this time Mr. Sparkes had no acquaintance within the rather narrow limits of Doulton's circle of friends. The time was not ripe yet, and the idea was forced to wait.

The next impetus came from a different and independent quarter. Edward Cresy had been shown by Henry Stacy Marks, the future R.A., an ancient Rhenish salt-cellar which he had picked up somewhere on the Continent. This was an example of the siliceous pottery made in the sixteenth century by the potters of Cologne, decorated with incised and applied ornaments, and enriched with cobalt-blue. This was the first example of *grès de Flandres 'kannetje'* which Cresy had seen, and it interested him extremely. About 1859, he secured a pot of this kind for his private collection, and pondered long on the best way to use it as an object-lesson. When he first suggested to Henry Doulton, as Mr. Sparkes had done a year or two earlier, that he should try to produce something of the same kind he was met at first with the same incredulity. It could not be attempted; it would be waste of time; Henry Doulton had other things to think of. He heard of *grès de Flandres* for the first time without any desire to emulate it. Cresy, however, did not abandon his notion. He looked up the history of Rhenish stoneware. He studied the story of how Jacqueline, Countess of Hainault, made pots in her prison at Feybingen in 1424. He came down to the moment when Napoleon, about 1812, impeded the art by putting a prohibitory duty upon salt. He perpended, and waited for his opportunity.

Meanwhile, Mr. Sparkes had been busy with his own tentative efforts. Failing to get a hearing at Doulton's, he employed one of his students who happened to be a workman at Stiff's pottery, to carry out a series of experiments.[19] In 1864, Mr. William De Morgan had set up a kiln in the cellar of his father's house in Fitzroy Square, and here he began to fire tiles with soft enamel colours. Mr. Sparkes set his pupils to draw on tiles, and to try various combinations and varieties of hue, and Mr. De Morgan fired them for him. Success was neither instantaneous nor brilliant, but still advance was made in a knowledge of what would and would not stand the heat of the kiln. In 1860 the Art Schools had been transferred to Miller's Lane, and wide attention to them was drawn by the circumstance that the earliest public act of the youthful Prince of Wales was to lay the first stone of the new building. To the cost of these schools Henry Doulton now contributed liberally, as a good citizen of Lambeth, but still he took no personal interest in them and had not conceived the idea that they would come to have a practical influence on his business.

All this while, Edward Cresy, without any knowledge of Mr. Sparkes' experiments, was persisting in his idea. He told Henry Doulton that it was not worthy of such a lover of poetry as he to

[19] By the mid-eighteenth century the most important of the Lambeth delftware potteries was one which lay between the Thames and Back Lane (now Lambeth High Street). It occupied part of a site of a former London residence of the Bishops of Hereford and was successively owned by Abigail Griffith, Griffith & Morgan and James Stiff & Sons. It later became part of Doulton's Lambeth factory. James Stiff had been a foreman in Doulton & Watts before launching out on his own about 1840.

confine himself to utility, but that he owed it to the world to try to add to beauty also. In 1862 he persuaded Doulton to allow one of his potters to copy his *grès de Flandres* pot as carefully as he could. The ornament was reproduced with a scratched line, and cobalt-blue put into the incisions. In the kiln, however, all the colour fled, leaving a dull surface of uniform brownish grey, with no other ornament than the scratched outline. However, for better or worse, this unattractive object was the earliest piece of Doulton Ware manufactured. The great potter, still unconvinced, gazed at it with irony; it was an ugly little thing, he very justly said. But he allowed it to appear among his goods in the Exhibition of 1862, where only one man recognised it as what it really was, the earliest glimmering of a new art.

That one man, however, was Mr. Sparkes, who started with surprise and pleasure at the sight of such an unexpected confirmation of his long frustrated hopes. He did not, however, see his way at once to making any further application to the Doultons. He pushed on with his own experiments in the firing of coloured pottery and early in 1863 some designs, painted by his students, offered such excellent results that he resolved to have the courage of his convictions and try Henry Doulton once more. He called at the pottery with some of his tiles, and the reception he received was in striking contrast with what he had met with six years before. The exhibition of 1862 had put Henry Doulton in a very different position from that which he had previously occupied. His name was now established as that of the most accurate and efficient of English stoneware potters. His works were now run on a system which ensured practical perfection in manufacture. The Lambeth School of Art, too, had secured a very different prestige. It was becoming acknowledged as one of the most vigorous of the new art centres of the kingdom. In 1862 it had produced two gold medallists in one year. Both Doulton's pottery and the Lambeth School of Art had passed out of their first tentative stages. They could ensure respect, and the time had come when each was prepared to look to the other for encouragement.

As an immediate result of their conversation, Henry Doulton invited Mr. Sparkes to dinner at Woodlands, and the only other guests were Edward Cresy and James Anderson Rose. The three men last-mentioned now met for the first time, and were consciously drawn to one another by an instant sympathy. The almost preternatural activity of Cresy's mind particularly and immediately struck Mr. Sparkes, and by a tacit understanding across the table, they entered into a compact for the conversion of their host. Accordingly, the talk was all of what could be done to restore the lost art of ornamental stoneware. Henry Doulton confessed his ignorance of the history of art pottery, but exhibited the greatest eagerness to be instructed, and his large eyes gleamed with the light of a revelation as his friends talked of the wonders of the past, of Nevers and of Henri Deux, of Delft earthenware and Nuremburg faïence, or most warmly of all, of the richly decorated Rhenish and Franconian stoneware of the sixteenth and seventeenth centuries. This little dinner-party of four was really the occasion of the renaissance of art pottery in Lambeth. From this moment the progress of the art might be slow, and might be uncertain in direction, but it had begun to move.

Before we pass on to the earliest experiments into which Henry Doulton, under the guidance of his friends, threw himself with increasing ardour, two branches of his more utilitarian business have to arrest our attention. As an annex to the drain-pipe manufacture, Henry Doulton turned his thoughts in or about 1862 to the improvement of filters. At the house of William Blades, the printer, he met a young man, who later became distinguished as the Waynflete Professor of Chemistry at Oxford, Mr. William Odling. Doulton had been much struck with Odling's *Manual of Chemistry* (1861), a book which was of remarkable influence in its day, and he turned to him eagerly for theoretical support in his new order of practical ideas. As he said himself, 'Everything told me that the filter trade was completely played out, but I was convinced that it was capable of resuscitation. The reason why this important branch of industry had languished was because it had not changed with the times. The crude, old-fashioned form of earthenware filter had been adhered to.' With the purpose of inventing a new and improved filtering medium, Henry Doulton consulted the late Dr. Bernays, who suggested manganous carbon. In the selecting of the carbon, Professor Odling's intuitions and experience were of the greatest service, and he was at this very time pursuing those investigations into the chemical change of carbon, which he gave to the world in 1869. In adapting to practical manufacture all the mechanical improvements in the arrangement of the filter, as to access and cleaning, the Doultons, of course, had no rival to fear, and in a short time they were offering to the trade by far the best filter that could be bought. The filter consisted of superimposed blocks of carbon, screwed to the bottom of a stoneware basket, the junction being absolutely watertight. This, it is safe to say, was a domestic innovation of extraordinary value.

About the year 1863, Henry Doulton announced in the private circle of his friends that he was going to extend his business in yet another direction. He had determined to manufacture plumbago crucibles and he believed there was a fortune to be made in them.[20] Edward Cresy was averse to the idea. Perhaps he thought that it would direct Doulton's mind from those studies in the history of artistic pottery in which he was just showing himself so eager a pupil. Perhaps the idea of the 'fortune' was an ambition unknown to Cresy, and foreign to his sympathy. He told his friend that he had enough to occupy his thoughts already, and, besides, that the crucible manufacture was already in the hands of certain firms, who ought to be left undisturbed. 'Don't poach,' Cresy said, 'on other people's preserves.' To this Doulton had an instant and effective reply. 'I propose,' he said, 'to try to make better and more accurately shaped crucibles than anyone has done before—crucibles exactly fitted to their purpose.'

Doulton devised, after much thought, a system by which the crucible was fashioned in a rotating plaster of Paris mould, down on to which came a steel arm so precisely adjusted that the thickness of the pot could be made absolutely accurate, the expensive material being slapped in and roughly moulded with the hand, before being compressed and sharply defined between the wall of the mould and the steel arm. From this invention or adaptation very large profits accrued.[21]

[20] Plumbago is a refractory material, composed mainly of a mixture of graphite and fireclay, used extensively for making crucibles for metal foundries. German manufacturers had a monopoly up to about 1856 when the Patent Plumbago Crucible Company (later the Morgan Crucible Company Ltd.) began to make them at Battersea. The manufacture of plumbago crucibles at Lambeth was discontinued about 1934.

[21] This was not an original invention but an adaptation of a shaping process (known in the pottery industry as 'jolleying') which was already being used in Staffordshire for making cups and other small hollow-wares. The first jolley is believed to have been used by Charles J. Mason, inventor of Mason's 'Ironstone China', in 1843.

In this, as in so many other cases, it is necessary to emphasise the fact that Henry Doulton, in a very great measure, owed his phenomenal and unfaltering success to his zealous determination to get good work done, and to his practical comprehension of what good work was. His shrewdness amounted almost to an art of magic. He knew by intuition what was going on in every part of his large and ever-spreading premises. He was scandalised by rough work; he simply would not allow what was scamped or unevenly finished to leave the place. One of those who knew him longest said to me, 'It was wonderful how bad potting used to "rile" Sir Henry; it made him quite ill.'

Often, as he went about his magisterial inspection, he would stop before a workman, caught by his instinct for almost invisible imperfections; and before the fellow knew what he was doing, the pot he had just made would be cut down with a wire in the accurate hand of the master, and an error in potting stand revealed. He would have an actual finished work broken if anything made him suspect that all was not proceeding with perfect exactitude. His clairvoyance often struck those about him as little short of miraculous. One, who had known him long, tells me that Sir Henry Doulton would be standing at a window in Lambeth, apparently in a brown study, when one of the hands would appear a long way off, carrying a load upon his shoulders. Something too impalpable to be defined would suddenly awaken Doulton's suspicions, he would give an order, the yard-chap would bring in the load and display its contents at his feet. Never, on these occasions—so they declare at Lambeth—would the master's intuition have been at fault. Something in that load would be sure to be as it should not. No doubt, this rather uncanny legend of the supernatural acumen of the chief kept the average of merit at the pottery remarkably high.

An important feature in Sir Henry Doulton's character was the definiteness of his aims. At any given moment, he knew exactly what he wanted, and on this and on nothing less did he concentrate his powers. Accordingly the stages in his career are remarkably simple. From his early apprenticeship to 1846 he wanted to be a sound and practised potter, and to comprehend the existing business to its innermost recesses. From 1846 to about 1856 he was introducing, in the face of every kind of prejudice and opposition, the drain-pipe system which he made practically universal in this

country. When that had taken hold of the public mind, he was able
to turn to another matter, the technical perfection, in accuracy,
smoothness and durability, of his various chemical manufactures. It
was this which really occupied him from 1856 to 1863, and each of
those ambitions absorbed him exclusively, giving him no respite,
making other schemes and prolongations of his business seem preposterous. Hence it was that, when the fine-art proposals were made
to him before the time for them was ripe, he rejected them without
consideration. Nothing in business existed for Henry Doulton,
except that which was appropriate to the immediate time and place.
He was akin in this to the boy in the old story, who, when he
accidently caught a salmon when he was dibbling for roach, flung
the prize angrily back into the water, saying, 'If I fish for roach, I
want to catch roach.'

The hours of Doulton's leisure were, through this period of his
career, as in those which have been already described, given to
music and literature. The removal to Tooting had not increased, it
had rather restricted, his social dissipations. He led, with his invalid
wife, and his circle of growing children, a rigorously domestic life.
A certain expansion of the old Lambeth Friendly Debating Society
had steadily gone on, and Henry Doulton had for several years been
permanent Chairman, when in 1860 it was thought advisable to
reconstruct the Society under a less lumbering name. Bacon happened
at the moment to be the object of Henry Doulton's particular
worship, and his works and his philosophic tendency had been
under discussion in particularly interesting meetings. It was accordingly suggested that the name of the Society should be altered to
the Verulam Club. The motto of the Club was to be 'The end of
our foundation is the knowledge of causes and secret motions of
things, and the enlarging of the bands of human empire'.

At a meeting on the 6th of November 1860, this change was
adopted, and the Verulam Club—a name so familiar in the ears of
every friend of Henry Doulton—came into existence full-formed.
Among those present on that evening were his brother Frederick
Doulton, M.P., John Hardcastle, Sir William and James Anderson
Rose, Joseph Pewtress, Edward Cresy, Sir Robert Rawlinson and
Mr. R. Ellington, all notable elements in the social and intellectual
life of their friend at this time. Theirs were the natures which
principally revolved about the burning centre of his enthusiasm and

versatile intelligence. The activity of the Society greatly increased with its formation into the Verulam Club, and the number of members also. The subjects chosen for discourse became more and more timely. Very soon after the publication of *The Origin of Species*, for instance, we find Darwin and his theory of evolution the subject of an animated session of the Verulam Club, parties being sharply divided on the burning controversy which that great book raised. The secretary during these years was Mr. John Hardcastle. On the 2nd of February 1863 the meeting of the Verulam Club was held at the Mansion House, Alderman Sir William Rose being Lord Mayor that year. The subject for discussion, on that occasion, was 'Should Dependency or Independency be the Future of our Colonies', a theme on which Henry Doulton was already beginning to hold what have since come to be called strongly imperialistic views.

About this time, or a little later, Henry Doulton began to slip away from the Liberal Party in politics, and especially from Mr. Gladstone, in whom his confidence was greatly shaken by the events which led up to the crisis of 1868. Baldwin Brown, on the contrary, was drawn close to Mr. Gladstone, of the wisdom and propriety of whose policy he saw no reason to entertain a doubt, and whose personal acquaintance he made, coming under the direct fascination of that seductive genius. Henry Doulton became, during these years, less and less concerned with party politics, though as we shall see, he afterwards resumed an interest in them. He drifted apart from his family, his father and his brother John remaining staunch radicals. Henry took more interest in the local life of Lambeth; it cannot be questioned that his action in parochial affairs was extremely public-spirited and useful. He used to point, with a just pride, to innumerable improvements which he had been able, in the course of his career, to introduce into the life of the parish of Lambeth.

Of his political convictions it will be convenient to speak later on. At present they were somewhat indefinite, although floating in a Conservative direction. As early as 1856, he began to be extremely interested in a matter which was to be of vital importance to him in his business, namely the degree in which it is the province of governments to interfere by legislature between capital and labour. His eldest brother, moved by the eloquence of F. D. Maurice and the new school of Christian Socialists, was anxious to encourage this. Henry Doulton thought such interference dangerous.

F

I differ from John, [he wrote], commerce, religion, and labour, too, are healthier if left to work out their own salvation with the exercise of honesty and common-sense, than if taught to expect the officious meddling of the State. Take care that you do not complicate our evils. We have arrived at a moment in our national history when we are invaded by a general passion for undoing what our fathers have done. But recollect what interests are at stake. Recollect that the infraction of a principle may give us a temporary advantage, but it is always attended with disastrous results. Go on if you like; produce your palliatives and your sudden changes, but remember that you must take the consequences, and that the weakest will go to the wall.

The man who wrote this might still call himself a Liberal, and might, as Henry Doulton did, strenuously deny that he was 'a party man' at all. But it is quite obvious that he was moving in a direction opposite to radicalism and that in heart he was already, as afterwards he avowed, a staunch Tory of the constitutional kind.

But about 1865 it was doubtless the question of education which moved him most, and this also away from any sympathy with the new Liberalism. He had no love for the uniformity of secular teaching. He was constitutionally averse from cut and dried plans of universal action. He thought that wisdom might be found in varied systems. The Dissenters of his youth had thought so too, and it had been part of their principle to oppose all forms of state influence. His friend Mr. Ellington became a heated supporter of the Gladstonian views on the subject, and had to endure endless jocularity from Henry Doulton, who had no patience with, and no pity for, that newly discovered and highly sensitive organ of the body politic, the Nonconformist Conscience. And so, without any cessation of the friendliest relations of life, he drifted more and more away from the views which had been more than popular, had been almost universal, in Lambeth, nor was it long before he could shake hands with Canon Gregory over the defeat of Mr. Gladstone at Oxford in 1868.

But his real enjoyment, now, as ever, was in poetry. His appetite for the great English poets grew as the years passed on. For Wordsworth, in particular, he knew no shadow of satiety, and the great sonnets or the 'Ode on Intimations of Immortality' were read by him for the thousandth time as if for the first. Among his rare notes on these subjects, which happen to have been preserved, I find (February 12, 1868) these words, jotted down with absolute simplicity:

> How real is Wordsworth's sentiment of life, how vivid the sensation he gives one! Truth is carried to one's heart by his passion for it. How he glorifies common things! All the gamut of poetic pleasure seems embraced by him; he rises as high as 'Paradise Lost', he comes down to the level of 'The Babes in the Wood'. His meditative pathos overwhelms me, and I approach his presence with an unconscious awe. Wordsworth demands the reverent spirit. But what a reaction it is from the artificiality of life to enter into his thoughts and his music.

At this same time, I see, he was reading with close study Coleridge, the Brownings, and Keats. As to Tennyson, he was positively steeped in his 'unfathomable sweetness', as he called it. But, after all, it was to Wordsworth alone he inevitably returned after every excursion in other fields. In Wordsworth alone, but in Wordsworth to the very end of his life, he found unfailing and ever-renewed poetical satisfaction. He did not keep this pleasure to himself, but was for ever trying to reconcile others of a more prosaic temperament to his own enthusiasm. The unwilling were held by his glittering eye, while, another Ancient Mariner, he kept them listening to quotations from his favourites. A quaint tribute to this trait in his character has been given me by one of his oldest employees—'It would have made any poet happy to hear Sir Henry recite his poetry. Why, he seemed to understand what it was all about!'

The first commission which the firm gave to the Lambeth School of Art was connected with the new General Factory, the great building begun close to the South-Western Railway's line, in 1864. Mr. Sparkes had trained Percival Ball, who was the first-fruits of the Lambeth Art School, and who, having taken the Gold Medal of the Royal Academy, was now apprenticed to Fontana, the sculptor. He suggested to Doulton: 'Let Ball make you a series of portrait heads of the great potters to ornament your façade.' Henry Doulton jumped at the idea; Mr. Sparkes, designed the medallion heads, and they were executed by Mr. Percival Ball, in terracotta, over life-size. These heads were completed in 1865, and this was the earliest art commission given by Messrs. Doulton and Co. The design was an alternation of the historical potter, with, in each case, a female head representing the country in which he worked— Palissy with a French girl, Wedgwood with an English one, and so on. In this same year Mr. Percival Ball attracted some notice with a statue of 'Elaine' in the Royal Academy.

At the Paris Exhibition in 1867 a demand was made on the skill and enterprise of the English manufacturers, and certain specimens from the Lambeth Pottery were exhibited. Mr. Sparkes had in the previous year taken to Woodlands a folio of things done in the sketch club attached to his School of Art. Amongst these were some designs by W. Christian Symons, a young Lambeth artist of remarkable talent. These sketches took Henry Doulton's fancy, and he proposed that Mr. Symons should see what he could do by way of scratching the green clay.[22] Accordingly the painter copied some of Flaxman's outlines, and an attempt was made to fill them up with colour. But no medium was known to anybody at Lambeth for making the colour stick to the clay, and in consequence it all went adrift in the chemical storm of the kiln. The scratched outlines remained, however, and a certain prettiness was secured by covering graceful forms of vessels with concentric lines of parallel 'runners'. To the ultimate success of these experiments, I shall return in the following chapter. It seems that, slight as were the examples exhibited in 1867, they attracted a remarkable amount of attention among potters, and this stimulated Henry Doulton to fresh experiments. He was now thoroughly interested in the idea of art production at Lambeth.

It was immediately after the Paris Exhibition of 1867 that a remarkable artist, whose work has been almost entirely identified with the Lambeth Potteries, became known to Henry Doulton. I have given elsewhere details of the career of that very remarkable man Mr. George Tinworth.[23] He was born near Camberwell Gate, Lambeth, on the 5th of November 1843. He was the only child of parents in a small way of life—his father a wheelwright, his mother a 'narrow' Dissenter. He grew up in a Biblical atmosphere, and for

[22] This is the potter's term for clay after it has been shaped but before it has been dried and fired.
[23] *A Critical Essay on the Life and Works of George Tinworth* by Edmund W. Gosse. (Published by The Fine Art Society Limited, London, 1883.)

the religious lines upon which his talent as a sculptor has developed, Mr. Tinworth's mother must be considered as wholly responsible. Without the least encouragement to indulge the artistic instinct which displayed itself in early childhood, Mr. Tinworth began as a boy to work at his father's trade and to help him in the shop. In 1861 he first heard that there was such a thing in Lambeth as an art school; he had the greatest difficulty in conquering his native shyness; but at length he was able to persuade himself to take a rough head of Garibaldi, knocked out of a lump of sand-stone by means of a hammer and a nail, to Miller's Lane.[24] Mr. Sparkes saw the youth's native talent in a moment, and Mr. Tinworth at once took a place as one of the most interesting students in the Lambeth School.

For the next few years, Mr. Tinworth, still engaged by day in the wheelwright's shop, was executing in the evenings at Miller's Lane work which won medal after medal, and he had even begun to exhibit at the Royal Academy. Now that Messrs. Doulton were raising their thoughts above the dead level of ginger-beer bottles, drainage pipes and Toby jugs, it occurred to Mr. Sparkes that, in the new art industry to which Henry Doulton was turning his attention, some handicraft might be discovered in which Mr. Tinworth might engage. The young sculptor was in desperate straits. His father was dead, and the business, such as it was, had fallen into his unaided hands. For the work of a wheelwright he had neither health nor aptitude. He could scarcely earn enough to support his aged mother and himself, and it made Mr. Sparkes' heart ache to see such a man digging out mortices in the nave of a wheel, or breaking his back over rickety barrows and broken-down cabs. He asked Henry Doulton whether it was not possible to find some modelling work for the young man to do in the Lambeth pottery. It was found that thirty shillings a week was the most that he was making as a wheelwright, and Henry Doulton at once said that he would give him at least as much as that to begin with. But for this, a very interesting and individual artist would probably never have been able to express his talent at all.

For some time, although from the first Henry Doulton took a lively interest in Mr. Tinworth, there seemed to be no very practical means of utilising his talents. He began by touching up old moulds

[24] Tinworth in his unfinished autobiography says it was a bust of Handel in Portland stone.

for use in the pottery, and presently went off into original work of a very modest kind by modelling filters. The first artistic productions which he carried out directly for Henry Doulton were some colossal medallions which he copied from ancient Greek and Sicilian coins, and executed in terracotta. Most of these were in profile; one, a head of Arethusa, from the British Museum, in full face, in high relief, gives some suggestion of the sculptor's later work. One of these great medallions, that of Hercules wearing the lion's head as a hood, from a coin of Camarina, particularly attracted the notice of Mr. Ruskin, who quoted it as the text for a lesson on the principles of relief. Mr. Tinworth also modelled some realistic heads, rather trivial in style, and in 1868 a large terracotta bust of Mr. John Doulton, which though scarcely a work of merit, was accepted that year by the Royal Academy. He had not yet developed his peculiar powers, but he was growing in knowledge and confidence, sheltered by the friendly chimneys of the pottery which had become his home.[25]

[25] Tinworth also designed some of the vases, with incised decoration, shown at the 1867 Exhibition.

5

The Doulton Ware
1869 to 1876

The success which Henry Doulton's products had enjoyed at Paris in 1867, in spite of their simple character as artistic objects, had greatly encouraged him. The French critics welcomed with generosity these attempts to ornament the green clay in graceful lines of an extreme simplicity.

Henry Doulton from this time forth never slackened in his determination to dedicate himself to the service of art. But it was not easy to make a start. Mr. Tinworth was beginning his sculpture, but in other fields of ceramic design little progress was made, the desultory impressing of the green clay with concentric lines of parallel 'runners' being the limit of experience. In 1870 Henry Doulton bethought him that he might try a little more definite design and asked Mr. Sparkes if he could not recommend another artist. It happened that at that precise moment Miss Rogers, the author of *Domestic Life in Palestine,* had introduced to Mr. Sparkes a young friend, Miss Hannah B. Barlow, who was thinking of adopting art as a profession. The connection of this eminent decorator with Lambeth, therefore, dated from 1870, but she did not at that time work at the pottery, nor had the peculiar manner in which her talent could be utilised occurred to her.

The outbreak of the Franco-Prussian War checked every species of artistic enterprise for the moment, and in the midst of it Henry Doulton was deprived, not merely of the most intimate and valued of his personal friends, but of the man to whom, more than to anyone else, he looked for encouragement in his artistic projects. The death of Edward Cresy was a blow which formed an epoch in

Henry Doulton's life. He spoke of it in the following terms in a
letter to his son, from Brighton, on the 25th of October 1870:

> The melancholy death of my dear friend Cresy has cast a gloom
> over our circle. How we shall miss him! He was the most accom-
> plished man I have ever known, and so good a judge as Professor
> Cheetham of King's College tells me that he was the best 'all-round'
> man he has ever met. His bright and piercing intellect, the extent
> and accuracy of his knowledge on all subjects, his genial kindly
> humour, and delight in giving pleasure to others, were appreciated
> by all his friends, but only those who knew him as intimately
> as I did, know how utterly disinterested and unselfish he was . . .
>
> He was very fond of you children, and I looked forward to
> your appreciation of his fine mental powers, and to the help and
> advice he would give you in your studies and conduct in life.
> Alas! Man proposes! . . . His illness and death were as sudden as
> they were painful. Indirectly his decease is a result of this fearful
> war, for he caught the disease, smallpox, of which he died, while
> he was travelling homeward in circumstances of great agitation
> and fatigue. He had to travel in carriages filled with those wretched
> Turcos and Zouaves.
>
> What an utter collapse this of 'la belle France!' I sincerely hope,
> though it seems hoping against hope, that Paris will not be
> bombarded. We receive balloon letters, or rather Ronald does,
> from Collet. He, with all Parisians and most Frenchmen, clings to
> the delusion that some fearful catastrophe will yet happen to the
> Germans, and that France will rise *en masse* and expel the intruder
> from her sacred soil.

Ronald was Henry's nephew, Mr. Ronald Doulton, who had
stayed on in Paris till the latest possible moment, leaving M. Collet,
the agent of the firm, to protect the interests of his employers,
which he did to the end of the war.

When the war was over, and business was quieting down again,
Henry Doulton's mind turned ever more and more to the artistic
development of his stoneware. It was as the result of several unsuccessful experiments that in 1871, greatly dissatisfied with the
slow advance of the methods of ornamentation, Henry Doulton
asked Mr. Sparkes very earnestly whether he did not think it
possible that a permanent variety of colours might be secured by

causing pots to be dipped in ochre or in cobalt-blue, and then having designs scratched upon them, in a line now thicker or darker, now lighter. The converse of this, the making the scratch first, and then rubbing in the cobalt-blue or the brown, also suggested itself, and in point of fact became the more usual process. To this, indeed, Miss Hannah Barlow definitely set herself in 1871, and she was joined by her brother, Arthur. The former had now given up the designing of birds, and had developed a really astonishing talent for the grouping of cattle, deer, sheep and other quadrupeds in slight conventional landscapes round the faces of pots.[26] Arthur Barlow's work was quite different; his ornament was described (in 1874) as 'a floating, tumbling wealth of vegetable form wreathed around the jug, now and then fixed by a boss, or pinned down by a point of modelled form'. He had been thoroughly trained as a modeller in the Lambeth Art School, and this was of immense advantage to him in dealing with plastic form. As was said in the report to the Society of Arts, 'the occasional use of a gouge, or carver's chisel, or other carving tool, gave frequent evidence of what resources were his. He like his sister, carried the system of bossing, or stamping with points, dots and discs, to its fullest development. His good taste and perfect mechanical ingenuity carried his art into fields of decoration of unexpected beauty.' Arthur Barlow, who suffered from constant ill-health, died in 1879.

There was a very fair little show of pots and jugs, decorated by Mr. Tinworth and the Barlows, at South Kensington in 1871, and again in 1872. Among those who greatly encouraged their efforts was the late Charles Drury Fortnum (he died in 1899), who was at that time exercising his extraordinary technical knowledge of the minor arts as an art-referee for the South Kensington Museum. 'Sgraffito ware' was his name for the Lambeth specimens, a name which long clung to the Doulton high-art production.[27]

[26] Hannah's sister, Florence, joined her and Arthur at the Lambeth Pottery in 1873. It is said that the two sisters made a pact that Florence would concentrate mainly on birds and Hannah on quadrupeds. Occasionally both their monograms and that of a third sister, Lucy (who was at Lambeth for a few years), are found on the same piece.

[27] From the Italian *sgraffiato* (scratched decoration). This term is usually restricted nowadays to decoration incised or scratched *through a coating of slip* to reveal the contrasting colour of the underlying body. Many of the Lambeth Doulton-wares were incised directly into the clay. See page 83.

Mr. Frederick Doulton, Henry Doulton's eldest surviving brother, died very suddenly at Tunbridge Wells on the 21st of May 1872 at the age of fifty; he had taken to public life, and for several years represented the borough of Lambeth in the House of Commons. He had amiable and generous qualities, and considerable ability, but the close of his life was agitated by business troubles and anxieties which, after his death, involved his father and his brothers in new responsibilities.[28]

To gain a complete rest which it was found he greatly needed after sorting out Frederick's affairs, Henry Doulton joined James Anderson Rose and two other friends in a trip to Florence. They were away for four weeks of unbroken delight. They spent three days in Paris, made Arles the centre for some exploration of Provence, and then on by Nice, Genoa and Lucca. At Florence they had certain introductions which opened the very pleasant society of that city to them.

In the summer of the same year Henry Doulton received a warning that he had no longer the power, in his fifty-third year, to devote himself without the slightest relaxation to the responsibilities of business. The disturbed state of the labour market in England during the early part of this year had doubtless accentuated the anxieties inevitably connected with a property so considerable as his, and so dependent upon a vast number of workmen. He had never thought, up to this time, of rest as a requirement. His very holidays, brief as he had always made them, were occasions of feverish excitement. He never rested; he tore from cataracts to mountain prospects, from galleries to cathedrals, and came back to Lambeth full of pleasurable impressions, indeed, but rather tired than refreshed. In 1872 he began to suffer from strange attacks of nausea, which were treated but without relief, as the result of dyspepsia. It occurred to his physician, at length, that they resulted rather from the brain than from the stomach. This proved to be the case, and

[28] Frederick had retired from Doulton & Co. in 1862. (Henry is said to have told him: 'You must choose between business and politics. One or the other.') John Doulton, Junior, the founder's eldest son, died the same year, in the prime of life, predeceasing his father by eleven years. As from 1st January 1864 a new partnership was formed between John Doulton, Senior (10/25ths), Henry Doulton (14/25ths) and James Duneau Doulton, the founder's youngest son (1/25th). Henry thus now held a majority of the shares.

Henry Doulton undertook to ride more constantly, and above all to take one day's holiday every week.

In the early part of August he was able to settle comfortably difficulties which had arisen with the men at some of the works but the incessant travelling and all the excitement exhausted him extremely. He was persuaded to go down to Hurtmore on a visit to his friend Pewtress, and there, the strain being removed, his health gave way to a serious extent. At Hurtmore in September he had two alarming attacks of cerebral nausea, and the doctors absolutely insisted on complete rest for three months. He sent for his son Lewis, who was being educated at Bonn, to join him as he passed through Germany, and at Dresden he found his elder daughter, who was staying there with an old schoolfellow. In company with his two children, he accepted the invitation of Count von der Recke to come to Craschnitz, in Prussian Silesia.

The visit to Craschnitz formed a delightful episode in Henry Doulton's life. The aged Count, in his eighty-third year, was a perfect specimen of the patriarchal Teutonic nobleman. His son, Count Leopold, after fighting through the Franco-German War, had returned to the management of his father's estates, and the entertainment of his guests. In this remote and romantic Silesian castle Henry Doulton enjoyed the exact refreshment that he wanted. The Count's daughters, highly accomplished women, spoke English perfectly. The estates of Craschnitz were vast, and every day Henry Doulton and his son took part in riding, shooting or fishing parties. In October, entirely recovered, Henry Doulton went to Breslau, and then back to England by Dresden, Heidelberg and the Rhine.

While he was away, his fame had grown in England. The Doulton-ware exhibited at South Kensington in 1871 and 1872 had produced no little sensation. The newspapers, from *The Times* downwards, had welcomed the Lambeth products as 'quite the most remarkable features of their class' in modern pottery. The Queen had purchased several specimens and the Commissioners for the permanent exhibition in South Kensington had bought a considerable collection of typical pieces.

A very large opportunity now presented itself in the external decoration of the new Natural History Museum in Kensington, the architect for which was Mr. Alfred Waterhouse, R.A. In November that gentleman came to Lambeth to inspect the terracotta work and to make inquiries. The result was somewhat a disappointment, for this undertaking—by far the largest commission for art manufacture which had been given for many years—was not entrusted to the Doultons.

The following interesting letter to John Hardcastle, dated 23rd of January 1873, speaks for itself:

Your letter of the 15th ulto reached me about a fortnight after date. I have delayed replying till I had an opportunity of asking Rose [James Anderson] to aid in your scheme for helping the young artist in whom you have taken an interest.

Rose thinks compulsory military service, or at all events some service of the kind, by which young men learn obedience and discipline, a good thing and he seemed disinclined to aid any project for freeing a young man from such obligation. I must say I have long held the opinion that we want something of the kind in England, and that, either as volunteers or in the militia, or in some other way, it would advantage the youth of England to serve for a stipulated time and under orders. We have done away with apprenticeship in England (or nearly so) and our youths, specially of the labouring and lower middle classes, grow up without learning those habits of order and obedience which are so desirable and in the weakening of which I think Society and the nation are suffering now, and are likely to suffer more in the future.

Still, I have no doubt you will do what is discreet in relation to the young man. His case, or something like it, is not uncommon here, and I have many applications for help of a similar kind, but if a subscription will be of any help I shall be pleased if you will give it for me, and I will repay you.

I called to see Waterhouse and gave him the information needed but we shall not do any of the work I saw him about. I think it was intended for someone else from the first. We would not do it at a price far beyond what is to be given, and unless we had such a price as would enable us to maintain our reputation as to quality of manufacture—and get a fair profit also—we are content it should pass us.

Waterhouse expressed himself surprised at our Art work.

There seems to be extraordinary appreciation of some things we are now doing and we cannot supply the demands at what are really prices *for Art work*. I am just launching out into a new manufacture in Art pottery, so you may suppose I am pretty well again. If all turns out as I fully expect during the next few months I shall build an Art pottery on some ground I have on the Southern Embankment.

Henry Doulton was troubled in the winter of 1872–3 by complaints made by the Archbishop of Canterbury as to the fumes caused by the salt-glaze kilns of the pottery. At one time the dispute seemed so serious that Doulton prepared for a law-suit; but he did his very best to abate the nuisance, and acted with so much urbanity and consideration that the trouble passed off, and relations became quite friendly again between the pottery and the Palace. Doulton had settled with the Board of Works years before, when they had accused him of causing the decay in the Houses of Parliament.[29] He disliked extremely the notion of doing anything unneighbourly, and being sincerely vexed that his omelette could not be made without the breaking of some eggs, he always tried to make them as few as possible. It is, however, certainly notable that while complaints were constantly made that the chlorine of the decomposed salt, as it poured out in fumes from the kilns, made the inhabitants of the district sneeze and choke to an irritating degree, it formed in reality a most potent disinfectant. It became a by-word with the doctors in charge of the poor of the parish of Lambeth that zymotic disease never spread within the influence of this searching vapour.

The Verulam Club was now at its height of success, and in its meetings Henry Doulton continued to find his main intellectual and even social pastime. About this time, in a succession of papers, to the preparation of which he gave the best of his leisure, he discoursed to the Verulam Club of the English poets, beginning with Cowper and closing the series with Tennyson.

In November 1872 Henry Doulton's only son, Henry Lewis, had entered the business, so that with his help and that of his nephew

[29] Henry Doulton argued successfully that the decay in the stonework was due to the choice (contrary to expert advice) of a type of stone quite unsuitable for standing up to the atmospheric corrosion caused by smoke and fumes from thousands of industrial and domestic chimneys much nearer to the Houses of Parliament than the Lambeth Pottery.

Ronald he could say 'we are getting new blood into the concern'.[30]

As far back as 1852, Henry Doulton had his attention drawn to the possibility of employing earthenware for stoves. He felt convinced, as long ago as that, that an earthenware stove, on a good principle, would be an immense advantage in England. He tried some experiments, and advanced some distance towards a solution of the difficulties, but his attention was presently called away to other and more pressing matters. When he was in Saxony in 1872, he looked into the question again. Henry Doulton, with an introduction from Count von der Recke, visited one of the best manufactories of these articles near Dresden, and he made a variety of notes. When he returned to Lambeth he started a series of experiments in this direction. He studied, not merely the construction of the German, but also that of the Italian stoves.

He came to the conclusion that something different from either was needed to suit English tastes and habits. Nothing could be more wasteful than the system in use up to 1873 in England, and Henry Doulton's instinct told him that dearness alone would soon force on manufacturers the necessity of a more economical mode of heating. He was alarmed about this time at the rise in the price of coal, an element of the highest importance to him as a potter. 'I have always urged', he wrote (February 25, 1873), 'that coal is the exceptional article, not to be increased by the skill, industry or ingenuity of man, that it is the main cause of the prosperity of England, and that it is foolish to export a million and a quarter tons of it per month, without levying even a one-shilling export duty. We waste it even by the wholesale destruction of tons at the pit's mouth.' These ideas were soon general, and a public inquiry into the supply of coal was ordered by Parliament.[31]

[30] Ronald Doulton was a younger son of John Doulton, Junior. Ronald's eldest brother, John, who had been in charge of the crucible section for some years, died in 1870 at the early age of twenty-five.

[31] The 'Radiating Tiled Stove', as it was called, although extensively advertised and exhibited, did not prove the success Henry Doulton had hoped. He had to confess that he had underestimated the difficulty of weaning conservative English householders from their sacrosanct methods of heating (or not heating!) their homes. He then turned his attention, with considerable success, to improving the construction of conventional fireplaces, and making them more attractive and easier to clean by the use of coloured, glazed stoneware, faïence and terracotta surrounds.

Miss Hannah Barlow gives me some pleasant reminiscences of this early time. There was no place set aside, at that period, for the art work, and she and her brother at length found a home for their wandering footsteps in the showroom at Lambeth, where they were provided with a large table and a screen to shut them off from the public. Miss Barlow recollects her first meeting with Henry Doulton. She was going downstairs early in 1871 and was met by a gentleman tearing up the staircase, two steps at a time, who, nevertheless, paused to take off his hat to her, and to give her a very charming smile.[32] 'I wonder who that is,' said Miss Barlow to herself, 'whoever it is, I feel sure he must be a delightful man to work for.' Very shortly after this, Henry Doulton came to her at her work and introduced himself. In a little while she learned to expect his daily visit, if only for a few moments; always brisk, courteous, enthusiastically encouraging, his suggestions and admiring comments made the work spring up and blossom like the rose. If, by chance, he was prevented from coming, Hannah and her brother Arthur would feel that it was difficult to get through the day. Later on, Doulton used to make a special point of constantly refreshing and stimulating Miss Barlow's invention, by describing to her groups of animals he had seen—cattle feeding in the field, or horses at play. 'He seemed,' says Miss Barlow, 'to bring these before me, right here, in the studio.'

Another crisis was marked in 1873. In company with Mr. Sparkes, Henry Doulton had been to visit an exhibition of 'art pottery' in one of the fashionable West End shops. Directly they got into the hansom to drive back to Lambeth, Henry Doulton began to expatiate on the poverty of what they had seen, its timidity, its tightness, its lack of all real beauty. 'Is that absolutely the best that English potters can do,' he cried, 'that thin, washy stuff?' And after a moment's pause, with his great eyes, brimful of eagerness, fixed upon Mr. Sparkes, 'Can't we make Lambeth the centre of a real art product? Don't you think we could work the matter out systematically and really do it properly? Have you the students? Can you send me a whole batch of them?' To each of these queries Mr. Sparkes gave a zealous and delighted affirmative, and that was how the second group of Lambeth artists came into being, and how the movement was actually made one of national importance.

[32] This would have been just after Miss Barlow came to the pottery from the Lambeth School of Art.

The first difficulty was to find a place for the artists. It was of no use to disperse them about, in holes and corners; they must have a definite home of their own. It happened that some twenty years earlier, the Doultons, in extending their property, had put up a block of workmen's dwellings with the view of helping their men to a better sort of habitation. In time, however, the project failed. The tenants had been found undesirable, and had been allowed to disperse, but these houses with their numerous little rooms had never been conveniently subjected to the general purposes of the works. They were practically unused, with their clusters of small, useless rooms, like a rabbit-warren. It immediately suggested itself to Henry Doulton that this was the place for his hive of decorators. Accordingly, these houses were put in perfect repair, made into comfortable little sets of studios, and all prepared for the installation. Mr. Sparkes, on a wet and dismal morning early in 1873, started from the Art School with a procession of students, male and female, all of whom were duly given more or less permanent engagements, and distributed throughout the little houses prepared for them. Miss Hannah Barlow and her brother were there already. Among those who arrived was Mr. Frank Butler, a deaf and dumb designer who soon developed, in this new work, a remarkable invention and became, of all the group, much the most successfully ingenious in squeezing the wet clay vessel into shapes other than circular.

Other notable members of the procession of 1873 were H. Bone Nightingale, Mrs. Eliza Banks, Miss Eliza Simmance and Miss Florence Barlow, each of whom developed some peculiar talent of his or her own. Henry Doulton did not attempt to direct them. He gave them the virgin pots of soft clay to make of what they could.[33] With the most enthusiastic gaiety and curiosity, he would hasten from one to the other, to see what each was contriving to do, and his praise was unstinted in its welcome of each successful experiment. He desired, from the very first, that each artist should affix his or her designation to each piece. At first, each piece—further to emphasise the individual character of the art—was dated as well. This, however, had to be given up because the dealers refused to buy, in 1875, a piece of stoneware, however beautiful, that was dated in 1874, on

[33] The leading artists sketched shapes they required the throwers to make for them. Each shape was given a reference number. By 1882, 1,600 different shapes had been produced and many times that number of different decorations on these shapes.

the ground that 'it was not new!' 'Not new,' Henry Doulton indignantly said, 'not new—and what does that matter with the most durable product that man's hand can make?' But the stupidity of fashion prevailed, and those collectors who possess a dated specimen of Lambeth stoneware have a rare object in their collections.[34]

At the close of 1873 the vitality and abundance of the stoneware art at Lambeth were so noticeable that at the request of Henry Doulton, Mr. Sparkes made an analysis, which was read at the Society of Arts, at a meeting on the 1st of May 1874, at which Mr. (afterwards Sir) Robert Rawlinson presided. The definition of the various kinds of work then produced at Lambeth, is so clear, that a repetition of Mr. Sparkes' exact words seems desirable here. After the lapse of a quarter of a century it would not be easy to improve this brief statement of the different methods open to the artist who set about to work in Doulton Ware:

1. By scratching in the pattern, while the pot is still wet, very soon after it is removed from the thrower's wheel. The line is scratched with a point which leaves a burr raised up on each side. This is useful, and serves to limit the flow of any colour that is applied, either within the pattern or to the ground that surrounds it.

2. At a later period, when the vessel has left the wheel twenty-four hours, the clay is too hard for this treatment. In this condition, a burr is not turned up, but breaks off and leaves a broken blurred edge. When in this state, the ware is scratched with an implement which scoops out a line, and delivers the clay that is removed cleanly away from the cut. It makes a clear incised depression with no burr; it too has its own beauty and subserves a use. Colour applied to the pattern, or to the ground, flows into it, fills it up, and is darkened by its deeper thickness at the place where a line crosses it.

3. Carving away a moulding or collar that is left on the ware by the thrower or turner is a fruitful source of excellent light and shade effects. This system is not only applicable to mouldings but also to flatter members, as for instance, where a row of leaves is first turned in a mass and carved in detail.

[34] Most of the dated specimens are of the period 1872 to 1877. Dates between 1877 and 1887 are less often found and after 1887 they are very rare.

G

4. Another method is by whitening the body. But the material used for this purpose is of too short a texture to allow of ornamentation by the first method, viz. by scratching the wet clay with a point when half-dry; however, it is tough enough to be decorated with patterns taken out with the excised line. In this body we observe a difference from the ordinary brown ware body. It has a less affinity for the soda, in the process of glazing with salt. It does not shine with the full glaze, as the brown ware does; and it has what is called a 'smear' by potters. On the other hand, it takes the blue colour much more kindly, from the circumstance that the yellow or burnt sienna-coloured body of the ordinary ware is absent, and also that a certain natural relationship exists between the blue grey of the body and the deeper cobalt blue with which it is decorated. There is a harmony of likeness between them.

5. Another system becomes imperative when a vessel of ordinary dark brown clay is dipped into a slip, or coating of a white colour. It is obvious that a cut made on such a vessel would expose the brown colour of the body made visible by the removal of the white covering. This method offers many varieties of treatment, with or without the addition of colour to the cut surface.

6. Now, in addition to those various methods, there is still another, which was extensively used by the old Rhenish potters; it is by the application of dots, discs, flowers, borders etc., by a process of sealing on a form of clay, usually of a different colour from the ground, from a mould, much in the same way as the impression of a seal is made in wax, with this difference, that the clay seal is made to adhere to the surface on which it is pressed; the clay being first spread on the seal.

7. Similar in principle is the method of cutting in patterns from a mould; such lines of sharp environment serve to set bounds to the little rivulets of flowing colours, when fused and fluid by the intense heat of the kiln; they seem to limit the flow, which if not thus checked, would run down the surface.

8. Again, it is quite possible to stamp on a disc or series of dots, with such a material that it will burn away with the fierce heat, and leave a small circular inlay of beautiful crystallised brown-grey substance, flush with the surface of the ware.

These eight heads of methods seem to classify the schemes of decoration applied to the Doulton Ware, but scarcely a kiln is burnt off that does not yield a suggestion of a new line of trial for new systems, and these are stored to be taken up in the future as the demand for newer methods is made.

It would be difficult to exaggerate the interest which Henry Doulton took in all these details. The new art work was the very apple of his eye. Not a day passed but he found his way up to the studios, chatting with the artists, suggesting ideas, heartening them up with his encouragement and complimenting them upon their skill. By talking of the ware outside the pottery, by inviting the leaders of taste to come and see it, by the infection of his own keen interest, he created a public demand for the products which his eager band of designers produced.

Mr. Ruskin, at this time Slade Professor of Fine Art at Oxford, had just published *Aratra Pentelici* and *Ariadne Florentina*. He was a supreme force in the tide now steadily turning to a reform in the cultivation of beauty in home life. With his niece, Mrs. Arthur Severn, Mr. Ruskin came down to Lambeth—very dubious, a little inclined to petulance, more than half-disposed to curse the whole movement. He remained to bless it in no measured terms. It is remembered that when Henry Doulton, after one of these visits of Mr. Ruskin's, asked him to accept whichever piece of Doulton Ware had pleased him most, the great critic, after much reflection, said, 'I will have, please, the jug with all the little piggies scurrying round under the handle.' This, it is almost needless to say, was one of Miss Hannah Barlow's animal pieces.

One of those who took the greatest interest in the early development of the Doulton stoneware was Professor A. H. Church, since universally known as an authority on chemistry as applied to the fine arts. On his visits to London from Cirencester, where he then held the chair of chemistry in the Royal Agricultural College, he rarely failed to look in at the Lambeth Works. He gives me the following notes of his early appreciation of the stoneware:

When decorative stoneware was first regularly made at Lambeth, though in small quantities, Henry Doulton asked me from time to time to be present, not precisely at the time when each kiln was drawn, but when the newly-fired pieces had just been set out for inspection. Frank criticism was invited by Henry Doulton; in reality my remarks, when not wholly congratulatory, were mainly directed to such points as these—the adjustment of the scale of the ornament to the size of the vessel; impracticably narrow necks, and excessively glittering glaze. But as to this last point the purchasing public in the early seventies—and now too I fear—insisted upon a shiny gloss and would not tolerate the matt surfaces in which I rejoiced. It was always pleasant to note the eager attention paid by Henry Doulton to my criticism and his satisfaction at my recognition of those merits in the pieces which I indicated.

These early visits of mine to the pottery when the kilns had just been drawn gave me the opportunity of securing a small but fairly representative series of specimens of the new ornamental stoneware. Henry Doulton often in after years assured me that he wished he had begun reserving such a typical set from the beginning. It is regrettable that the earliest pieces are not dated, and that the later specimens likewise bear no year-mark.

I remember the particular delight I felt on more than one occasion (I believe in 1872) in intercepting certain pieces of the white or 'C' body marked in pencil 'for New York'. Henry Doulton allowed me once and again to circumvent his sales manager.

On the 21st of May 1873 old Mr. John Doulton died; he would have completed, in six months, his eightieth year. A little before his death, he had the misfortune to break his ankle, and there were other circumstances which combined to trouble his serenity. From a letter to Mr. John Hardcastle, I quote these words, which show the honour in which the father of the family was held. Henry Doulton says (May 26, 1873):

Our deep sorrow is mitigated by much that tends to solace and to cheer us. We feel irreparable the loss of the revered and beloved Head of our House. We only knew the noble generosity of his nature, and his high Christian character. The testimonials I have received from those associated with him in public life and charitable work have surprised me. I knew he was esteemed and revered, but I had no idea of the depth of the love he inspired, or of the veneration in which he was held, by so many able and good men. It seems the general feeling that his place cannot be supplied in Lambeth, and that the sick, the aged and the poor have lost their best friend.

He was ill with bronchitis for some weeks before his death, but no danger was apprehended till a few days before he was taken away. He took to his bed *for the first time in his life,* only two days before he died. His end was most peaceful and happy; it was a privilege to be in the room; he seemed just on the verge of heaven. Not a cloud obscured the setting of his pure and holy life. For many years, I, and others, have noted how much he was growing in richness of character. He was vigorous, and showed no signs of either physical or mental decay until within a week of his death and then only of the former.

This spring, with the same companions as before, Henry Doulton travelled in Normandy, and these annual continental tours now began to be an institution, and always an immense pleasure. In the late months of 1873 a fresh extension of the artistic work at Lambeth was undertaken. By the picturesque accident of Mr. Sparkes' seeing him at work on a plate in a window, it became known that a man in Lambeth was attempting to revive the manufacture of painted faïence.[35] This proved to be Mr. John Bennett, a very clever and original worker, who had been trained in the porcelain potteries of Staffordshire. He was induced to enter the pottery at Lambeth, and to instruct a new bevy of artists in the mysteries of faïence and impasto-painting upon plaques and pots.[36] A great number of ladies, among whom Miss Florence Lewis was perhaps the most distinguished, undertook this species of decoration with great success. The faïence work became exceedingly popular with the public, particularly in consequence of the gaiety of its hues and designs, two pigments of different fusibility being often combined to form harmonies of a very attractive character. I believe, however, that I am right in saying that connoisseurs were never so much interested in the specimens of faïence as they were in those of the original Doulton stoneware.

[35] Faïence, maiolica and delft are all names for tin-enamelled earthenwares, the main differences being in colouring and styles of decoration. These wares were coated with a lead glaze containing tin oxide, which gave them a white finish.
[36] Bennett was said by his fellow artists to be 'imperious and touchy' and did not remain very long at Lambeth. Henry Doulton said of him, 'You can buy even gold too dear.' Bennett later went to America where Tiffanys sold some of his pots.

Mr. Tinworth became so much more widely known as a sculptor than as a decorating potter, that there is a special interest in recording that his successes in the latter province were at this time most brilliant, and gave the keenest pleasure to Henry Doulton. Mr. Sparkes wrote in 1874:

When the demand for artistic stoneware came, Tinworth's general grasp of the intention enabled him to do works that were more than equal to the occasion; and since that time he has done some of the best pieces the factory has produced. He prefers the clay soft from the thrower's wheel, so soft as to be too tender to handle. His delight is a spiral band or ornament ribbon, sometimes deeply interdigitated, or elaborately frilled. The ornament usually covers as much surface as the ground, and creeps or flies over the surface in wild luxuriance; bosses, belts, or bands or plain or carved moulding keep this wild growth to its work, put it in its place, and subject it to its use. No two pots are alike, and although he has done many thousands, all different, he will still produce them in endless variety out of the same materials. Of course no one could produce such ever new combinations, unless he had invention. He is an exponent of religious art, such as seldom arises in any community in the present day.

This year he exhibited a large jug, in which he has worked a kind of gallery round the shoulder, and placed alternate groups from the history of the Passion of our Lord, and small niches of single figures from the Old Testament, which have a bearing on the groups they separate. The earnestness of the actors in these little scenes, and the expression of their faces and hands will repay close examination. Apart from the detailed richness of the high art work on this jug, the vessel, as a whole, is perhaps the finest piece of decorated stoneware that has ever been produced in modern times.

In February 1876 the Doulton Ware had arrived at such a condition of abundance and perfection, that Henry Doulton instituted a private exhibition of art work at Lambeth, to which all prominent connoisseurs were invited. He did not anticipate any special success, but the show happened to be opened at a moment when everyone was talking about the salt-glaze pottery. Originally only 250 invitations were issued, but the works were so bombarded with requests for admission that in the long run 2,000 visitors were received. In a letter to Mr. John Hardcastle (February 25th, 1876) he says:

We kept the exhibition open for two days on purpose for Ruskin. He came at last, and expressed himself warmly as to the merit of the work. He declared that Tinworth is 'an indubitable genius'. Of course he was critical, but he explained that this was because he was so immensely interested. *One thing this exhibition has taught me, that in art-criticism there are many mansions, for equally good judges and authorities had very different opinions as to which were the most excellent specimens.* Happily, all seemed to agree that the work was good.

We had some of the best people in England to visit us. Gladstone made himself very pleasant, and was both cordial and interesting . . . Of all our visitors Sir Garnet Wolseley was, I really think, the warmest and the most discriminating.

I am bound to acknowledge that I am proud of this offshoot of my business which was taken up, as you know, all for love and nothing for reward, but which I think is going to prove successful from every point of view.

The instructed interest which Lord Wolseley takes in the ceramic arts is known to all his friends. He was one of the connoisseurs who early secured specimens of the Doulton Ware for their collections. To my inquiry whether he recollects the exhibition of 1876, Lord Wolseley sends me a very cordial reply (May 28, 1899), from which I quote the following passages:

I remember very well the visit my wife and I paid to Sir Henry Doulton's potteries. I remember all the little incidents of his taking us round afterwards to see the men and women, and even boys and girls busy on what was real artistic work.

What is most impressed upon my mind is Sir Henry's genial kindness, not only to me, his visitor, but to all those whom he employed. Each little object had imprinted upon it the individuality of the *artist* who shaped it, or engraved upon it, or otherwise decorated it.

Doulton did very much to develop the artistic talents of those whom he employed. It was no mere question with him of making beautiful pottery in moulds; he appealed to the genius of the worker as well as to his or her nimbleness of fingers. I learned much from him during my long visit to his Lambeth Works in 1876, and to this day I never pass them without thinking of him, and of what he did for art, and of what he did to help those with any artistic talents.

I cannot but think how these words, so delicately discriminating in their praise, so absolutely just and deserved, would have gratified my old friend, coming as they do from a man whose public career he followed with a peculiarly enthusiastic admiration.

Another valued acquaintance of these years was George Eliot, who was then living at Witley, near Godalming, not very far from the spot where Henry Doulton was already searching for a country home. She and Mr. Lewes paid several interesting visits to the works at Lambeth and was on terms of much cordiality with the potter. From a letter of hers to Henry Doulton dated August 8, 1878, I extract the following lines:

Just before we left town I was telling Mr. Burne Jones of the interesting Tinworth, whose name I hope will by and by need no such reporting. Such indication as I was able to give of the works we had seen gave our friend Mr. Burne Jones a strong desire to see the artist, and he said that he would, as soon as possible, make a journey to Lambeth for that purpose.

Pray be so kind as to recall us to Mr. Tinworth's recollection, and assure him that we have not yet lost the cheering benefit of our interview with him.

Indeed, our visit to Lambeth ranges with me beside our visit to Murano, with the added ground of delight that the Doulton Establishment belongs to our own country, and is benefiting the workers near our own doors. And I think you will agree with me that we are bound to care more for London even at its ugliest than for Venice in its utmost beauty. But you are helping to spread beauty in London too.

6

A public figure

In the autumn of 1876 Henry Doulton became one of the protago-
nists in a great public struggle which attracted universal attention,
and has its place in the history of social life in England. He was
successful, for the first time, in checking Unionism in its more
exacting and unreasonable forms.

The trades unions were then forces, the exact direction and limita-
tion of which were but little understood. They had been created to
check the tyranny of capital, and had been hailed by most of the
liberal thinkers of the time as wholesome and at the same time
ingenious methods by which labour could legitimately protect itself.
But it is not unfair to say that many of those who most warmly
welcomed the trades unions had omitted to observe that labour also
had its responsibilities and its duties. The success of the unions had
startled the labour leaders themselves out of their discretion. They
thought their dictation absolute, and having met with no vigorous
opposition, they expected to meet with none. It was time that the
trades union rules should be adapted to the general interests of the
community, and Henry Doulton, by the exercise of a great deal of
courage and determination, was able to make a successful appeal
against the narrowness of class selfishness.

The firm was engaged in building two large establishments on
the Albert Embankment and a smaller and more elaborately
decorated one at the corner of Lambeth High Street. These buildings,
especially the latter, are of distinct architectural pretension; to this
day, with the shifting of taste in a quarter of a century, they cannot
fail to provoke admiration. The great chimney, in which the red

brick blossoms out into a pedestal that distinctly recalls the Palazzo Vecchio in Florence, is really a very noble thing. There is, perhaps, no handsomer chimney in London, old or new.[37]

In the execution of these new buildings, Henry Doulton took the most enthusiastic pleasure, and he was extremely anxious that every part of them should be as nearly as possible perfect. The walls of the new buildings were to be ornamented with terracotta, and the fixing of the decorative work was a matter of considerable anxiety. The peculiarity of terracotta is that no piece of it is ever *exactly* square, due to slight variations that take place in the formidable heat of the kiln. The fixing of each individual piece has to be done on its own merits, with a skilled consideration of its relation to the next piece. But the bricklayers' union was unable to recognise any such niceties as these, and it considered that every ordinary bricklayer was quite competent to fix terracotta. The union found a spokesman in the Rev. Henry Solby, then a prominent advocate of advanced Unionism, who laid it down that 'terracotta is a hard-burnt substance made into blocks like bricks, and built into walls with mortar, in precisely the same manner as brick-work', and that therefore bricklayers ought to fix it.

Henry Doulton, however, had practical knowledge of the skill required in dealing with terracotta. In the rebuilding of his own house at Tooting, the terracotta ornament had been so badly done by the bricklayers that the more prominent parts of it had to be reset by competent terracotta fixers. Consequently, when the High Street building came to be finished, Doulton had his eyes open to the possibility of this part of the work not being properly carried out. But he warned the bricklayers to take particular care, and as they seemed impressed with what he said, he let them go on with the fixing. It soon proved however that though very good men undertook the business, from inexperience they were not able to carry it out properly. The delicate terracotta ornament, which required the most careful balancing, and in which every piece

[37] The two large buildings and the great chimney have now gone (see Note 8). Much to his disappointment, Henry Doulton was never able to buy the freehold of the site on which they were built. The smaller building on the corner of Lambeth High Street and Black Prince Road, with a panel by Tinworth over the entrance, is still there (1970), although no longer in the possession of Doulton & Co. Limited, who moved to new headquarters on the Albert Embankment in 1939.

needed to be considered in relation to each of its immediate neighbours, was dabbed in with the most unsightly irregularity, and presented no sort or appearance of style. The two men, a father and son of the name of Spinks, who had so successfully revised the work at Tooting, were called in to exercise their knowledge at Lambeth. They had for many years been employed in this particular species of work and very clever at it they were.

The correction was made in a most conciliatory way. The Spinks were put by themselves, for two days, on one of the Embankment buildings, to fix terracotta bases and pilasters. Henry Doulton's idea was that by this means the bricklayers might gain an opportunity of seeing how work of this kind ought to be executed, and they were asked to watch how the two men contrived. As is so often the case, the bricklayers had no idea that their feelings were being outraged until somebody from outside was so kind as to point it out to them. At first, they watched the plasterers very good-humouredly, caught the trick of it, and immediately began, by copying their processes, to fix the terracotta soundly and properly. All seemed to be going for the best in the best of all possible worlds.

Somebody, however, described the incident to the secretary of the bricklayers' society, and it was thought that this was a capital occasion for teaching the capitalist his place. Accordingly, like a bolt out of the blue, on the 20th of September 1876 one of the executive council of the bricklayers' society came to the office at the works 'to know when the two plasterers setting terracotta were going to be discharged'. The manager, Mr. John Phillips, submitted the startling question to Henry Doulton, who replied, 'Never—so long as they do their work so satisfactorily as they are doing it at present.' About ninety men were being employed on the building works, some sixty of whom were bricklayers or their assistants. It was extremely important to proceed rapidly and steadily with the work, which was just in the condition when regular progress is essential. It was, therefore, no small blow to the firm when, a few days later, two of the bricklayers asked to see Mr. Phillips and informed him that an order had come from their union that all the bricklayers should cease working until the two plasterers were discharged.

The expense, the difficulty and the danger which were involved by this strike will be best comprehended by those who are acquainted with the risks by which a great contract is hemmed in, and who realise the fatal stagnation of business involved. But the awkwardness of the position was vastly increased by the fact that in those days very little was known as to the limitations of the power of the unions. There was practically no restrictive legislation on the subject; employers had not learned what they could do to protect themselves. A great many people were fatalistically in terror of the societies, and considered that it was useless to attempt to withstand them. As a matter of fact, no big strike in the building trade had been successfully faced, and it was thought that to hesitate to give way to the union was to court disaster, and merely to prolong the agony of ruin. The bricklayers' society had carefully chosen their moment. They knew that nothing could possibly be more provoking or likely to lead to more severe loss than the stoppage of these huge and complicated works at exactly this stage of their construction. They looked for an easy triumph; it would be a very small thing to sacrifice the two plasterers; the union would have scored another victory of 'principle'; and the Lambeth Works would be completed without delay.

But they reckoned without Henry Doulton. He never wavered for a moment. He refused, instantly and finally, to commit an act of injustice to two servants of his merely to gratify the tyrannous caprice of a union of workmen. In a vigorous letter to *The Times* he placed the situation lucidly before the public, and announced his intention of fighting it out. He stated his view in clear words: 'I think the principle insisted on by the bricklayers' trade union not only involves an interference with the freedom of the workman, but interposes difficulties in the introduction of improvements.' For these two reasons he absolutely declined to yield an inch to the union, and in consequence all the sixty bricklayers at work on the three new buildings went out together on strike. The two plasterers, who were the innocent cause of all the trouble, offered, as Henry Doulton explained on the 6th of October, 'to leave their employment, on the ground that we should suffer serious loss and inconvenience if they remained. We have requested them to stay, urging that it would be as cowardly for them to succumb to the dictation of the bricklayers' union, as it would be for us to discharge them.' Accordingly, during the whole strike, Spinks and his son remained at their work.

Throughout the extremely difficult time which now began, the temper and action of Henry Doulton were in the highest degree admirable. He became Argus and Briareus in one, the chief with a thousand eyes and a thousand hands. He pervaded the works with his eagerness, he thought for everyone, he provided against every emergency. To each suggestion of yielding made by those around him of lesser faith than he, to every premonition of failure and exhaustion, he confronted a cheerfulness and courage which were perfectly splendid. It must not be forgotten that, as has already been indicated here, the strike was a test one. Hitherto the societies had had it all their own way. No resistance, save of the weakest and most half-hearted kind, had been offered to their demands. Flushed with success, and supported by inexperience, they believed themselves to be quite impregnable. They thought that if they were to tell the Queen to get out of Buckingham Palace she would have to go. They prided themselves upon their moderation, and if capital would allow them exactly their own way, it might, for the present, go on supplying them with wages. But it lay in the hollow of their hand.

This was what Henry Doulton had the pluck to bring to the test. At the very outset of the fight he characteristically amused himself by adapting a stanza of Tennyson to the case in point:

> Should banded Unions persecute
> Opinion, and induce a time
> When single thought is civil crime,
> And individual freedom mute

then, Henry Doulton considered, England would cease to be a country where Englishmen would care to go on living. In the particular case of the Lambeth plasterers, there were happily no features which could confuse popular judgment on its rights and wrongs. The terracotta fixers, on account of the superior skill required in their work, were paid more highly than ordinary brick-layers. Moreover, the employment among them of two very old servants of the firm, who were nominally plasterers, involved on Messrs. Doulton's part no innovation on the customs of the trade, for it had been for many years the habit to use skilled artisans as terracotta fixers without question, and this new fiat of the union was a perfectly gratuitous one.

Meanwhile the strike began in earnest, and throughout the country its progress was watched with extraordinary interest. It was the general opinion that the Doultons would be forced to give way. The Operative Bricklayers' Society instituted an effective system of picketing, and every man who presented anything of the appearance of a bricklayer was intercepted as he approached the works. A few words sufficed to prevent some from going on to work, whilst others had to be taken to one of the adjacent public houses, and more effectually dealt with there. The customary features were repeated. Many of the men took private opportunities of saying that they would be willing to work, but that they dared not brave the wrath of the union: 'It is no matter to us who is wrong or right, but we cannot go to work on a building when a strike has been ordered by our union.' Four bricklayers belonging to the society actually asked for employment with a full knowledge that the strike was going on; they asked, however, if the buildings were picketed, and, learning that they were, they declined to go to work, saying that they should have been glad to do so if the works had not been picketed. This circumstance particularly impressed Henry Doulton, and long afterwards he was never weary of insisting that picketing was a weapon deliberately made use of for purposes of intimidation, and that it ought to be made illegal.

Another instance of what Henry Doulton considered tyrannical behaviour on the part of the union was that of two bricklayers belonging to the Operative Bricklayers' Society, who were employed as foremen at the buildings, and who refused to leave work when the others struck. These men were summoned to attend a meeting of the Lambeth Branch of their society, and to 'explain their conduct in not obeying the orders of the members'. At this meeting the two foremen were ordered not to return to work after the following Saturday unless the two plasterers were discharged; and, as they hesitated, they were told that if they refused to obey, they would be 'dealt with at some future time'. All these particulars, which Henry Doulton was careful to communicate to the press, and which no attempt was made to deny, produced a considerable sensation throughout the country.

For seventeen weeks the strike continued, and all through that time the pickets stood and walked in the street opposite the works 'watching' the non-union bricklayers at work on the scaffolds, and

gathering close round the gates of the works at meal-times, scruti-
nising the features of the bricklayers as they came out and went in.
Many of the latter left, because, they said, they did not like to be
constantly 'watched', and some discharged themselves while giving
as their reason that they were afraid to continue at work lest they
should be struck against at other places. All these facts were commented on very widely and not at all to the advantage of the
bricklayers' union. The matter was taken up by the Royal Institute
of British Architects, and other bodies in various parts of the
country. It raised an echo even in France, where the celebrated
political economist Michel Chevalier noted the strike to French
sociologists as an economical incident worthy of their closest
attention.

At length, in January 1877, the late Mr. Mundella, already
prominent as the radical member for Sheffield, considered that the
scandal had gone on long enough. He went to the London Trade
Union Committee, and told them 'to stop the strike, or they would
disgrace themselves'. 'Mr. Doulton,' Mr. Mundella had the courage
to say, 'has done very good service to his country. I think the
bricklayers' union has used Mr. Doulton very hardly, I entirely
concur with him in the line he takes up about piece-work. What
we want is conciliation boards established in the building trades,
and when that is done, there will be no more strikes on such trum-
pery pretexts as these.' The Stonemasons' Society gave it as their
opinion that the bricklayers were in the wrong. Thus abandoned by
their own friends, the Operative Bricklayers' Society determined to
yield and on the 30th of January 1877 at length withdrew their
pickets.

A feeling of indignation was irrepressible when the works began
to be examined after they were resumed. This was supposed to be
a 'friendly' strike, yet the evidences of rancorous ill-feeling were
only too obvious. Before the workmen went out, it was found, they
had taken care to do all the mischief that it was in their power to do.
After the buildings were finished, scores of openings had to be made
in the solid walls to dig out the obstructions which the intruding
strikers had caused by throwing bricks down the chimneys and
then pouring cement on top of them, with the ingeniously foreseen
result, of course, that when the first fires were lighted, not one of
these flues would work.

The entirely courageous stand taken throughout these seventeen weeks by Henry Doulton produced a great effect throughout the country. His resistance was very widely commented upon, and almost universally commended. He became a prominent public character from this moment forth, and was looked upon as a man powerful enough to help to hold the balance a little straighter than it had of late been held between employers and employed. Almost the only serious attacks which were made upon him originated with certain clerical politicians whose craze it was that the working man could do no wrong. The behaviour of some of these persons somewhat incensed Henry Doulton, who roundly told them that they 'looked at the question from a sentimental point of view, ignoring economical laws', and that they 'were not alive to the serious consequences of the position they took'.

As a direct result of the controversy which thus began, a clerical conference was held in the Chapter House of St. Paul's Cathedral at the end of the month of June 1877, with the Rev. John Oakley in the chair. Various well-known figures took part: the late Dr. Littledale, the Dean of Ripon, the late Dean of St. Paul's. A young clergyman was prominent, then curate of St. Matthias', Bethnal Green, who later became widely known as the Rev. Stewart Headlam. Among those who came down to see that all was fair were Mundella, Tom Hughes, and the hero of arbitration, Mr. W. R. Cremer. At the meeting the first place was given to Henry Doulton, who delivered an eloquent and characteristic speech, of which a portion may be quoted here, because the sentiments expressed were those which the speaker had now thoroughly adopted, and which he entertained with strenuous conviction during the remainder of his economical life. The clerical friends of the unions had to listen to very plain speaking on this occasion. Henry Doulton, in the course of opening the discussion, said:

I hold as a fundamental principle of individual liberty the right of every man and woman to do the very best with the talents Providence has given them. That principle is at stake and I felt it inconsistent with my self-respect to give way. I have given instructions that the men engaged on the work should be treated with the utmost fairness, and be paid the best wages; but I certainly would have resisted to the last penny any dictation of the Trade Union as to the men I employed. In the interests of the workmen, I maintained their right to sell their labour in the very best market . . .

One of the evils of the Unions has been their opposition to piece-work. I have never known a case in which a person who had changed from day-work to piece-work, has not done half as much, and in some cases, double as much as before. Is it to the advantage of the community that a man should take an hour to do what he could do in half-an-hour? Instances have come under my notice of an ordinary unskilled labourer, who by day-work earned 21s. per week, earning on the same work 30s. at the least per week at piece-work. Having learnt my trade myself, I saw the possibility of this at once, but I have had great difficulty in getting my men to see it. There are three classes of workmen; the exceptionally intelligent, clever, and skilful; the ordinary or medium class; and then the thriftless and idle. Are all to be put on the same footing? All rules which limit individual exercise of skill are injurious to the community . . . A very serious declension in the pace at which work is done has also taken place, the weakest and poorest workers setting the pace for the rest where day-work was the rule.

This is a convenient place to mention another public controversy in which Henry Doulton took a leading part, and which extended, in one shape or another, over many years. We have already had occasion to mention his love of horse exercise and the important place which it held in his daily life, after his taking up his abode at Tooting. The commons of Tooting Bec and Tooting Graveney, comprising nearly 200 acres in all, lay at his doors, and it was the greatest possible pleasure to him to start away at once over the turf and gallop off at his heart's desire. It soon appeared, however, that this privilege was threatened, and Henry Doulton found himself involved in a long and costly legal contest.

About the time of his first arrival in the parish, the Lord of the Manor made an application to the Enclosure Commissioners for permission to enclose part of the common of Tooting Graveney and possibly to build upon it. This act was strenuously opposed by the inhabitants of Tooting, who appealed to the Commissioners, with

H

but faint encouragement. One of them said frankly that the law affecting commons and other open spaces was 'a virgin soil which the courts of law had yet to plough'. The Lord of the Manor was not amenable to sentiment and instituted six actions for trespass against the inhabitants of Tooting. At a public meeting Henry Doulton was appealed to for advice, and he suggested a compromise. This was that half of the Tooting Graveney common should be devoted to the public use for ever, while the other half was to become the freehold of the Lord of the Manor, with this important condition, *that for twenty-one years it should neither be enclosed nor built upon.*

The Lord of the Manor acquiesced, and the actions for trespass were withdrawn. But this pleasant state of things did not long continue, and after a short delay the Lord of the Manor intimated to Doulton, who had been obliged to complain of excessive gravel-digging and other infringements, that his counsel had advised him that it would be unsafe for him not to enclose half the common, since otherwise he could not hold his own in severalty. He further announced that he should in future consider it 'unwise' to permit cricket or any similar game to be played on the common. Doulton was extremely indignant at this, which he held to be a distinct breach both of the letter and the spirit of the previous agreement, and he made a very strongly worded protest to the Lord of the Manor. He used to say that, cost what it might, he would be a little village Hampden and fight for the liberties of Tooting. With the help of a few neighbours, he collected a sum of about £1,000 to defray expenses, but this was exhausted at an early stage of the proceedings and owing to what Henry Doulton hotly described as 'a disgraceful apathy on the part of the people most concerned', no help could be obtained either from the Metropolitan Board of Works or any other body representing the interests of the public.

The Lord of the Manor now saw that he had his own way, and he proceeded to enclose. In November 1865—to the rage of Henry Doulton, who used to chronicle these invasions to his friends with indignation and horror—twenty-five acres of the common was enclosed, a fence put up, and, the ground having been ploughed up, the greater part of it was later sown with oats.

This conduct was appealed against, particularly by Henry Doulton, and much vain negotiation and correspondence ensued. The

whole matter remained in an entirely unsatisfactory condition until
the 22nd of May 1868 when Doulton convened a public meeting
'to consider the recent enclosures by the Lord of the Manor and to
discuss what measures, if any, ought to be taken with reference to
that enclosure'. This meeting was largely attended, and a resolution
was passed, desiring the rector and churchwardens to protect the
rights of the commoners. Principally by dint of Henry Doulton's
unwearying zeal and eloquence, Tooting had now begun to wake
up, and not only this, but public opinion throughout England, which
had hitherto been extremely slack and languid with regard to
common rights in general, was now becoming aroused. By the
lovers of open spaces and free parks, the test case of Tooting
Graveney common was watched with extreme interest, and Henry
Doulton, too, was conscious that much more was now involved
than a mere local contest between landlord and tenant.

The existing Lord of the Manor, Mr. Thompson, had originally
bought the common, together with seven copyhold cottages, for
the merely nominal sum of £3,650, from Mr. R. Goring Thomas,
the late Lord. In talking the matter over with his committee, it
occurred to Henry Doulton that the family of the former possessor
might have preserved deeds or other records which would facilitate
an examination of the conditions on which the common was held.

Accordingly, in the summer of 1868, he called on Mr. G. Goring
Thomas Treherne, the son of the former Lord of the Manor, at his
office in Bedford Row. Thus one of the most valued friendships of
Henry Doulton's life began. Mr. Treherne was impressed by the
freshness and geniality of manner, the sprightly loquacity, the eager
and indomitable fervour of the visitor who surprised him that
summer day. Instantly he became interested in the dispute; it was
found that he did possess documents which threw a useful light on
the conditions; and he soon entered hardly less actively than Henry
Doulton himself into the whole escapade of reclaiming Tooting
Graveney common from the hands of the Philistines. The Common
Preservation Society had lately come into being, and at their offices
also Doulton was an assiduous visitor.

It soon became apparent that the Lord of the Manor was impregnable unless an action could be brought against him by someone
who had indubitable common rights. This did not describe Henry
Doulton, nor Mr. Treherne, nor any other of the prominent

conspirators. At last a genuine commoner was found in the person of a sturdy old butcher of the name of Tom Betts, whose family had been settled in Tooting for more than a century. This Mr. Betts was a great 'character', humorous, bluff, with a considerable spice of adventure about him. He entertained Henry Doulton hugely, and he really added a farcical element to the whole concern. Tom Betts was persuaded to lend his name, under promise of course, of complete indemnification, whatever turn events might take. The Lord of the Manor was shrewd enough, however, to lie low, and the army of revolt had some difficulty in knowing how to start on their campaign. Henry Doulton was advised that an overt act on their part was necessary. Hence on a certain afternoon in June 1868, Tom Betts might be observed conducting a small party of navvies to the precincts of Tooting Graveney common, now blossoming with the undulated oat. A barrel of beer was brought to the battle-field and broached. In the middle distance, forbidden to take an active part, but a delighted spectator, Henry Doulton was to be observed, almost distracted with anticipation and animal spirits. Tooting soon sent forth the younger portion of its populace in large numbers, and the navvies, having refreshed themselves with the beer, sawed off the posts which surrounded the enclosure and built up with them an effective bonfire.

This was the necessary act of overt remonstrance, and the Lord of the Manor was thereupon forced to begin an action of trespass. On the 10th of July a bill was filed by Mr. Thomas Betts, 'on behalf of himself and all the owners of freehold lands and tenements within the ambit of the Manor entitled to commonable rights', against Mr. W. J. Thompson. That defendant filed his answer on the 15th of February 1869, and the cause came up for hearing before the Master of the Rolls (Lord Romilly) on the 8th of June 1870. The judge reserved his opinion, but finally on the 21st of July 1870 he pronounced a decree in favour of Betts, with costs against the Lord of the Manor. He gave the parishioners leave to break into the enclosures.

Meanwhile, the posts had been replaced by iron railings, more of the land levelled and dug up, the furze cleared off and oats sown again. When the oats blossomed it was announced that the public would once more enforce their rights. At a given day and hour the inhabitants assembled with their cattle, one of the posts nearest

Streatham Lane was sawn through at the level of the ground and kicked inwards; then the cattle were driven in. This demonstration was perfectly quiet, the police merely taking the names and addresses of those principally concerned.

Henry Doulton had in the meantime discovered that a spirited action had been taken in the year 1815 to prevent the enclosure of the commons by the then Lord of the Manor, and with complete success. This greatly strengthened his hands, and he left no stone unturned to ensure final success. How active he was, how unceasing in his labours in this cause, may be gathered from the testimony of his friend Mr. Treherne, who has kindly supplied me with the following recollections:

Throughout this business I had an intimate and constant knowledge of all that happened; I can truly say that without Mr. Doulton's invaluable and unfailing support and influence with his neighbours it would have been impossible to carry the work through. He was always at hand with advice and assistance, was indefatigable in obtaining the necessary evidence and in stirring up the enthusiasm of his neighbours, several of whom had a far larger interest in the affair than he.

That the value of our Metropolitan commons and open spaces as 'the lungs of London' has come to be regarded as an axiom in municipal economy is due to the efforts of those public-spirited men (Mr. Doulton prominent amongst them) who had the foresight and courage to stand forward as leaders of what at the commencement of the struggle was regarded by many as a forlorn hope.

I am speaking of facts within my own knowledge when I assert this—that not only have the inhabitants of Tooting to thank Doulton for the preservation of Tooting Graveney common, but the English people at large owe him sincere gratitude for having, at very great expenditure of time and of money, taken the lead in establishing a precedent which has been most useful in subsequent cases where commons in all parts of the country have been threatened with spoliation. The public mind, in the early sixties, was just beginning to awaken to the importance of preserving those metropolitan commons which had hitherto been given up without scruple to the builder and the investor. Sir

Henry Doulton was one of the very first to recognise the importance of this movement, and he did not hesitate to identify his
wealth and his energy with it.

The Lord of the Manor was curiously persistent, and appealed
against the decision of the Master of the Rolls. The appeal was
carried before Lord Hatherley, the Lord Chancellor, and on the 2nd
of August 1871 he elaborately and decisively confirmed the judgment. The victory, therefore, for the inhabitants of Tooting was
complete. A dinner was accordingly given to the intrepid Mr. Betts
early in 1872, and a jovial evening was devoted to mutual congratu-
lations. It is said that on this occasion Tom Betts surpassed himself
as an orator and as a wit, and finally, in his chronicle of the high and
puissant deeds which he had done in Tooting, gave so heroic an
account of having once beaten the parish bounds by carrying the
rector round in his arms, and whacking his head against salient
objects at intervals, that Henry Doulton was rendered absolutely
helpless with laughter, and at one time threatened to have to be
carried from the table if the worthy butcher would not desist from
being so funny.

In 1874 Henry Doulton was riding over the neighbouring common of Tooting Bec, in company with his friend and neighbour
Mr. P. W. Flower, of Tooting (the father of Lord Battersea), when
it occurred to him that a group of residents might purchase this, so
as to prevent it from being enclosed. The opportunity, he thought,
was a favourable one, the greatly reduced and juster estimate of the
real value of the manorial rights having become apparent in consequence of the recent action concerning Tooting Graveney common. His proposal received encouragement, and the rights of the
Lord of the Manor of Tooting Bec were eventually purchased for
£12,000. The common was then dedicated to the public use and
transferred to the Metropolitan Board of Works, on condition of
the repayment of the purchase money.

But no sooner had the Board of Works become the owners than,
in 1875, they attempted to pass a by-law interfering with some of the
most valued privileges hitherto exercised by the inhabitants of the
neighbourhood, and in particular by the village Hampden himself.
The Board of Works dared to lay a sacrilegious hand on the bridle
reins of gentlemen riding on horseback across either of the Tooting

commons. Undaunted by Henry Doulton's just indignation, the Board of Works began to put up posts with a swinging chain uniting each pair, to prevent this exercise. Henry Doulton, though wearied with years of fighting, instantly shook off repose and entered the fray with all his former ardour. With the utmost energy he drew up a protest from the householders of Tooting, and in a very few hours had it signed, not a single person refusing his consent. Once more, victory attended Henry Doulton as the tribune of Tooting. The Metropolitan Board of Works showed fight, but was ruthlessly snubbed by the First Commissioner, Lord Henry Lennox, who vetoed the by-law, and bade the Board to clear away its obnoxious posts.

It is difficult to know why the Metropolitan Board of Works has so grounded an antipathy to the horse. In 1879 it made a bold plunge and set up the posts again. Meanwhile, by an Act of 1877 (40 Vict. Cap. S. 8 6), it had been provided that a proposed by-law requires confirmation by one of Her Majesty's principal Secretaries of State. The representatives of the parishes of Tooting Graveney and Tooting Bec had no idea of this change in the legislation and were within an ace of losing the benefit conferred by it. Once more it was through the vigilance of Henry Doulton that the state of things was discovered a day or two before it was too late, and an application made to Mr. (later Lord) Cross, who decided, on the 15th of April 1879, that 'it is not necessary to impose restrictions on riding on Tooting Bec and Tooting Graveney commons'. Once more the defeated lictors were ordered to carry their sheaves of 'posts' away.

Amazing to record, they refused to do so. In spite of the cancelling of their by-law, in spite of the decision of the First Commissioner, the Board of Works would not move a post. Nor was it until defeated, point by point, in an ignominious and unaccountable struggle, that the Board at length acknowledged itself beaten, and churlishly readmitted horsemen to the commons.

It would be tedious to recount the petty interferences which continued for many years to be used as a weapon to annoy the residents of Streatham and Tooting, so that the very body which was supposed to be instituted to defend the liberties of the parish came to be looked upon as the most obstinate of its enemies. Almost to the end of his life, certainly until 1893, Sir Henry Doulton was engaged in resisting what he and his neighbours conceived to be insidious attacks on their rights by the petty tyrants of official bumbledom. It would be to give a very poor and truncated sketch of Sir Henry Doulton's life to omit to describe the efforts which he made, through more than a quarter of a century, to preserve for public use the commons and open spaces of the part of Surrey in which he lived. In the prosecution of this scheme he spared neither time nor money; his unselfish energy never flagged, and his persistency was crowned with success after success. In the history of the remarkable revival of an interest in the preservation of open spaces, a matter of immense importance to the future comfort of our great population, Sir Henry Doulton deserves an honourable page for his life-long and often almost single-handed defence of the common lands of Surrey.

7

Arts and handicrafts
1880 to 1885

It was, I think, in 1880 that I first enjoyed the privilege of Mr. Doulton's acquaintance. I am unable to recollect, or to discover, to whom I owed my introduction to him, and I am almost sure that nobody acted the amiable part of go-between. I believe that he wrote to me about something which I had written, and that my reply led him to invite me to Lambeth, and, almost immediately afterwards, to Tooting. I cannot, in fact, recall any relation between us more distant than friendship; there were no transitional steps. I know that I liked him immensely, from the first, and that his cordiality never slackened to the end. His manner with young men who attracted his sympathy was perfect. I remember that I did not realise, and afterwards found it very difficult to believe, that he was nearly so old as he actually was. In 1880, of course, he was sixty years of age, but in his ways, his appearance, his quickness and buoyancy of mind, he might have been no more than forty-five. Although he lived so sedentary a life, taking but little physical exercise except his daily rides, his figure was slight and his gestures elastic and mercurial. His gentleness, vivacity and ardour were the qualities of a prolonged and innate youthfulness. If it is not absurd to say so there was something almost innocent about his graceful enthusiasm.

The great surprise, I remember, was to find in this celebrated man of business, this active manufacturer, such an obsession of poetical ideas. Not merely was his conversation saturated with literary illustrations and images, but it was impossible to converse with him for a quarter of an hour without seeing that he was essentially a man of imagination. He had lived a retired life, except in the world of affairs, and he had not had the edges of his talk rounded away by the practice of social conventions. His companions had mainly been the poets, and he talked their language, often, half-unconsciously, weaving his thoughts into a canto of reminiscences of the great English writers. He was, in fact, what used to be called a *virtuoso,* a man who, without himself wishing to write, has cultivated by means of literature a strong natural sense of what is graceful and becoming. No type is rarer, nowadays, when poetry, art, the cultivation of beauty in any one particular form, is either more and more severely specialised, or else worn as a mere conventional trick of speech. Henry Doulton belonged to an earlier race than ours, to the 'little clan' that Keats so wistfully desired to address, who gather round the poet for the anguish and ecstasy which he can give them, without any critical or comparative *arrière-pensée.* To hear him talk about Wordsworth was to realise what is the use to the world at large of such people as Wordsworth. Henry Doulton listened to the poets exactly as lovers listen to the nightingale—in a tremor of moral ecstasy.

The combination of this poetic sensibility—so absolutely unaffected, so abiding in its freshness—with the keen pursuit of business, was very piquant. The qualities seem diametrically opposed, and yet in Henry Doulton they met without a clash. He would start from Tooting in the morning, riding across his beloved and re-conquered common, with his mind and memory full of romantic reminiscences, apparently the very type of a dreamer, and he would arrive at Lambeth with his attention ready to resume the duties of his vast establishment, in all its details, with the most lucid and astute practicality. There did not seem to be any conscious transition from the one mood to the other. Prolonged meditation on an ode of Keats did not weaken his almost preternatural acumen in facing some economical problem, nor render him a whit less alert than the plainest 'City man' in forming a clear judgment on some difficult piece of commercial tactics. Indeed, it was one of the most interesting features of his character that while, when once released from business cares, his mind escaped directly to the domain of fancy, when it was in its normal state it acted with extreme decision and a sort of accurate clairvoyance. It was the secret, no doubt, of his mercantile prosperity, that he never hesitated and that the practical conditions were always at his command. The double existence certainly gave him a charming originality.

He was now becoming more and more accustomed to be told on his arrival that this or that company of more or less distinguished visitors proposed to pay the works a visit that morning, and that they would have to be immediately prepared for. Nothing pleased Henry Doulton more than to accompany such visitors through all the varied stages of the life of a pot. He liked to begin at the very beginning and take the party out into the yard, where the cartfuls of raw clay and other ingredients were deposited. Then their attention would be directed to the grinding by machinery, which reduced the material to a uniform texture; then they watched the 'wedging' of the clay by boys whose business it was to see that the air was all pressed out. The next process always gave the great potter extreme pleasure to explain. Before the eyes of the visitors a man would throw the clay on the wheel, and afterwards turn it to a true face in the lathe. 'The most primitive industry in the world,' Henry Doulton used to say in his little sermon, 'and one which comes down to us practically unaltered from the very dawn of time.' The roaring kiln at the centre of the works would then be pointed out, from afar off, as the ultimate destination of the modelled product. If the visitors were there late in the week, he would point out the 'salting' of the ware, salt being poured in through holes in the crown of the kiln, where it was decomposed and the chlorine constituent went off in smothering clouds of white fumes.

To the general visitor, the attractions of Lambeth culminated in the studios, devoted to the decoration of the partially dried ware on its way to the kiln. The art department had now vastly increased, losing, perhaps, in its expansion, a little of the freshness which it had displayed in its earliest developments, but still extremely interesting. Early in 1881 the number of skilled young women, decorating and modelling, under the general direction of Mr. Wilton Rix, had passed the figure of 200. In each room from six to ten girls were now employed under the supervision of an artist, who was herself occupied with decorated work of a higher and more independent order. I quote the report of the Conference of Architects, 100 of whom went over the pottery on the 12th of May 1881:

In some rooms patterns were being pencilled on and then incised into the surface of the jug to be ornamented; in others small points, discs and bosses, leaves and flowerets were being stamped

in clay and applied in decorative lines to vases; in others, parts of
the patterns were being brought out by colour, the pigments
being clayey solutions of closely-allied drabs and greys, un-
suggestive to an untrained eye of the ultimate brilliant appearance
when fired; a higher form of work was seen in the *pâte-sur-pâte*,
where a second clay in delicate forms and outlines was being
applied to the modelled surface by highly-skilled workers.

In one of the rooms, we saw the Misses Hannah and Florence
Barlow at work; the latter lady was executing paintings of finches
by the *pâte-sur-pâte* process in coloured clays; while her sister was
etching in upon a vase a group of Suffolk cart-horses, in which
by a few rapidly-drawn lines the peculiar heaviness and strength
of the animals were portrayed with accuracy and spirit. In another
room we found Mr. Frank A. Butler, a deaf and dumb artist,
who was keeping four assistants busy by sketching the first
portions of interlacing disc patterns on vases. In yet another
studio we found Mr. George Tinworth actively at work.

Throughout the works, visitors were always struck by incessant
evidence of the anxiety of Mr. Doulton to encourage as far as
possible the development of the originality of each individual artist,
which was further promoted by the practice of signing in monogram
every unique piece of art work, and by the prominence accorded to
the name of any worker who displayed special talent or skill. This
was a feature of the Doulton art work which claims conspicuous
notice in any sketch of the career of its originator.

The public action of Henry Doulton was not a little modified at
this time by his close friendship with Sir Philip Cunliffe-Owen,
who on the retirement of Sir Henry Cole, had been appointed
Director of the South Kensington Museum. Cunliffe-Owen was a
great believer in the merit of public exhibitions. He had been, in
1875, the Executive Commissioner to the Centennial Exhibition at
Philadelphia, and he came back more assured than ever of the value
of these attractive shows. When he became acquainted, at South
Kensington, with Henry Doulton, Cunliffe-Owen found in him a
man after his own heart, a manufacturer as anxious to exhibit as he
himself was to collect and display manufactured articles. They
encouraged one another; each fed the other's enthusiasm. Sir Philip
Cunliffe-Owen used to say that no exhibitor gave him so little

trouble as Henry Doulton, who raised no difficulties, secured just as much as could be given to him and tried for no more, never 'badgered' the unfortunate Commissioner, and, what was most to the purpose, never demanded a *quid pro quo*. The two men thoroughly liked one another, into the bargain, and the result of all this was that Cunliffe-Owen encouraged Doulton to exhibit as much as he possibly could, and delighted in facilitating all his arrangements.

It was he who attracted the attention of the royal family to the Lambeth Pottery, and led the way to the series of visits which were not merely interesting and advantageous in themselves, but which all through the eighties, tended to make Doulton's works positively fashionable. Sir Philip Cunliffe-Owen used to tell his patrons that Doulton's was 'the finest show in London'. Of these royal visits, one of the earliest was that paid, in July 1881, by the Crown Prince of Germany, afterwards the Emperor Frederick. He was so much gratified by what he saw that his example was presently followed by the Crown Princess, who came attended by Dr. Ernst Ewald, the director of what answers to the South Kensington Museum in Berlin, and two other eminent German officials. This was a highly memorable occasion. Henry Doulton was inclined at first to be shy of his august visitor, and he summoned Sir Philip to his support. But scarcely had the Empress Frederick (as she later became) cast her eyes round the first room at Lambeth than he recognised in her a kindred spirit. The fire of his enthusiasm met with an equal flame in her. The Empress had an open eye for everything, and Dr. Ewald was kept incessantly on the alert as the details of the art work were explained to her. 'Have you taken a note of this?' or 'Just notice that!' were her constant ejaculations; and as Henry Doulton's zeal increased at the same ratio as the Princess's curiosity and pleasure, he entirely forgot, and she entirely forgot, the formalities of court etiquette. Her astonished suite saw, with horror, the potter grasp the royal lady's arm to emphasise the point of some explanation, and, with even more horror, observed that she was too deeply interested to have noticed this unusual act of *lèse-majesté*.

This little anecdote is characteristic of Henry Doulton's temperament. He was extremely sensitive to sympathy, and if he did not meet with that intelligent response which the Empress Frederick so eagerly gave on this occasion he was capable of withdrawing into an icy shell. It would be easy to cap this little story by telling how

persons of the most illustrious order have found their way to Lambeth, and, not entering into the spirit of the master, have been taken
round in a cold and perfunctory way by a stolid Henry Doulton
who appeared to be struggling with internal pain. This sensitive-
ness, these contrasted moods, used to afford the greatest entertainment and some little apprehension to Sir Philip Cunliffe-Owen,
who was accustomed to say, 'I never know beforehand whether you
will fold people in your arms or snap off their heads.' But the second
alternative did not quite meet the truth of the case. If the august
personage was unsympathetic, it was Henry Doulton's head that
seemed to have been snapped off.

He was worried during these years by successive and unaccountable fires at Lambeth, some of them rather serious. The first did a
good deal of damage because the men did not know what to do, and
in the absence of trained firemen ran about in a distracted way to
fetch engines which they did not understand. After this, Doulton
was careful to have a trained and exercised brigade about the place
but fires continued to break out at strangely brief intervals and some
of them proved very awkward.

In the early part of 1881 Henry Doulton had been again attacked
with alarming illness, the result of excessive attention to business.
One of his ears was growing steadily deafer and deafer, and he was
troubled with a recurrence of the old, alarming giddiness. He was
rather peremptorily ordered to go out of England, and to take a
complete rest. Accordingly, in company with Messrs. Rose, Sparkes
and Todd, he went to Florence and Rome in April. Soon after their
arrival in Rome, the friends had the advantage of making the
acquaintance of Dr. Steele, the well-known Scots physician, to
whom so many British visitors have, during the past two generations, owed a great part of their enjoyment of Roman antiquity and
landscape.

Dr. Steele, an enthusiast for things of art and of the mind, had
then just recently discovered, in miserable lodgings in the Vico dei
Miracoli, a young English sculptor, who had left the studio of
Cavellier in Paris, and had come on to Rome in the vain hope of
obtaining work to do. He had striven and had failed, and now, in
deep indigence, with a wife and two children to support, had almost
come to the very confines of his courage. Dr. Steele, full of enthusiastic sympathy, had no sooner seen Henry Doulton and listened

to his conversation than he bethought him that here was the man whom he must bring to see his young, struggling sculptor. By this time, Mr. Alfred Gilbert—for it was no one less—had secured, by Dr. Steele's help, a not incommodious studio in the Via S. Basilio. Thither Dr. Steele brought his English friends, and there Mr. Alfred Gilbert's friendship with Henry Doulton began.

Mr. Gilbert's art, at that time just breaking away from the traditions of the French *atelier,* and leaning towards more romantic forms, was precisely calculated to please Henry Doulton. In his first conversation with his visitor, Mr. Gilbert discovered that he was full of enthusiasm for the sentiment of the early Tuscan sculptors, that in Florence he had succumbed to the genius of Donatello and Della Quercia. The English friends had already seen the newly opened Bargello, with its revelations of Florentine art. Henry Doulton's stimulating geniality, his simplicity of mind, his rapidity of movement, struck his new acquaintance in a moment. Here was a man seeking to live up to the highest ideal, by helping in a direct and practical way what he thought stood in most need of help. At their first interview, Henry Doulton saw, admired and gave a commission for the statuette by which Mr. Gilbert first became generally recognised in London and Paris, the now well-known 'Perseus'. He inoculated Mr. Rose with his own enthusiasm, and that gentleman also gave a commission. These permitted Mr. Gilbert to break away from his bondage at Rome, and to go to Perugia, where improved conditions and a far better air awaited him. The sculptor had no hesitation in saying, and in wishing me to say, that the visit of Henry Doulton to the little studio in the Via S. Basilio was the turning point in the tide of his fortunes.

In this spring of 1881 Mr. Gilbert had many talks with Henry Doulton whose visits to his studio were frequent. He had been struck, at once, with that remarkable quality in Doulton's character which we have often already had occasion to notice, his mixture of hardness on the practical and softness on the emotional side. Suffering or injustice always touched him, and the sculptor ingeniously compares him to one of those matrices found under the scoriae at Pompeii, which have no tale to tell, unless liquid plaster is poured into them; then, and then only, cooled and broken up, the image of life is perceived at its perfection inside them. Mr. Gilbert found Henry Doulton greatly occupied with *The Stones of Venice,* of which he would even quote long passages by heart, and he talked much of style, confounding a little, perhaps, literary style with the distinguishing features of plastic art—in this, doubtless an obedient disciple of Ruskin. Led by the light of *The Stones of Venice,* he had been visiting the stones of Rome, and the sculptor was interested at the instinctive way in which he responded instantly to any part taken by ceramics in the architectural harmony. In talking of the Campaniche it was the inlaid bosses of pottery which had irresistably attracted him; he longed, he said, to climb up somehow and examine them closely. What did not appeal to him in some such distinct form as this passed quickly out of his memory; but what he did retain he retained for ever.

Before dragging himself away from Rome, Henry Doulton gave Mr. Gilbert a commission for the noble group of a mother displaying a scroll to the child at her knee, which is one of the rare works which Mr. Gilbert has executed in marble. This visit brought to Henry Doulton great pleasure and a wealth of interest. He returned to England greatly benefited in health and spirits.

On the 26th of April 1882 there was a large gathering of persons connected with the firm of Messrs. Doulton & Co. to witness the presentation to Mr. Henry Doulton of an address from the ladies engaged in the Lambeth Works. To what those works had now grown may be realised from the fact that this address was signed by 250 women and girls. The movement was entirely spontaneous, and was the result of strong, genuine feeling among the artists themselves. The excuse was the fact that ten years had now elapsed, since, in April 1872, women had first been employed in the Lambeth Potteries. Mr. Sparkes took the chair, and made the meeting an occasion for recounting, briefly and simply, the history of the art movement at Lambeth ever since the Doultons first took it up. Miss Hannah Barlow, as we have seen, had been the nucleus around which this great system of art work had formed. Amidst loud applause, Henry Doulton, excessively moved and touched by so unexpected a mark of friendly consideration, accepted the vellum address, with all its signatures attached, and made an appropriate speech in reply. In the course of it, he said that in his youth he had been horrified in the potteries of Staffordshire to see the coarse and degrading work in which women were employed, and that this had given him a prejudice against women's work.

The text of the letter, which was signed by the 250 ladies, should, perhaps, be given here, as it was a document which Henry Doulton held among his greatest treasures:

TO HENRY DOULTON, ESQ.,

Chevalier of the Legion of Honour

Dear Sir,

Ten years having now elapsed since the introduction of Female Employment into the Lambeth Art Pottery, we the undersigned being the whole of the Lady Artists and Assistants now engaged in the Studios upon the work, desire to take this opportunity of expressing our obligations to you for the origination of an occupation at once interesting and elevating to so large a number of our sex.

We also desire to record our very high appreciation of the arrangements made for our comfort and convenience in the various sections.

Each year since the opening of the Art Studios has seen a large increase in our numbers, and an extension of the variety of decoration.

There has also been an extended patronage and appreciation on the part of art critics and the public, while the continued demand for our productions leads us to the conviction that we are fully justified in congratulating you on the marked success of the undertaking.

We would express our hope that the Department which has so auspiciously completed its first decennium, may long continue to prosper and assure you to this end no effort on our part shall be wanting.

Wishing you continued health and prosperity,

We are, dear Sir,

With much respect,

Yours most faithfully, etc.

Throughout these years, Henry Doulton became more and more an exhibitor of his manufactures, both artistic and utilitarian. In this he was aided and abetted by Sir Philip Cunliffe-Owen, although often opposed by his own agents and managers, who thought that it was a mistake to allow his rivals to see everything that he invented and adapted, in all its attractive novelty. These objections Henry

I

Doulton overruled, and when he was entreated to recollect that his fellow-potters would find out what he was doing he replied, 'That's exactly why I wish to have it done. While they are trying to imitate us, we shall be spending the time in inventing something fresh.' Accordingly, during all these years, not an exhibition of the least importance was opened at home or abroad but Doultons had their section or at least their stand at it. They exhibited more freely and more abundantly than any other manufacturers, perhaps, in the whole of Europe. They were strong enough to brave the dangers of such publicity, and, in return, they became known in every country of the globe. This was the great epoch of exhibitions, and Doulton was in the forefront of those who competed in this way in the open arena. He was warmly supported by such friends as Sir Philip Cunliffe-Owen and Sir George Birdwood, in whom the genius of organisation was strongly developed. Times have changed, and exhibitions are not the commercial factor that they were twenty years ago, but it would be more than rash to suggest that Henry Doulton, with his astonishing *flair,* did not know perfectly well what he was doing in being well represented in every World's Show from China to Peru.

Among new productions of 1883 and 1884, much was expected from what was called 'Nature-printed Pottery'. This was produced by impressing fresh leaves or blossoms on the pot or vase when it was just fresh from the potter's wheel. When the objects adhered smoothly to the surface, the whole pot was covered with a thin coating of coloured clay, which was allowed to dry, after which the flowers or leaves were removed, leaving an exact imprint. To emphasise these forms, they were often delicately *repoussé* from within. This was, perhaps, a not very artistic contrivance, but the public likes variety. A new sort of manufacture was introduced about this time, called 'Silicon'; this was pottery of great hardness, the body being highly vitrified, and colours infused into the mass. What was called *'painting in appliqué'* was also tried as an alternative. It is doubtful whether any of these kinds of skill could compete with the original development of the 'sgraffito' stoneware, in the hands of the artists who first employed it in the early seventies; they added, however, to the sense of profusion and fertility which was so characteristic of the Lambeth Works all through this period of stimulus and varied prosperity.

The artist who displayed the most pronounced talent during these years at Lambeth, and the one in whom the public found most to attract and amuse it, was obviously Mr. George Tinworth. His earliest sketches in sculpture had been made, not in terracotta, but in stoneware. In 1871 he designed and executed a salt-cellar, the sides of which were covered with figures in high relief, representing four scenes from the last hours of the life of Christ. In 1872, he finished a cabinet in ebonised wood, with twelve little stoneware panels of Scripture subjects; this was thought a great curiosity, and was bought by the South Kensington Museum. These panels were each eight inches by four, crowded with figures, and illustrating such themes as 'Balaam meeting the Angel' and 'Zaccheus'; they were executed very rudely in the plain green clay with some rough admixture of blue and when they left the kiln they looked like quaint productions of some old German potter, struggling with a material which he had but poorly understood. It is amusing to compare these primitive conceptions of Biblical narrative with the sculptor's later treatment of the same scenes. Almost all of the subjects in these first panels are rude sketches of compositions which Mr. Tinworth has since carried out in more perfect form.

In 1875 Mr. Ruskin discovered, and in 1876 the famous architect, George Edmund Street, began actively to encourage, the talent of Tinworth. Each year, now, he had his scriptural panels in the vestibule of the Royal Academy, and the public began eagerly to look for his work as a matter of course. Henry Doulton took the most animated interest in the preparation of each dramatic conception, and he tried to persuade Street to combine his own architectural labours with the sculpturesque inventions of Mr. Tinworth. It did not, however, seem at that time possible to employ stoneware in architecture, and the three men had many consultations as to the material in which Tinworth should work. Street recommended carving in wood, but the sculptor and the potter equally declined to entertain this suggestion. Street then came forward with a definite commission. He proposed that Mr. Tinworth should produce a reredos for York Minster, and that he should sketch it in terracotta and execute it in wood. This again, Mr. Tinworth refused to do; the scheme fell through for eight or nine months, but Henry Doulton had not abandoned it. He made a variety of experiments in improving the colour of terracotta, and when these had at length resulted in a satisfactory tint, he asked Street to come and inspect it at Lambeth. The architect was so highly delighted that he gave Mr. Tinworth the commission for the York reredos on the spot. Years later the figures in the reredos were coloured and gilded to look like painted wood. This did not represent any change of front on Mr. Tinworth's part; he was not consulted and the responsibility for these remarkable changes probably lies with the local clergy.[38]

Early in the eighties, Mr. Tinworth, encouraged by the large ecclesiastical work he had been doing at York, began to produce compositions on a much larger scale than any he had attempted before. Two of these were seen at Burlington House, the 'Going to Calvary', in 1880, and the 'Triumphant Entry into Jerusalem', in 1881. The latter was so large that space for it was with the greatest difficulty found at the Royal Academy, and when, in 1882, Tinworth sent a still more enormous 'Preparing for the Crucifixion', the Academicians, with the best will in the world, simply could not find a wall large enough to contain it. He had started an equally huge 'Leaving the Judgment Hall' for 1883. These, therefore, could not be seen by the public, and, in the face of the great curiosity and interest awakened by Tinworth's sculpture, Henry Doulton found himself baffled by the artist's ambition, which he was unwilling to check. In the winter of 1882, then, he took me into his counsel, and asked me to suggest to him a mode in which Tinworth's new panels should be seen. After a good deal of consultation, it was determined that a complete 'one-man show', representing the evolution of Mr. Tinworth's talent from its earliest evidences, should be brought together and exhibited in Conduit Street, and I was commissioned to prepare a biographical and critical essay on the subject.

Eventually all this was carried out, with Henry Doulton's customary and astounding energy. The *Critical Essay on the Life and Works of George Tinworth* duly appeared in the spring of 1883, a long vellum quarto, illustrated by thirty plates in Goupil photogravures of a kind never till then attempted in England. These had, as a matter of fact, to be manufactured, to their last touch, in Paris, no English firm in those days knowing the least of the mysteries of the process. The volume was a triumph of book production.

[38] The reredos which depicts the Crucifixion is now in the St. Stephen's Chapel of York Minster. There is a detailed description of it in one of the *York Minster Picture Books* series entitled 'The First Hour of the Crucifixion'.

Unhappily, almost the whole of the edition was destroyed in a fire at the Fine Art Society, and the volume, which was not reprinted, is therefore of the utmost rarity. In the preparation of the literary part of it, I was brought into the closest relations with Henry Doulton, whose interest in the minutest details of the work was unflagging, and I had opportunities, by these means, of observing his methods of thought and action, which years of mere acquaintanceship would never have supplied. I recollect, too, in connection with that piece of literature, immense talks at Lambeth, and still more in the garden at Tooting, in which the conversation slipped far away from stoneware and sculpture to wider themes of speculation, until we found that we had strayed unconsciously

> In Lessing's track, and tried to see
> What painting is, what poetry.

Strange that of the intellectual life's most vivid pleasure, the free talk of friend with friend, so little should remain, even to the most careful, in the crucible of memory!

In the course of May 1883 the works of Mr. Tinworth were brought together and arranged on the walls of the galleries in Conduit Street. The delight of Henry Doulton was unbounded; he told me that he had never enjoyed an exhibition so intensely, which meant much on the lips of one with whom exhibitions were a passion. The succession of pale panels, with their multitudes of figures in relief—perfect microcosms of Biblical vitality—looked extremely well. They excited curiosity, and they certainly repaid it richly. When all was ready, the world was asked to see. The Prince and the Princess of Wales came first, to a private view of their own, and the Princess was so much entertained and fascinated by the endless succession of animated Scripture scenes, that she was scarcely to be torn away to other social duties. She passed to her carriage at length, protesting against having to go so soon, with the vellum volume in her hands. Then a selected public came, and took an almost childish pleasure in the groups of gesticulating figures. Society accepted the occasion as a kind of glorified Sunday-school class—piety and fine art combined. Then the general public, and the thing became a furore; again and again, after the stated period of exhibition was over, Henry Doulton was wheedled into letting the show remain open a few days longer. Everybody, except some very hypercritical sticklers for conventional principles of statuary, enjoyed the series of terracotta illustrations to the Bible without restraint. And art has many chambers, and there are more kinds of sculpture than were known in Athens.

At the International Health Exhibition in 1884 Henry Doulton outdid himself in lavish and ingenious display. The collection of pottery was the finest that had ever been brought together, and it was enclosed in a building, popularly known as the 'Doulton Trophy', which was itself a triumph of ceramic construction. It stood at the end of the central gallery, and was, in fact, a highly ingenious and spacious pavilion, with an Indian dome, supported on intersecting arches, the whole built from designs by Mr. Sparkes. The outside was decorated by sixteen panels of glazed Doulton Work —views of Lambeth, places of industrial art, famous potters, and the like. The interior was really extremely pretty, divided into four rooms, each profusely fitted up with Doulton Ware, and the inside of the dome brilliant with encaustic tiles. The corners of the 'Trophy' were utilised for the exhibition of filters, stoves and sanitary ware. Mr. De Morgan started the name of 'The Big Potter' for Henry Doulton, and it was immediately taken up. The Doulton Trophy was the rage, and rather threw the rest of the International Health Exhibition into the shade. There was pottery—pottery everywhere; new applications of pottery that no one had ever dreamed of, the whole thing designed and carried out on a very daring scale. It is a great pity that the Doulton Trophy of 1884, which cost over £2,000 to construct and arrange, was not preserved, for in several respects it was a unique thing; and nothing which Henry Doulton had up to that time conceived had made his name so universally popular. There was a rage for Lambeth pottery. Some wag gave out that Mr. Doulton had invented a salt-glaze umbrella, and that everyone of fashion was wearing enamelled porcelain next the skin. It seemed as though the millennium of pottery had set in. The furore reached its height on the evening of the 23rd of September, when Henry Doulton entertained the Prince and Princess of Wales in his pavilion, to the light of the then novel incandescent lamps.

One of Henry Doulton's most valued friends at this period was James Nasmyth, F.R.S., the inventor of the steam hammer, and

eminent both as an astronomer and an engineer. An anecdote is,
perhaps, worth recording as illustrative of Henry Doulton's outlook
on money. James Nasmyth arrived one day at Lambeth in a ferment
of excitement, 'I have a wonderful invention,' he said. 'I have
discovered how you can make a mould, pervious to the air, in which
you can put in the clay, stir it round, see it adhere, and turn out your
pot in five minutes. It will revolutionise pottery. Why! there's a
couple of hundred thousand pounds in it.' Henry Doulton grasped
his arm, and said, smilingly, 'What should I do with a couple of
hundred thousand pounds? I have enough to occupy my thoughts
from morning to night, and more money than I need.' 'You are
quite right,' said Nasmyth, 'of course you have, of course you have!'
and his enthusiasm faded away. 'Money is not everything,' Doulton
was constantly saying, and it was sincerely said. His first interest in
life was good potting, the best and soundest potting that a strict
attendance to every aspect of the processes would secure. If, in
consequence of this, the money flowed in—as it did—that was very
agreeable, but it was never the first object. Some parts of his business
were not lucrative; the art work, for instance, never paid its way,
and yet this was the department which he loved the most. He was
no doubt rewarded for his comparative indifference to money for
its own sake, since it prevented him ever being snared into speculation.[39]

A subject which greatly absorbed the attention of Henry Doulton
in the winter and spring of 1884–5 was the engagement of his only
son, Mr. H. Lewis Doulton, who was married to Miss Jessie White
on the 18th of April 1885. This event was the occasion of a spontaneous outburst of friendly feeling among his workpeople, which
gave the enthusiastic 'Big Potter' extreme pleasure. The employees
at Lambeth, Rowley Regis, Smethwick, St. Helens, and Burslem
united to show their esteem for the head of the firm and for his son

[39] Nasmyth's invention sounds like some form of 'slip-casting'—casting with
liquid clay in plaster moulds. This process, as Doulton would certainly have
known, was already used in Staffordshire. Probably he did not want to hurt
Nasmyth's feelings by telling him so. Tinworth's studio alone often involved a
loss of over £1,000 a year. Although it is probably correct that, so far as the
accounts could show, the Lambeth art wares as a whole generally produced little
or no profit, their prestige value, which made the name Doulton famous all over
the world, was incalculable.

by giving various, and in several cases, costly gifts to the young married couple. These were presented by deputations who met, on the 9th of April, in the lecture hall of the Lambeth Works. In order to celebrate the occasion among his own people, Henry Doulton then invited the whole of his staff to a series of simultaneous entertainments. The London one, which was attended by more than 1,000 employees, was arranged at the Alexandra Palace. At the same moment, 650 people sat down to supper in the covered market of Burslem. At these and at all the other festivities staged in honour of the marriage the cordiality was so natural and so universal that Henry Doulton was extremely touched by it. I remember his saying to me at the time, in his ardent way, 'I don't suppose that there is another manufacturer in England who has such nice people to work for him as I have. I think that pottery makes people wonderfully warm-hearted.' He despaired of thanking everyone individually, and so he sent this round robin to everybody in his five great factories:

To the Clerks, Managers, Travellers, Foremen,
and Workmen of Messrs. Doulton & Co.
My Dear Friends,
The marriage of my son has called forth such a warmth of kindly feeling to my family, and our firm, on the part of all associated with us in business, that I feel I cannot rest content without sending you a few words of thankful acknowledgment.
That my son in his responsible and difficult position has won your esteem, is to me a source of pride and gratitude. I know that he has striven to be just, and I am sure he has been kind, and that he has succeeded, you have shown not only by the splendid presents you have given him, but still more by the hearty and cordial addresses and good wishes that have accompanied them.
For the growth of our firm, and for the honours we have won in the peaceful rivalries of Commerce, we are indebted in no small measure to your earnest efforts and cordial co-operation.
Looking forward, I am cheered by the thought that those loyal personal relations, which I am happy to know still subsist between us, are the best guarantee for our mutual welfare in the future.
Wishing you and your families every blessing,
I am, yours very truly,
Henry Doulton

The reputation of Henry Doulton went up by leaps and bounds all through these years, and reached its culminating point in 1885. Subsequent rewards and distinctions, though gratifying, could but be subsidiary to the extraordinary honour paid him by the Society of Arts in awarding to the Potter of Lambeth their Albert Medal. This medal was struck 'to reward distinguished merit in promoting Arts, Manufactures or Commerce', but as a rule it had been used as a supreme form of recognition of the services of eminent men of science. An idea of the rarity with which it is awarded may be gained from glancing at a list of the successive recipients. The immediate precursors of Henry Doulton had been Sir Joseph Hooker, Pasteur, James Prescott Joule, Lord Kelvin, Lord Armstrong, J. B. Dumas. It was with men like these that the Society of Arts now determined to measure Henry Doulton and the compliment seems to me unquestionably the greatest that he ever received. Nor was he indifferent or unmoved by it, himself.

A confidential letter from Sir George Birdwood to the council seems to have set the project in movement on the 19th of April 1885. In this letter, which I have been permitted to see, the attention of the Society of Arts was officially drawn to 'the great impulse given by Mr. Henry Doulton to the production of art pottery in this country, by the revival in Lambeth since 1871, of the manufacture of ornamental salt-glazed stoneware, of the kind that has become universally known as Doulton Ware'. With this were combined, in a secondary sense, the business carried on by the firm, 'since 1834, in stoneware chemical apparatus, and, since 1846, in stoneware drain-pipes and other sanitary works'. Sir George Birdwood proceeded to give a brief summary of the history of pottery in Lambeth from the earliest traces of those immigrants from Delft who settled round the Archbishop's Palace in the seventeenth century, down to the revival, or creation, of ornamental salt-glazed stoneware by Henry Doulton and Mr. Sparkes. He gave a particular account, too, of the development of the Lambeth Potteries, from 1834 down to 1885, and closed as follows:

It is not, however, on this account that Henry Doulton's work is chiefly deserving of the recognition of the Society. Nor is it because of the opening he has made for the occupation of steadily increasing numbers of educated women in a handicraft in which

they are so happily fitted to excel—and in a neighbourhood where
such employment of female labour has been previously altogether
unknown. What we are called upon to honour in him above
everything else is his sustained devotion to the principles on which
he has acted in organising the revival of the old ceramic handicraft
of Lambeth, and through the fruitful operation of which it has
so rapidly assumed a genuinely indigenous and national type.
These simple principles are two: the first (inspired by the love
which Mr. Henry Doulton acquired in early life for the use of the
potter's wheel) being to make every piece intended for decoration,
or all that can be so made—and there are few that cannot—on the
wheel, by which alone living pottery can be made; the second,
also derived from the personal experiences of Mr. Henry
Doulton, to give the utmost scope to the individuality of the
designer into whose hands the piece, as thrown on the wheel, is
at once passed in its soft state for ornamentation. . . . It is in this
way that Mr. Henry Doulton has created a school, or, rather,
several schools of English pottery, the influence of which is being
felt in the revival of the ceramic arts in all the countries of the old
world, where they had become degraded during the last fifty
years by the use of machinery in their production. The influence
of his example in the United States has been quite marvellous,
this country now producing—and it has all been done since 1871,
—the most artistic common pottery made in any country in the
world. Moreover, all the arts which refine and elevate human life
being connected with one another, the improvement of any one
of them leads in the end to the improvement of them all; and the
marked advance in recent years of every branch of higher industrial work in England, which has now placed us at the head of the
art manufactures of the West, may be distinctly traced to the
influence of the Lambeth art-pottery, and particularly to the now
widespread application of Mr. Henry Doulton's principles, of
relying as much as possible on actual hand work, and on the
natural artistic instincts of each individual hand worker.

In June the Albert Medal was duly awarded to Henry Doulton,
and the Prince of Wales consented to present it. In announcing their
decision, the Council of the Society of Arts remarked that they 'felt
that the establishment of the new industry of artistic stoneware fully

justified' the distinction, but 'while recording this opinion, they wished it to be understood that in making the award they had also in view the other services rendered by Mr. Doulton to the cause of technical education, especially the technical education of women, to sanitary science by the productions of his firm, and, though, in a less degree, to other branches of science by the manufacture of appliances of suitable character'.

It is usual for the recipient of the Albert Medal to proceed to Marlborough House to be invested with it. The Prince of Wales, however, had on this occasion one of those luminously tactful inspirations which have done so much to make him popular. He observed that it would be far more interesting that Mr. Doulton should receive him at Lambeth, in the midst of his work-people, and with the evidences of his various industry around him.

Accordingly, on Monday the 21st of December 1885, Lambeth was lifted to the seventh heaven of patriotic satisfaction by seeing the Prince of Wales, accompanied by Sir Henry Ponsonby and Lord Sudeley, arrive at the showrooms on the Albert Embankment, where Henry Doulton, supported by Sir Frederick Abel, as chairman of the Council of the Society of Arts, and by Archbishop Benson, as the most distinguished inhabitant of the borough, were waiting to receive him. There was a large and distinguished company present. The choir from Westminster Abbey had come over the water to give a musical grace to the occasion. The showroom did not know itself in crimson draperies and a velvet dais. The Prince's address was brief, pointed and appreciative. Henry Doulton, unable to trust his memory at such a moment, read a capital little essay in reply, in which he characteristically remarked that his motto had always been *Le beau est la splendeur du vrai*. The close of his speech was certainly happy:

> As illustrating the continuity of English history, may I, in con-
> clusion, be permitted to remind your Royal Highness that the
> place in which we are now assembled is in the Prince's Ward—or
> as I prefer to call it by its old name, the Prince's Liberty of the
> Parish of Lambeth—forming part of the Manor of Kennington,
> of which your Royal Highness is the Lord? It might be called the
> cradle of the Princes of Wales. The arms of your Royal Highness,
> with its plume of feathers and its noble motto, was first assumed

by one of the most illustrious and best beloved of his race, Edward the Black Prince, who is specially associated with the manor. Tradition says it was in Prince's Liberty that the Black Prince gave a grand and sumptuous banquet when he returned home fresh from the honours of Crecy and Poictiers. The conquests of your Royal Highness have been on other fields, but 'Peace hath her victories no less renowned than war'; and in the paths of artistic and industrious progress, in international exhibitions, and in all humane enterprises for the welfare and happiness of Her Majesty's subjects throughout her vast empire, your Royal Highness has been a leader whom all good men have been proud to follow.

It was peculiarly characteristic of Henry Doulton that at this moment, when he stood on the very pinnacle of success, he should, with an irresistible instinct, call Lambeth in, as it were, to share it with him. His life had been a part of Lambeth, and he did not wish to be known, he did not expect to be remembered, except as a portion of the little commonwealth or peculiar with which he was so intimately associated.

It was characteristic of him, too, that when the Prince of Wales' visit was first announced to him he had eagerly asked whether his people might not have a practical share in the matter. This had been most graciously acceded, and consequently when the potter had ended his discourse of thanks, the senior foreman in the works, Mr. Edward Bryon, stood forward, and presented to the Prince an address from 'the craftsmen, artists and workers employed in the various branches of Messrs. Doulton and Co.'s Lambeth Potteries', to which His Royal Highness made an appropriate reply, and was then conducted in state through the various ateliers and work-shops.

This ceremony attracted a very wide attention, the occasion of it being something singular in the history of art in this country. The press was highly complimentary, and some remarks in *The Times* leader next morning (December 22nd, 1885) summed up the situation excellently.

It is impossible to dissociate such a ceremony as that of yesterday from the discussions that are now so frequent upon technical education and its effects both on artistic progress and commercial prosperity. The success of the Lambeth works, as Mr. Doulton yesterday fully admitted, is largely due to the efficiency of the Lambeth School of Art. Founded twenty-five years ago by the Prince of Wales,[40] then at the very beginning of his public life, this school has flourished amazingly, and has produced on the one side a large number of artists, in the more generally accepted sense of the term, and on the other an unfailing supply of 'artists and workers' for the Lambeth Pottery. The two institutions have reacted upon one another. Students entering the school know that, if they show any talent for design there is a remunerative opening for it close by; and the pottery finds an unfailing supply of young men and young women to draw upon for its designing room. The example of this double organisation might well be more widely followed. The success of Messrs. Doulton's productions are a standing proof, to put the matter in the bluntest possible form, that artistic training pays.

A proof of the sincerity of the local response to his parochial patriotism—if such a phrase may for once be used in none but a good sense—was offered by a fact which greatly touched Henry Doulton. By some unfortunate accident, for which no one was willing to claim responsibility, the Bishop of the Diocese was not invited to the meeting nor in any way informed of it. The first intimation which Henry Doulton received of this omission was contained in a letter from the Bishop of Rochester himself (Dr. A. W. Thorold, afterwards Bishop of Winchester), saying that he wished to convey to Henry Doulton his 'cordial sympathy in this gratifying and well-deserved recognition of your distinguished services not only to Art, and to civilisation, but also to our own country, and particularly to South London'. The Bishop went on to regret that he had not been offered the opportunity of expressing, by his presence, 'my personal acknowledgment, as Bishop of the Diocese, of all you have done for the poor and populous neighbourhood around you'.

This communication—while it could not fail, in one sense, to vex the potter—deeply gratified him in another. He remained on friendliest terms with Bishop Thorold, until the death of the latter in 1895. But of all the letters which arrived to cheer the approach

[40] This is incorrect—see pages 59 and 61.

of Christmas 1885, certainly not the least valued was one from the
enthusiastic and cordial Sir Philip Cunliffe-Owen:

To Henry Doulton   21, Dec. 1885
My dear Friend,

   I must ask you to have the goodness to present my very kindest
regards to Mrs. Doulton and to ask her permission, as her husband's friend, to congratulate her upon the exceptional honour
which has been conferred upon you and your dear family, by the
world-wide acknowledgment of your sterling worth as a man,
as an employer, and as a friend of the Working Classes.

   Never did the Prince of Wales do *himself* more honour. In this
Mrs. Doulton, who knows you best, will agree with me.

   I never took my eyes off the bright faces of your dear daughters,
and it was a picture never to be erased from my memory to
watch their loving and proud expressions while they witnessed
the honour so deservedly conferred upon such a tender Father.

                              Your affectionate Friend,
                              Philip Cunliffe-Owen

THE BURSLEM POTTERY

*(Editor's note: Although it is evident from Gosse's remarks on pages 122 and 169
that one of his original drafts included a section on Doulton's Burslem pottery,
there is no trace of this in the final version. Henry Doulton's activities in building
up the Burslem enterprise were of such importance that no account of his life and
work could possibly be considered complete without some record of this phase of
his career. I therefore append at this point an extract from my book* Royal
Doulton: 1815–1965 *(Hutchinson 1965) in order to some extent to fill the gap.)*

In 1877 came another unexpected development which, although regarded
at first with a certain derision by many of the Staffordshire potters and
with scepticism by some of the Lambeth managers, was to bring added
renown to the firm and to influence profoundly its whole future. This
arose from a decision by Henry Doulton to acquire an interest in a small
Burslem factory in the heart of the North Staffordshire Potteries. Before
describing this new venture it is necessary to consider briefly the background against which it arose.

Speed's list of Staffordshire manufactures in 1625 does not even mention pottery. There had been potters in Burslem and adjoining districts since Roman times, and even earlier, but probably no more than elsewhere. Today, on the other hand, 'the Potteries'—without any geographical qualification—denotes for china-buyers all over the world a concentrated area in North Staffordshire, covering some forty square miles, with about 300,000 inhabitants, of whom perhaps half depend for their livelihood on pottery-making and ancillary industries supplying machinery, colour pigments, lithographs, silk-screen transfers and other essential materials.

Up to the Industrial Revolution there was no reason for potters to congregate in one area. Almost every village had its potter and, in many parts of the country, a farmer and his family, in the winter evenings or other periods not devoted to agriculture and livestock, would make simple kitchen crocks for their own needs; any surplus was sold at the nearest market-town, and brought in a small additional income. Pottery-making had its origin literally in the soil—the same good earth that provided sustenance for man and beast. The question thus arises: how did it come to be concentrated to such an astonishing degree in this particular district?

Many factors contributed to this outcome. They include the availability of good plastic clays for making the red and drab-coloured earthenwares which prevailed up to the mid-eighteenth century; the presence of abundant coal supplies which enabled local potters to increase their output at a time when demand was increasing and the shortage of wood for firing kilns had become a problem in many places; the discovery by the Eler brothers that local hematite clays were ideal for making redware teapots in imitation of the imported Yi-hsing wares so popular with the late seventeenth century tea-drinkers; and the deposits within easy reach in Derbyshire and Cheshire of lead ore for one type of glazing and of common salt for another. It has been suggested that a certain impetus was also given by the Dissolution of the Monasteries when monk-potters from Hulton Abbey in Burslem parish became laymen-potters to earn a living. With the growing use of steam power and machinery, the proximity of the area to midland foundries and engineering firms became another advantage.

Over and above all these factors was the human element itself—the independent, dogged and even stubborn streak in many of the local enfranchised copyhold farmers, used to overcoming difficulties in their own way and peculiarly fitted to deal with a refractory medium such as clay. And from this native stock the district engendered gifted sons to carry on the traditions of their forefathers—men such as Astbury,

Whieldon, Twyford, Wood, Wedgwood and Spode, who combined skill in potting with astuteness in business transactions. It is not without significance that some of these names have a dynastic ring, and that to this day one hears references, for instance, to Ralph Wood I, Ralph Wood II and Ralph Wood III.

Even now in North Staffordshire one meets comparatively few actual clay-workers who were not born in the district. The non-Staffordshire element is found mainly among technicians, designers, artists, modellers and sales staff. Thousands of workers in the various potteries can trace back their connection with the craft for several generations.

There was, however, one foreign element to which the Staffordshire pottery industry, in its early days, unquestionably owed an incalculable debt. This was the advent of the Eler brothers, former Dutch silversmiths turned potters. The difference between the tea- and coffee-pots, tea- and coffee-cups, tea-canisters and mugs made by them and the crude wares which preceded them is nothing short of revolutionary. The forms are new and refined—thanks no doubt to the Elers' training as silversmiths; the body is made from well-levigated and finely sifted clays—an innovation of the utmost importance for subsequent tableware developments; the fine-grained wares are thin, light in weight and delicately made, many having been turned in a lathe after being formed on the wheel or cast in moulds; the stamped relief decorations of Chinese-style plum-blossom, foliage, birds and figures are exquisitely done. It is not surprising that teapots in this style sold at a guinea a piece—a high price in those days— and that people travelled to Bradwell to try to discover how they were made. The Elers introduced into English pottery-making a degree of precision and refinement which had never before been known.

The popularity of their wares led to Staffordshire potters gradually adopting similar techniques, and between the beginning and the last third of the eighteenth century redware was being made by Astbury, Whieldon, Wedgwood and others. Perhaps the most important of all the Elers' influences was the fact that they drew attention to the existence of an important new market—the growing community of tea-drinkers. (It has been said that the prosperity of 'The Potteries' was built up on tea-drinking.) It is sad to think that the Elers enterprise itself ended in bankruptcy!

The Eler wares marked the beginning of a long process which led to the evolution of fine cream earthenware and, towards the end of the eighteenth century, of translucent bone china—two superb materials which gave the English potters pre-eminence in the world-markets both for good quality tablewares for everyday use and for the more expensive china services which, at first, only the wealthy could afford. In these developments, Whieldon, Wedgwood, Minton and Spode played leading parts.

Among the many earthenware manufacturers in Burslem, the 'mother-town' of the Staffordshire potteries, in 1877, was a firm in Nile Street known as Pinder, Bourne & Company. Pottery had been made on the site of this works since the beginning of the eighteenth century. The previous occupiers, Pinder, Bourne & Hope, also owned part of the former Enoch Wood factory at Fountain Place, and had bought some of the Wood moulds from which they continued to make for a time figures decorated in typical Victorian fashion. The main products of Pinder, Bourne & Company, however, were medium-quality earthenware tablewares, either plain cream colour or decorated with monochrome landscape prints (orange being a favourite colour); decorative jugs with randomly disposed 'Japanese sprays'; red terracotta garden ware: jet ware; telegraph insulators; and sanitary earthenware.

Doulton had occasionally bought sanitary earthenware from Pinder, Bourne, and Mr. Shadford Pinder, the sole proprietor, had visited the Lambeth Pottery. He was impressed by the phenomenal success Henry Doulton had achieved with the salt-glaze stoneware and faïence, and the latest productions which he saw being prepared for the Paris Exhibition of 1878 convinced him that Doulton was about to strengthen the claim that was already being made for him that he brought new life and inspiration into English ceramics.

Pinder had long wanted to lift his somewhat mediocre vases and tablewares into what he called 'the region of higher ceramics'—of the kind associated with such names as Wedgwood, Spode, Minton, Worcester and Derby. He decided to approach Henry Doulton and suggest that he should join him in partnership, invest an initial £12,000, and help him with his enterprise, knowledge and capital to achieve his ambition.

Fired with enthusiasm by the success of the Lambeth art-wares, Henry Doulton was intrigued by the idea of extending his interest in ceramics into the field of fine earthenware, the manufacture of which had been largely confined for over a century to that district of North Staffordshire familiarly known today as 'The Five Towns'. (There are in fact six—Burslem, Fenton, Hanley, Longton, Stoke and Tunstall—but Arnold Bennett, who made the term famous, omitted Fenton!)

Doulton was also influenced by the fact that Pinder, Bourne were making two other products in which he was greatly interested—sanitary pottery and insulators. He decided to agree to Pinder's suggestion, although he pointed out that with all his other commitments he would have to limit his interest to technical and artistic advice from the Lambeth staff, occasional visits, and a financial investment. It was agreed, rather

K

against James Duneau Doulton's better judgment, that Pinder should be the managing partner and that the firm should continue to trade as Pinder, Bourne & Company. Henry, whom James sometimes teasingly referred to as 'my brother, the Lambeth Maecenas', was by now much less commercially minded than thirty years previously and was content to leave the bulk of the business administration in the hands of James although, as in this instance, he did not always take his advice.

For the first few months the Doulton incursion into the Staffordshire stronghold of English ceramic tradition appears to have gone more or less unobserved by the local potters. Its significance can hardly have been realised by the correspondent of the *Staffordshire Advertiser* who, on 23 March 1878, reported on Doulton's success at the Paris Exhibition in these words:

Doulton Ware is certain to become a lasting name in ceramic annals, and if you in Staffordshire do not bestir yourselves, Lambeth will in truth become *'The Potteries'*, and you will have to choose a subordinate designation.

The editor perhaps had some qualms about printing such a critical comment for he tried to protect himself by adding the words: ('The which *we* do not believe.') To question the supremacy of Staffordshire must have seemed almost like blasphemy to those of whom Henry Doulton once remarked: 'In their view, we Southerners know little about God and *nothing at all* about potting!'

The Doulton influence at Pinder, Bourne's factory had in fact already had some effect by the time of the Paris Exhibition. With the help of Henry Doulton's now considerable experience of international expositions, the Burslem firm staged, in its own name, with no reference to the Doulton connection, the most impressive display of their fine earthenware products which had so far been seen. It was awarded a silver medal—an honour which, although overshadowed by Doulton's *Grand Prix* and two gold and four silver medals, was the highest granted to any earthenware-maker.

Within a year or so, the Doulton 'invasion', as it was called, had become common knowledge, as had a rumour that things were not going too well at Nile Street. Rumour for once was right. The Doulton investment had been spent unwisely; the rate of progress was disappointing; serious differences had arisen between Pinder and the Doultons. In short, it looked as if the new venture was not going to prove a success.

Henry Doulton's advent in Burslem had led to some sarcastic comments in the clubs and taverns where local pottery-owners foregathered. The heads of long-established family firms looked on him as an overweening interloper—'that stoneware fellow from London who thinks he can teach us to make pots' being one of the milder remarks. (Even today you will find people in Stoke-on-Trent who refer to Doulton as 'comparative newcomers'). There was some ribald comment also on the fact that when Henry Doulton visited the painting-room, where women were at work, he invariably took his hat off—a gesture unprecedented in their experience and one which did not, as one might think, raise him in their estimation; it merely confirmed the allegation that he was 'a bit of a fop' and quite out of his depth in Burslem. They were always willing to imitate French designs, if they were likely to sell, but to introduce French *politesse* was going too far!

The suggestion that he could repeat in Staffordshire the success he had achieved in Lambeth seemed to many almost ludicrous. The aura of the great period of the second half of the eighteenth century still hung over Staffordshire, giving rise to complacency. Making techniques had progressed but in design the wares were often sadly mediocre and garish or, at their best, imitative of French, German, Italian, Spanish, Etruscan, Greek and Oriental pottery. All the old styles were blatantly copied, including fantastic mixtures of styles. As long as the cry for 'ornament and more-ornament' was met all was thought well.

William Owen, writing in 1910 of this period, said: 'The mid-Victorian times were distinguished not merely by a neglect of beauty but by a positive cult of what was ugly. The utilitarianism of the period seemed to preclude not only the endeavour, but the hope, of reconciling use and beauty, and in all departments of life, in costume, furniture, architecture, and in the decorative and industrial arts, the artistic impulse was almost wholly absent. *And in no art was this poverty of the artistic sense more profound than in that of pottery.*'

In Burslem and the other pottery towns dwelt a population with an inherited aptitude for pottery-making and the skill which seems almost to be inborn when, for generations, a community has pursued a specialised craft in a certain measure of isolation. This isolation, however, had begun to have its dangers as well as its advantages, and many of the wares shown by the Staffordshire potters at the Great Exhibition of 1851 revealed the low level to which the industry had fallen.

The threat of failure in his new venture, far more than the possible loss of his investment, was just the spur which Henry Doulton needed to make him throw himself whole-heartedly into the task of putting the Nile Street pottery on its feet. He was prepared to lose much more than £12,000 over the first few years—provided there was some hope of achieving the ultimate object.

He decided to spend some months at Burslem personally investigating every aspect of production, for it was here that the trouble mainly lay. In 1881, differences between him and Pinder reached such a stage that the matter had to be taken to arbitration, the outcome of which was that Pinder accepted a settlement and retired from the business, and the name was changed in 1882 to Doulton & Co., Burslem, with Henry and James D. Doulton as the proprietors. By a deed dated 2 April 1884, Henry Doulton's son, Henry Lewis, also became a partner, the proportion of shares being Henry Doulton three-sixths, James D. Doulton two-sixths and Henry Lewis Doulton one-sixth.

During his investigations Henry Doulton had satisfied himself that the art director, John Slater, of whom more will be said later, was the right man in the right place. What was badly needed was a competent manager who could act wisely on his own initiative, be entrusted with a considerable measure of authority, and be relied upon to act on Doulton's dictum: 'Forget, for heaven's sake, most of what was done here in the past; we are going to make a new beginning and I intend, come what may, to bring the Burslem products up to the standards we have set in Lambeth.'

The news that a young man of twenty-three, John C. Bailey, of whom Doulton had come to form a favourable impression during his visits to Burslem, was to be appointed to this responsible post caused a sensation second only to that to which Doulton's original incursion had given rise.[41] The local wiseacres were now convinced that it was only a matter of time before the whole enterprise would have to be abandoned.

About the time that Henry Doulton first took an interest in the Pinder, Bourne Company, a young man named John Slater had been appointed Art Director—a rather grandiloquent Staffordshire expression for what at that time, in such a small pottery, would more correctly have been described as a Design Manager. Slater's father and grandfather had been artists at Derby and he himself had served an artist-apprenticeship at Minton's under the famous French Art Director, Léon Arnoux. There he had also come under the influence of another great French artist, M. L. Solon, whose name will always be associated with his beautiful *pâte-sur-pâte* work.

While with Minton, Slater had two years running won first prize for china painting at the Hanley Exhibition, in competition with the whole of Staffordshire. At the International Exhibition of 1871 his work had gained an honour. So far as the art side of the Burslem enterprise was concerned, Doulton felt that Slater, with the right guidance and encouragement, including visits abroad to widen his horizon, would prove satisfactory; what was now needed was to build up an art department under him.

[41] See pages 169–71.

Slater, as events proved, was a man who could appreciate Doulton's ideals and put them into effect. He had the faculty of selecting and training others and encouraging them in their particular gifts. He helped Doulton to follow out the policy, already so fruitful at Lambeth, of drawing upon the best available talent, both locally and further afield. Within a few years a distinguished staff of ceramic designers, artists, modellers and other craftsmen was gathered together, to whom were accorded freedom and all possible encouragement to develop and express their talents.

In this way, the danger of keeping to hackneyed, stereotyped designs, even if these included some of the best of the past—a practice which could only lead to sterility—was avoided. By the time of the Chicago Exhibition in 1893, the new Nile Street group of artists were distinguished by the same range and versatility as their colleagues at Lambeth. In achieving this end, Slater was greatly helped by his deputy, Robert Allen; by his first apprentice, Leonard Langley, who later became his invaluable personal assistant; and by Charles J. Noke, who came as a modeller in 1889 and succeeded Slater in 1914 as Art Director.

One of Slater's earliest successes, while he still had only an earthenware body at his disposal, was a revival of the old Near Eastern and Hispano-Moresque technique of lustre-painting. Here his study of chemistry as well as art enabled him to develop the beautiful iridescent effects which characterised the earlier wares while using them to produce entirely original designs. Some of these, for example the mermaids, lobsters and birds on a yellow background, are singularly attractive. The lustre effects were obtained by using certain metallic oxide compounds, especially copper and silver, for painting on the glaze. During the final firing the oxygen was 'reduced' and part of the oxide changed into the metal, copper producing an attractive ruby red, and silver a yellowish grey with a somewhat bluish reflection.

In years to come, Slater was to win numerous diplomas and medals for his designs—at the Paris, Brussels, Chicago, St. Louis, Turin, Ghent and many other exhibitions. His successor, Noke, wrote of him:

To the true potter the all importance of pots is an inspiring ideal. In that ideal he lives and breathes and has his being; he is impelled to express it visibly in form or colour, or to break his heart in impotent endeavour. . . . And so, amid the smother and smoke of the potters' ovens, John Slater worked and strove for his ideal. . . . [His] breadth of outlook assured the development of original minds, and gave each man when signing his work the chance to feel a real personal interest in every piece made. . . . John Slater, art director and artist, has left an impress upon the character and quality of Doulton pottery that will not soon be forgotten.

Slater, besides being a designer and artist, was of an inventive nature. As early as 1883 he was experimenting with a photographic process to transfer designs to pottery, and in 1889 he took out a patent for 'improvements in decorating china and the like by means of which paintings and designs are printed on a photographic plate to obtain a negative, and from the negative a gelatine printing surface produced, from which the design can then be printed on transfer paper in any of the colours commonly employed for china painting'. Further patents for improvements upon this method were taken out in 1894 and 1896.

Another Slater patent was for a process he began to develop about 1884, in which fine lace and other fabrics were used to form patterns on pottery. This process was used not only at Burslem but also, on a more extensive scale, at Lambeth.

Up to 1884 earthenware only was made at Nile Street, and, helped by the artistic experience gained at Lambeth, particularly in decorating faïence, an extended range of products gradually began to make some impact. Some of the Lambeth artists were seconded to Burslem to help in the new developments. The limited range of colours available for underglaze decoration on earthenware precluded any attempt to rival the effects that could be attained with the on-glaze enamel painting of china at some of the French, German, Danish and English factories. Slater and Bailey both hankered after a bone china body to show what could be accomplished by the new group of artists. They made several attempts to persuade Henry Doulton to agree to build a china-works but, faithful to his policy of 'one thing at a time', he refused to hear of this until satisfied that the existing productions were on a sound basis.

Between 1877 and 1880 the number employed at Nile Street had already increased from 160 to 300, and in the next four years rose to over 500. The sanitary-ware and insulator sections were doing well but the decorated earthenware had hardly begun to pay its way, although some £20,000 had already been poured into its development by 1880. At Lambeth, Bailey and Slater were regarded as something of a danger to the whole Doulton 'Empire', and one manager scornfully described the Burslem Works as 'a bung-hole without a barrel'. Fortunately the third member of what was called 'the Burslem triumvirate', Henry Doulton himself, refused to be discouraged. 'It needs time,' he would say.

For some years Doulton & Co. marketed, in addition to their own tablewares and art-wares, a wide range of products obtained from other potteries. These, which were always sold unbranded, included Sunderland, Newcastle, South Yorkshire and South Derbyshire wares, Rocking-ham teapots and ironstone china. Glass bottles and glasses for hock, claret, sherry and other wines were also sold.

Bailey and Slater evidently persisted in their attempts to persuade Henry Doulton to sanction the making of bone china, and eventually he agreed to their buying some undecorated china from another Burslem firm, Bodley & Son, to be painted by Doulton artists. He stipulated, however, that none of this was to be sold with the Doulton trade-mark, and reminded them that Josiah Wedgwood II's brief dalliance with bone china (between 1811 and 1815) had proved disastrous.

A difficult situation for Bailey and Slater arose some time in 1883, when Doulton's principal oversea traveller, Sam Mawdsley, returned from a visit to the United States with a valuable order for new tableware designs by Fred Hancock, provided these could be supplied on a translucent china body instead of on earthenware.

It happened that, shortly before this, Slater had been sent to France by Henry Doulton to study the ceramics in the famous collections there, and to visit the Sèvres, Limoges and other potteries. 'You must not grow so practical,' Doulton told him, 'as to forget the theoretical. The moment a man ceases to be a student he begins to be rusty as a teacher. Go to France and see for yourself what it is they have which we have not in Staffordshire.'

During this visit Slater met many French ceramic artists and one night was invited to a party which went on into the small hours and at which the wine flowed freely. He awoke the next afternoon in a hut on the outskirts of Barbizon, in the Forest of Fontainebleau, having, as he con-fessed, 'no recollection whatever' of why he was there. What had hap-pened was that a French ceramic painter, Georges Léonce, famous for his beautiful bird-studies, had taken him to his studio hut in the forest and looked after him until he recovered from the stupor brought on by the heady French wines to which he was unaccustomed.

A discussion arose between the two artists as to whether or not Léonce could produce as good results on English bone china as on hard-paste French porcelain. The outcome was a wager. When Slater returned to Burslem he was to send over an undecorated bone china dessert-set, to be obtained from Bodley & Son, and if Léonce could equal on it his painting on porcelain Slater would pay him £50. Léonce's results were in fact superb and Slater kept to the bargain. His only criticism was that Léonce had not signed a single piece. Back came the curt reply: 'They are signed all over. There is no man can paint birds like Léonce!' This famous dessert-service, or part of it, eventually found its way to Australia and three pieces are now in the Sydney Technological Museum.

This meeting with French potters gave Slater what he fondly thought was a brilliant idea when the opportunity for the American order arose. He persuaded Bailey to send Mawdsley to Limoges to order a consignment of white glazed porcelain for Hancock to decorate. This was done and samples were prepared to send to New York so that the order could be confirmed. By some mischance the Doulton trade-mark was printed on these samples without Bailey's knowledge and, to make matters worse, the day they were being packed, Henry Doulton arrived from London and decided to go on a 'grand tour' of the factory, ending up in the warehouse. With his intuitive flair for finding weak spots he noticed the samples and saw at once by their greyish tinge that they were not English bone china. On turning over a saucer he was horrified to see the Doulton mark. 'And where did this come from?' he demanded.

It was a wet and stormy day and as the works were rather scattered he was carrying a large umbrella. When Bailey told him that he had bought the ware from Limoges he went into a fury such as nobody at Burslem had ever thought him capable of, for ordinarily he had remarkable control over his feelings. The storm raged inside as well as out, as he brought his umbrella down again and again on the samples, smashing some of them to smithereens and sweeping the remainder from the packing bench. The unfortunate Mawdsley, who had been called in to give an explanation, was dismissed on the spot; Bailey and Slater were suspended and told they would hear more. Doulton then called for his hansom, which had been waiting a quarter of an hour, and when he arrived at Stoke station the train for London had already gone, so that he had to stay the night at the North Stafford Hotel.

The following morning, to everyone's amazement and consternation, he was back at Nile Street. Bailey and Slater thought this was the end of the Burslem venture or that, at best, the whole place would be turned into a sanitary-ware and insulator factory, where reasonable profits could be expected without so many problems.

'Good morning, Bailey; good, morning, Slater,' said Doulton. 'Will you be so kind as to send for our architect? I have decided to build a china works.'

He had seen the beauty of Hancock's work on a translucent body; he had more money already than he would ever need; he had thought the whole thing over during the night and decided he was as much to blame as anyone for having so long frustrated Bailey's and Slater's aspirations which were, after all, the outcome of a desire to do credit to the name of Doulton.

Mawdsley was reinstated forthwith and for many years afterwards played an important part in extending Doulton's export markets; Bailey and Slater were forgiven and Henry Doulton never again referred to their temporary fall from grace. It was not his nature to rub salt into the wound.

From then onwards the earthenware body was reserved more or less for good-quality tablewares for everyday use. China was developed for more expensive tableware and for the vases and other decorative wares so popular in that era. A much larger group of designers, artists, gilders, etchers and modellers was gathered together. Some already at Nile Street, such as Fred Hancock, Herbert Betteley, Charles Hart, Walter Slater and William G. Hodkinson, had been trained elsewhere in china decoration. To their ranks were now added many names already famous or destined to become famous in English ceramics: Edward Raby from Worcester; David Dewsberry and Edward Ernest Parry from Cauldon; John Hugh Plant, Joseph Birbeck and Enoch Piper from Coalport; Thomas D. Bott from Worcester; Charles Brough from Copeland; Louis Swettenham from Minton; George White from Lambeth and South Kensington Art Schools; Charles Labarre from Sèvres and many others who had been trained at London and Staffordshire art schools or apprenticed at famous potteries. Most important of all for the future direction things were to take, came Charles J. Noke, who had been trained under Charles Binns at Worcester and had worked there for sixteen years. Under their guidance promising young students such as Joseph Hancock, Harry Tittensor, Edward Birks and Percy Curnock grew to maturity.

Seldom, if ever, before in Staffordshire had such a large and gifted group of creative artists come together at one time in one centre. Never before had a ceramic studio been so little tied to a particular school for, among this array of talent, were artists who were able not only to draw upon the inspiration of the Classical, Renaissance, Baroque, Rococo, Adams, Geometrical, Oriental and other styles but who could also open up new paths of their own, bringing a different approach to floral painting, a chaster use of gilded embellishments and a new conception of figure design.

The Doulton artists began to create a school of their own, the originality of which was expressed by a writer in the *Pottery Gazette* in these words: '. . . the artistic quality, though easy to recognise, is not readily definable, and though with some wares a means of expression may be found by reference to this, that or the other country or period, this is not the case with Doulton art, which is distinctly original, and is not to be regarded as derived from any country or century. It is just "Doulton" and to the cognoscenti that implies a very high degree of artistic conception and accomplishment.' Obviously many external influences played their part, especially in the early days, but these were gradually absorbed and transmuted and something that people could recognise and say 'That's Doulton' began to emerge.

Charles J. Noke was once asked how it was that he and so many others had been willing to give up assured futures with famous china firms to throw their lot in with the at first somewhat suspect Doulton enterprise. His reply was significant. 'Not for the money, which was much the same as elsewhere in those days, but for *the freedom and the promise*. Henry Doulton was like a fresh sea-breeze. We had seen what he had done with the salt-glaze in a few years—more new inspiration, more real originality than [other] potters had produced for the past sixty years. It is impossible for anyone of the younger generation [this was in 1937] to begin to conceive just what an impact Doulton made on Staffordshire. To talk to him was invigorating, challenging, demanding the best one could give. He was just what the industry needed. The others had "to pull their socks up". Imagine their feelings when at the time of the Chicago exhibition an American critic wrote: "Doulton's have completely outstripped their rivals and are today the leaders in English potting." What the Elers, Whieldon, Wedgwood and Spode had done for the industry in the eighteenth century this man by his tremendous vitality, his irrepressible enthusiasm, and his genius for inspiring others, did in the nineteenth. Strange, isn't it, that he too came to Burslem from Vauxhall, like the Elers? Why did we throw our lot in with him? I suppose in some way we sensed all this and felt he was the man we had been waiting for.'

While Doulton was ready to subsidise the Burslem enterprise for a reasonable time out of the profits on the utilitarian wares of the other factories, it was his aim that it should stand on its own feet as soon as possible. To this end, he paid great attention to the development— alongside the *tours de force* for exhibitions and the exquisitely hand-painted, gold-embellished china service-plates and game-plates for the wealthy American market—of a wide range of more simply decorated and comparatively inexpensive, yet well designed, fine earthenware tablewares. He always insisted that everything that went out from the Doulton kilns, whether it were a plain cream-glazed ink bottle, a moderately priced dinner-service or an elaborately moulded and painted vase should be the best of its kind, well potted from the best clays, glazes and other ceramic materials. He was pained by scamped, slipshod or meretricious workmanship.

Apart from the tablewares and art-wares, a large section was developed for producing china and earthenware lamps, of which by 1893 Doulton had become possibly the largest, certainly one of the largest, manufacturers in England. Another profitable branch of the earthenware business was the many different designs of toilet-sets. Before bathrooms and, in the more expensive types of houses, wash-basins in bedrooms, became more general after the First World War, these sets were a basic necessity both in cottage and castle; many of the Doulton designs were so attractive that the jugs are still used today for flower arrangements.

In 1877 the Nile Street Pottery had employed 160 people. By 1889 there were 1,200. At the same time as the new wing for china was built in 1884-5, the earthenware and insulator departments were doubled in capacity. The 'utilitarian feature' was certainly not being overlooked! In 1887 an adjoining works in Sylvester Street, together with two acres of vacant land, was bought, and two years later further extensions had to be made.

8

Last years
1885 to 1897

In the autumn of 1874 Mr. Doulton and Mr. Sparkes were visiting a friend at Tooting who possessed a water-colour drawing by Harry Hine, representing the view from Coneyhurst or Pitch Hill. Each of them was struck by the beauty of this prospect, and Doulton expressed great surprise at finding that it existed within his own county of Surrey. It stands, in fact, in what was not so long ago one of the wildest bits of unspoiled England, in the parish of Ewhurst, west of Dorking and east of Guildford, but a good deal to the south of each. Mr. Sparkes found a lonely bit of ground, a cluster of six or seven fields, which he bought in the autumn of 1875, and he rebuilt the house on it which had an old wild garden sloping away to the south. This was just under the cornice of the range of heathery hills running from Holmbury to Hindhead, and about five miles west of that celebrated eminence, Leith Hill. From every turn of the sharp hillsides could be seen the Weald of Sussex, with the Downs dim in the distance, crowned by the spectacular shape of Chanctonbury Ring.

During the autumn of 1876 Henry Doulton stayed with Mr. Sparkes at Heathside. It was his earliest visit to the country which he was to make his own, and in which, to the very last, he was to experience the most enthusiastic pleasure. It is recollected, however, that on his first appearance he was indifferent to all the attractions of scenery, and blind even to a bevy of particularly charming young ladies. He had got hold of Björnson's pastoral story of *Arne* and until he had finished it he lay on his back in a hammock in the garden, dead to social responsibilities of every species. After this tribute paid to the genius of literature, Henry Doulton awoke to the hour and the place. He announced with a conviction which he maintained to the last, that there was more beauty of scenery in the parish of Ewhurst than was to be found, equally composed and combined, in any other parish in England. When gently reminded that he had not seen all the English parishes, he admitted it, and said that, after seeing Ewhurst, one would not want to see them. Something permanently bewitched him, and he determined, with all his pertinacity of purpose, to get a foot-hold for life under the shadow of Pitch Hill.

For nine or ten years he was mooning about among the heather and skirting the high plantations, before his wish was finally granted to him, but during all this time his purpose never swerved. He was the creature of immediate impulse; he liked the *mise-en-scène* of his actions to be perfect. Hence when at last he had an opportunity of buying the beautiful Elizabethan farmstead of Coneyhurst, he saw it on a wet day and refused it. About 1883, he visited it again, and fell in love with it, but all he could now do was to rent it, and a higher farm called Rapsley, for a period of twenty-one years. He determined to make Rapsley his provisional house, and in a short space of time he had so reconstructed the old homestead as to turn it into a charming country-box. I used to wonder that he was not satisfied with Rapsley, with its delicate lawns and knolls, and its long sweeping view across the woods. But he wished for a 'place', for a great property and a fine new house wholly designed for him and made to suit him.

Further to the east, there was a broad valley or combe in the broken slope of the range, which had been leased to the Radical politician, Mr. Lock-King, who did nothing with it. Henry Doulton found that the lease was falling in, and would revert to the trustees of the Abbot's Hospital in Guildford. He made an offer to buy it, and in 1885 it passed into his possession; flanked by his leased estates —Rapsley and Coneyhurst, and by his subsequent purchases, Barhatch and Parkhouse—it formed a considerable extent of property which took him down almost from Shere on one side of the Pitch Hill to Cranleigh on the other. It had the great advantage of being five miles from a station, Gomshall and Ockley dividing the honour of connecting the place with civilisation. The name of the farm on this estate had been Woolpit and was retained.

While the house at Woolpit was being built and the grounds 'laid out', Henry Doulton was living, as much as the claims of business would allow, at Rapsley. I have several times thought that these were among the happiest months of his existence. It was true that one extreme disappointment was prepared for him. He had hoped that Mrs. Doulton, now a confirmed invalid, would enjoy them with him. She did, in fact, once make the journey to Rapsley, but she was so greatly fatigued, was with such difficulty got back and was so ill after the excursion, that the experiment was never repeated. Woolpit, indeed, she was never able to visit. With this one great exception, Henry Doulton's satisfaction while his house was a-building, was refreshing to see. The height of his pleasure was reached in the evening, when, after an active day spent in tramping over his fields and ascending his clumps of orchard for fresh points of view, he would dine alone, or with one choice friend, and withdraw to the little library which he had filled with the poets. If I recollect aright, there was no prose at Rapsley, but all was verse; and under the lamplight one might see Henry Doulton stretched on the sofa, beating the measure with his paper-knife, and bursting every now and then into irresistible elocution, when the melody of Keats or Coleridge was more than could be endured in silence.

In arranging his 'grounds' he placed himself in the hands of an elderly landscape gardener of repute, in whose taste and ingenuity he had unbounded confidence. This gentleman belonged to the old, eighteenth-century school of the pupils of Le Nôtre, who comb out the tangled locks of nature, and seek to improve landscape by judicious composition.

Variety and expression were infused into the upper copse by introducing clumps of mahonias and rhododendrons. The lawns were inclined to an ogee form in softly adjusted slopes. Obtrusive hedges were swept away, and herbaceous plants, described as 'chastely decorative', were planted in their stead. The coarseness of some of the sky outlines was delicately corrected. An artificial sheet of water, crossed by bridges, took the place of a small brook that had flowed for centuries without dignity through the lower part of the estate. An enroofed gazebo crowned the bosom of the hill.

In permitting these costly and laborious alterations to be made, it is impossible to say that Henry Doulton was supported by the approval of all his friends. There were some, who, when he eagerly insisted

> . . . this is an Art
> Which does mend Nature—change it rather; but
> The Art itself is Nature . . .

could but shake their heads, and sigh for the old informal undulations and the coarse hedgerows which were in such sad disgrace. On questions of this kind there is an infinite variety of opinion, and time may be trusted, at last, to cope with the most active and ingenious of landscape gardeners. When, however, all the attractions had been made, and the lawns of Woolpit were stretching, in the exactest sense of the words, swept and garnished, I have sometimes thought that in the vehemence with which Sir Henry Doulton insisted upon our acknowledging the beauty and fitness of each change, there lurked an uneasy consciousness that Pitch Hill, unadorned, had really been a very agreeable corner of the globe.

In the centre of this estate Messrs. George & Peto, from designs by the well-known architect and etcher, Mr. Ernest George, began in 1885 to build Henry Doulton a house. It was 'constructed of thin red bricks, with rather profuse dressings in creamy-coloured terracotta, of a slight pinkish tinge; a tower of fitting character' was added. A panel in terracotta, by Mr. George Tinworth, of 'Abraham receiving the Angel's visit', was placed above the porch. This was not, however, to be taken as a symbol that the visits of Sir Henry's guests were few or far between. On the contrary, as soon as Woolpit became habitable, he was accustomed, during all the brighter months of the year, to exercise a profuse hospitality, and he was never so happy as when the house was full of his friends.

A word may be said here on the nature of Doulton's enjoyment of the country, which was exceedingly vivid, but had its peculiarities. He was not a sportsman in any particular, except in his great love of horses. He neither shot, nor golfed, nor played any game; his indomitable will, indeed, made him persist in riding on horseback on into his seventy-eighth year, and up to two months before his death. Hence his activity at Woolpit was principally exercised in strolling about; he liked to explore every corner of the estate, and always in the pursuit of landscape effects. He never had any scientific interests; he was neither zoologist, botanist nor geologist. He scarcely knew one bird from another, nor could he distinguish between a fern and a hawkweed; stratification left him perfectly indifferent. What he took an untiring pleasure in observing was the composition of landscape and the effects of colour, light and shade. Ruskin had originally opened his eyes to atmospheric beauty, and he had studied with some care the composition of landscape. But it was to the last a sentimental and almost a literary pleasure which he took in it. I am not sure that he would have found much satisfaction in anything that he could not find expressed in the poets. And he definitely preferred Wordsworth, in this connection, to Tennyson, because he was in much closer sympathy with the broad intellectual impulses of Wordsworth than with Tennyson's minute observation. He once said to me that he thought if Tennyson had a fault it was that his fancy was 'too scientific'.

About this time he was very much interested in the portraits of Wordsworth, about which, in 1886, he entered into correspondence with Professor W. Knight, of St. Andrews', who in consequence came to stay with him, and became one of his most valued acquaintances. Henry Doulton had become possessed of a very interesting painting of the poet, executed from life by Margaret Gillies, of whom he had some amusing stories to tell. Miss Gillies reported that she was staying at Rydal while this portrait was being painted, and that on one occasion, while she was walking with the poet, darkness overtook them. Mr. Wordsworth said he knew the way, however, and all would have been well, but, unluckily, he had forgotten the presence of a small disused quarry on their route. Into this they both fell, but Miss Gillies, though rather scratched herself, was reassured to hear the voice of the poet at her elbow. He had fallen on his face, not at all hurt, and he was continuing the sentence he had begun when they fell together into the pit.

This serenity is mirrored in the painting, which Henry Doulton took great pride in possessing. The face is curiously like that of an aged, but highly intellectual horse. There was no good reproduction of it, and Doulton had an exquisite copper-plate engraving produced, which he distributed among his friends. Besides the ever-green recollection of his interesting personal interview with Wordsworth in 1849, Henry Doulton, although no great collector of such things, possessed several objects connected with this, the poet of his peculiar worship, and, in particular, a lock of Wordsworth's hair, which had been given to him in 1860 by Mrs. Ward, the sister of the marine painter E. W. Cooke, R.A., who had known the Wordsworths. He was not, on the whole, addicted to the amassing of rare things, for their rarity's sake. I recollect only the collection he possessed of specimens of ancient pottery, in which he took an independent or professional interest; and this he bought complete from Robert Ready of the British Museum. There were some unique things in this cabinet. But, although he bought books freely, he did not care about them bibliographically; he had few 'first editions', and he was a timid buyer of pictures.

By this time, Henry Doulton had gradually grown to be what in his youth he had never showed any signs of becoming, rather a keen practical politician. He had begun by being a great admirer of Gladstone, and he had dropped the Hawarden faith, not at once, but in a slow and unwilling process, tenet by tenet, shred by shred. His interests, very early indeed, had been Imperialist. From early middle life he had deprecated the motion that the colonies should be left to take care of themselves. On imperial and colonial policy there is no question that Henry Doulton was a whole generation ahead of his time. Quite early, at the debates of The Verulam Club, he had fought almost alone against the sectarianism of allowing party interests to interfere in the proper maintenance of the Empire. In 1883 Professor (afterwards Sir John) Seeley published his book *The Expansion of England,* and Henry Doulton could not contain the ecstasy with which he read it and made the whole circle of his acquaintance read it. 'Here,' he said, 'is to be found stated with perfect power and knowledge, what I have been trying all these years, without the requisite equipment, to urge upon other people. This book justifies me in all my ideas and all my intuitions.'

About the same time, he became acquainted with Mr. G. R. Parkin, who later became principal of the Upper Canada College, Toronto, but who then was doing a great national work as the secretary of the Imperial Federation League. Henry Doulton went to one of his lectures, introduced himself to the lecturer, and for some time threw himself very warmly into Mr. Parkin's work. The teaching of the League brought Doulton's political convictions to a point, and he became an ardent propagandist. He had maps of the Empire painted for Mr. Parkin, and helped him in a variety of ways. The views of the Federation League were those which he had long before independently adopted, and he now began to be himself a speaker on the imperial aspects of defence, emigration and trade. As early as January 1885 he was invited to contest West Newington in

L

the Conservative interest, the election agents guaranteeing that he should be returned. But his health was not equal to the strain of the night-work in the House, and he declined. Mr. C. W. Radcliffe-Cooke was invited, and succeeded in winning the seat, and in retaining it in 1886. Henry Doulton was several times earnestly begged to contest Metropolitan constituencies, but the nocturnal life of a member of parliament would have disturbed all his habits, and have given him little satisfaction. He steadily refused.

He often spoke, however, at meetings in his own neighbourhood, and he was an effective political orator. At starting he always found a little difficulty in pitching his voice and in finding his words, but as soon as he was warmed up to his argument, all this disappeared. Often he was very impassioned, and carried audiences with him against their will. He rarely spoke outside Lambeth, however, and there he had the confidence born of being known to every person present, and the object of unbounded local respect. As an orator, his splendid memory greatly aided him; he had a taste for apt quotation and no difficulty in fitting the passage accurately, at the proper point, into his discourse. His political speeches would not have been his, if they had not been largely diversified by poetical citations. I suppose that, at one time or another, the indifferent citizens of Lambeth have heard the greater part of 'The Happy Warrior' from the lips of their eminent potter. He supported General Sir Charles Fraser when he stood for North Lambeth in 1885, and had a great deal to do with getting him in. He spoke at the Conservative Club at Stockwell and at other centres in the borough, and a favourite place for non-political addresses was the 'Old Vic'—the Victoria Hall in the Lambeth Cut.

One of his discourses, that delivered on the 16th of November 1885, in the lecture room of the Art Pottery, to some hundreds of his own employees, was much noticed in political centres. Lord Iddesleigh pointed to it as to a type of what was wanted, at that critical moment, to stir the most patriotic feelings of Englishmen. 'Mr. Henry Doulton's excellent address,' said Lord Iddesleigh, writing a day or two after its delivery, to Colonel Sussex Lennox, 'is just the sort of thing for intelligent working men, who mean what is right, but who require instruction upon topics with which they are not familiar.' Henry Doulton, however, was most gratified by a letter from Lord Salisbury, telling him that he had read the report of his address with deep interest and satisfaction. Now, once more, Doulton was urged to enter Parliament, but again he declined the laborious honour. Instead of himself accepting, he helped General Fraser and again, in 1886, had the satisfaction of seeing his majority largely increased.

It was felt by more than one of his influential friends that the time had now come when Henry Doulton's services to art and industry should be recognised. Both from the political and the professional side, as he was afterwards made aware, representations were put forward on his behalf in high quarters. These representations were conducted without his approval or cognisance, and it was only a very short time before the Jubilee of 1887 that his friend Sir Philip Cunliffe-Owen informed him that something had been said—that, in fact, he would do well to be prepared. Henry Doulton took no step that might seem to encourage whatever application had been made, and so completely put it out of his thoughts that it was almost a surprise to him to receive, on the very morning of the Jubilee Procession, a note from Lord Salisbury, dated June 20th, 1887, in which the Prime Minister announced that Her Majesty had been pleased to confer on him the honour of knighthood. His friends were not entirely pleased. They had hoped for a baronetcy. One of them described the honour as 've ry late in coming, and not enough of it, now it had come'. But Sir Henr y only smiled, and could never be induced to discuss the matter. He insisted that the honour of being associated with the Queen on su ch a day, in whatever capacity, was far greater than he deserved. He 'put on no side' of any kind, and Sir Henry was not distinguishable fr om plain Mr. Doulton of the Lambeth Pottery.

In the autumn of 1888 a crushing blow fell upon Sir Henry Doulton. The health of Lady Doulton had for many years been exceedingly precarious, to say no more. Her husband and her children had become accustomed to see her bear with fortitude a weariness and suffering which no remedies seemed able to alleviate. Nothing, however, warned them of any particular modification of her state of health, until the autumn of 1888. But with the beginning of October her condition grew worse. For three weeks she lay in a crisis of great weakness, to which, on the 26th of that month, she succumbed. Their married life had lasted nearly forty years, and it had been unclouded by any misunderstanding or strain of feeling.

No husband and wife ever existed who were more devoted to one another, or to each of whom the welfare of the other was more dear.

No one can blink the fact that the prolonged ill-health of Lady Doulton, practically cutting Sir Henry off from all those chances of exercising hospitality on a large scale, or even of accepting it, which would have been so congenial to him, was an extremely trying element in the life at Woodlands. The potter would have enjoyed seeing his house thronged with friends, his table presided over by an admired and vivacious hostess. But as soon as it appeared that this could never be, he accepted it with absolute philosophy and good humour; no expression of annoyance ever passed his lips; and he redoubled his efforts to make his wife enjoy to the full what few and thin pleasures her unfortunate health still allowed her. Often, when he came home exhausted on a summer evening, he would pull himself together, and be discovered smilingly pulling Lady Doulton's bath-chair round the gardens. If a friend dined with him at Tooting, now and again during the evening he would start up, with an apology, and disappear for a moment: 'You won't mind my just seeing how my wife is getting on?' To the very last his unselfishness never flagged.

Lady Doulton was buried at Norwood, in the mausoleum which was eventually to receive her husband's ashes also. A little while after her death, Sir Henry was wandering among the monuments of the beautiful priory of Christchurch, in Hants, when his eye fell upon this triplet:

> From her it never was our fate to find
> A deed ungentle or a word unkind—
> The sweetest manners with the bravest mind.

He considered them singularly apt to the character of his own wife, and he ordered them to be carved upon her tomb.

The death of Lady Doulton broke the last tie with Tooting. He had hoped, indeed, about this time to withdraw from business. His dream was to wander among his lawns at Woolpit, and, like Jean Chapelain, to pass the remainder of his days in innocence, with Apollo and with his books. But, oddly enough, the very summer of 1887, which had been marked for a partial retirement, was burdened by a recrudescence of responsibility. Instead of business slackening, it absorbed him more and more. Of this immense industry he was still, and more than ever, the brain and motive power. Problems continued to rise before him, and, instead of growing easier, they proved harder and harder to solve. Competition increased, and was every day more formidable. It was far less easy to conduct the world-wide affairs of the firm than it had been thirty, or even fifteen, years earlier. The consequence was that, just as he hoped to cling to shore and climb out of affairs, the vortex made a fresh swirl and dragged him round with it again. Nor can it be said that he ever escaped until ill-health broke down the powers which old age was unable to tame or slacken.

Three great international exhibitions occupied the energies of Sir Henry Doulton through three successive years. They marked the highest point in the exhibitional fervour of his work. These were the monster shows of Liverpool in 1886, of Manchester in 1887 and of Glasgow in 1888. The Liverpool Exhibition was opened early in May 1886. A very special interest was given to it by the fact that it was opened by the Queen in person. She arrived from Windsor on the preceding night, slept at Newsham House, and, having rested, drove to Wavertree Park, where the buildings had been raised on some ten acres of what was known as the Edge Lane Hall Estate. The occasion was one which awakened unbounded enthusiasm in Liverpool, where the Queen had never stayed before. The late Lord Granville was the Cabinet Minister in attendance, and it was he who, standing at the Queen's right hand, was commanded by her to declare the Exhibition open.

The first object which caught the eye on entering by the western entrance was the Doulton 'screen' consisting of nine arches, the central one being the loftiest. This introduced a colossal trophy of potter's ware, in the form of a terracotta cupola supported by pilasters, with naval compositions painted on tiles between the pilasters. The opening ceremony took place opposite this trophy, and when the Queen had been conducted through the principal sections of the Exhibition, she returned to the back of the Doulton pavilion, and rested there. The Lambeth Potter received her and Princess Beatrice, and conducted them to chairs opposite the grand entrance. Then, close to Her Majesty, a potter threw a vase upon the wheel, Mr. A. E. Pearce decorated it on the spot, and Henry Doulton showed it to the Queen, to whom the finished object was later presented. Her Majesty, who had seemed fatigued by her long walk, recovered her strength as, with marked interest, she watched the graceful processes of manufacture, and she expressed herself much gratified. When on the 12th of August 1887 Sir Henry Doulton went down to Osborne to be dubbed, the Queen briefly referred to her pleasure in having seen his work in process of being made at Liverpool.

In face of the astounding abundance of the show of Doulton work in the Liverpool Exhibition, it was a proof of remarkable energy to contrive that the display at Manchester in the following year should not be a mere repetition. As a matter of fact, Sir Henry Doulton was particularly solicitous that his contributions to this, which was essentially a Jubilee exhibition, should in the main be new. The show was opened early in May 1887. The Doultons were represented by four quadrant arches of richly decorated terracotta placed round the arches of the dome, a large shallow basin, with shrubberies arranged about it, being disposed as a fountain in the centre. The arcades under the decorative frescoes of Ford Madox Brown were filled with a profusion of Lambeth ware. At the south-west end of the great hall were large kilns and, in front of these, Messrs. Doultons erected a pavilion, decorated in glazed terracotta, which formed a magnificent showroom sixty feet by thirty. There was a hexafoil fountain in yellow, grey and blue; and several of Mr. Tinworth's largest Scripture panels, in particular 'The Release of Barabbas' and 'Christ's entry into Jerusalem', found adequate places.

Nor was it in the artistic only, but in the more prosaic and utilitarian departments, that the Manchester Exhibition of 1887 showed the industry of Lambeth to an advantage hitherto un-approached. The adaptation of glazed earthenware to sanitation had never been displayed to anything like the same extent, and the profusion and ingenuity of the self-adjusting joints, the interceptors, the water waste preventors, the syphons, the flushing tanks, the valves, the taps, won the admiration of architects and engineers. The applications of glazed ware to fireplaces, mantelpieces and fender kerbs were very novel. In their pavilion, the Doultons showed, during the whole exhibition, the entire chain of successive processes in connection with the manufacture of pottery including firing; this had never been attempted before, and proved excessively popular among the visitors who were able to purchase specimens direct from the kilns. One of the products was a china tumbler, of a delicate biscuit colour, with a design of the Queen's portrait in 1837 and in 1887, of which not fewer than 100,000 were manufactured by Messrs. Doulton & Co. at Burslem, 45,000 of them as a Commission from the Prince of Wales. These were ultimately distributed at the Children's Jubilee fête in Hyde Park in June.

During the summer of 1887 the Burslem business of the firm was found to be developing so rapidly that it was no longer possible to conduct it on the existing premises. Sir Henry accordingly purchased two acres of adjoining land, with the factories existing on them, and entered into occupation on the 6th of August.

The third of the trio of exhibitions was held in Glasgow in 1888. As early as January of that year they began to build in the grounds of the exhibition, where the slopes of rhododendrons descended to the banks of the Kelvin, a monumental fountain on a scale hitherto unattempted. It was forty-six feet high, and measured seventy feet across the outer basin. It was designed, in what is called the style of François Premier, as a group of decorative and symbolic sculpture, crowned by a terracotta statue of Queen Victoria. It was intended to tell the history of the Empire, and Sir Henry Doulton was carefully solicitous that due prominence should be given to the imperialistic and federated ideas which he had taken up so warmly. The colonies were prominent in large figure groups at the base of the monument. It was, unquestionably, the most highly elaborated structure in pure terracotta which had, up to that time, been executed in England. The statue of the Queen at the summit was afterwards smashed to bits by lightning, and a new one had to be made. It gave so much pleasure to the inhabitants of Glasgow that, at the close of the exhibition, Sir Henry presented it to the city.

The Glasgow Exhibition was opened by the Prince and Princess of Wales on the 8th of May 1888. The Doulton exhibit was contained in a rich and spacious 'Indian' pavilion manufactured at Lambeth, composed entirely of glazed and enamelled terracotta. This was an interesting example of the use of this material for permanent decoration. It contained the usual profusion of every description of Doulton Ware, but the specimens were, in the main, what had been seen before, and especially at Manchester. The Glasgow Exhibition had, however, an important influence on the development of the Doulton business. Sir Henry was much struck with the high level of education and intelligence among the Scots workmen, and being urged to open permanent showrooms in that city, he was induced to study the economic conditions.

In the end it was not at Glasgow, but close by, at Paisley, that he instituted a section to start in Scotland the manufacture of sanitary ware. In particular he discovered that he could make metal taps and fittings cheaper and better here than in the south, and he developed the casting of baths in his new Paisley works. A great effort was made to induce him to bring some of his art manufacture to Scotland. A Scots wag, in the Glasgow press, made a piteous appeal to Sir Henry Doulton to free Caledonia from the 'brown jennies' of Alloa and the blacking bottles of Portobello. But he was not encouraged to believe that the time had come to invade the solid history of Scotland with his delicate ceramic art.

Sir Henry Doulton had long since settled down into a churchman and a Conservative. But he was latitudinarian and liberal in his conduct of his views; in other words he was individual. No one was ever less of a party man; he insisted on having his own interpretation of public as of private questions, and he would not boast of the hard-and-fastness of what obstinate people call principle. He liked to judge each case on its own merits. In religion he supported the incumbents of the Lambeth parishes, but he was on friendly terms with most of the other ministers, no matter of what denomination. One of his most distinguished neighbours was Charles Haddon Spurgeon, who had been connected with Southwark ever since 1853. As a young man, Henry Doulton had sometimes attended Spurgeon's services at New Park Street, and later at the Surrey Music Hall. But since the opening of the Tabernacle in 1861, Henry Doulton had not thought it necessary to visit Spurgeon's services. He was therefore greatly surprised and touched to receive the following letter:

> Westwood Beulah Hill,
> Upper Norwood,
> 1890, March 20

Dear Sir Henry Doulton,

In the name of myself and co-trustees, I write to ask a favour of you. Will you be so good as to take the chair at our Orphanage Festival, June 19, this year? It will be my 56th birthday, and we hope to have, as in former years, a vast open air assembly. You may speak as briefly or as much at length as you wish. The duties need not be heavy. For the sake of 'auld lang syne' for good neighbourhood, and for esteem to yourself personally, I invite you. I was by your father's death-bed, and before that had many tokens of his Christian love to me. I have not been burdensome to you all these years; and, now I make a request, I do so with a full conviction that I am asking it of a hearty friend, who will gladly aid me in work for orphan children.

Yours very sincerely,
C. H. Spurgeon

To this cordial letter, Sir Henry Doulton instantly replied by an acceptance of the invitation. The meeting on the 19th of June proved a delightful one. The Stockwell Orphanage had been founded by Spurgeon in 1867, and had been by this time so enlarged as to accommodate 500 children. But the sight of the day was the enormous concourse of people gathered in the grounds of the orphanage, all turning like sunflowers towards Spurgeon as he circulated slowly among them. I remember Sir Henry Doulton's vivid impression of the kindly force and varied, masterly tact of the great Baptist minister. 'I knew he was a good man,' he said afterwards, 'but I had no idea he was such a clever one. They followed him as if he had been the Pied Piper of Hamelin.' Henry Doulton was much affected by this visit to the domains of Spurgeon.

On the 5th of July 1890 died, in his ninetieth year, Sir Edwin Chadwick, with whom Henry Doulton had for a great many years been somewhat closely associated. Chadwick considered himself the most indispensable human being that ever breathed. He adopted the name of the 'Father of Sanitation', and used to boast that his inventions had saved more lives than Napoleon and Wellington put together had destroyed. For this able, but grotesque and absurd being, Henry Doulton had a curious feeling of mingled aversion and respect. He admitted Chadwick's remarkable powers, but deprecated his egotism and obstinacy. Chadwick's interest in sewerage was astounding, and led him into adventures which could scarcely be told by any later chronicler than Sir John Harington. Nothing connected with sanitation seemed to Chadwick common or unclean, and his conversation opened up abysses of horror for the unwary. It was impossible that Henry Doulton should not listen to a man whose interest in sewer pipes was so enthusiastic, yet he was often dreadfully bored by his conversation. He easily permitted Chadwick, however, to air his fads to him, and would even carry out experiments at his suggestion, but at moments of social relaxation, the sight of the Father of Sanitation at a distance approaching, filled him with a paralysing terror. I recall walking with Henry Doulton in Lambeth one afternoon, while, as he liked to do to his acquaintances, he held my elbow in his hand. He was talking cheerfully and profusely, when he suddenly stopped, and painfully gripped the flesh of my arm. The next moment he had bolted with me down a side lane. I was greatly alarmed, but it was only that Doulton had seen Chadwick advancing upon us.

The comic stories which Henry Doulton used to tell about Edwin Chadwick were without number. On one occasion the sanitary philosopher arrived breathless at the Lambeth Pottery and must see Sir Henry Doulton without a moment's delay. 'I have made a great discovery,' he explained. 'A pig that is washed puts on one-fourth more flesh with the same amount of food as a dirty pig. We must have automatic, and if needful, compulsory washing for the English lower classes. I have devised an apparatus by which a man may be completely washed, against his will, in five minutes, a woman in four, and a child in three. It can be done, with the help of apparatus which you will manufacture for me, at the rate of ten a penny. England clean and fat, my friend, at the laughably trifling cost of one penny for ten adults!'

He was so bent on this glorious scheme being carried out that Sir Henry positively indulged him with the machine he described. On a given day Chadwick came to Lambeth to experiment upon it, and at once demanded that the staff at the potteries should lend their bodies for the purpose. But this is a free country, and one and all they declined to be made a sanitary spectacle. Even the little boys refused, weeping, and threatened to 'tell their ma's'. At last, frustrated by the cowardice of man and boy, the Father of Sanitation withdrew in dudgeon and nothing more was heard of 'washing for the million'.

This is but one example of Chadwick's fantastic and visionary but strangely ingenious schemes, and of the patience with which Doulton bore with them, in virtue of the old man's unquestionable talents, and his long services to science. He allowed Mr. Tinworth to make a bust of Chadwick who was of an appearance the least sculpturesque imaginable. This did not prevent Sir Edwin, while he sat, from urging the artist to be sure to give the portrait the aspect of 'a saviour of mankind'. His self-concentration, indeed, and his imperturbable confidence in himself were a power. He used to attend the services of a certain preacher, whose delivery was as dull as his message to mankind was insipid. Henry Doulton tried to induce Chadwick to go to a livelier place of worship. 'No,' said the sanitorian, 'Mr. —— is just the sort of preacher I like. He never says anything that interrupts the current of my own thoughts.' He was reported to owe to pity the title which gladdened the last months of his extended life. Some wicked wags announced to Chadwick that he was to be knighted. He was overjoyed, and spread the news on all sides. When the cruel hoax was exposed, the poor old man was so excessively chagrined that it was thought that he might die; his friends made lamentable representations to the proper authorities, and a knighthood, genuine this time, graciously prolonged his life to the borders of ninety.

It was part of the genius of Sir Henry Doulton that he kept a watchful eye upon all the remote provinces of his business, and allowed the prosperity of no one to make him indifferent to the progress of the others. In 1889 he saw an opportunity for greatly increasing the usefulness of his works in Rowley Regis, and he threw himself into this work with all his old energy. As we have seen, the Doultons had possessed pottery works in the little dependency of Dudley for a great many years. Since 1870 the Birmingham group of works, including Rowley and Smethwick, had steadily increased in value and output.

Every few weeks or so, over a long period of years, Doulton would pay a visit to the group of factories. He had a great dislike to 'surprise visits', and made it a point of honour to acquaint Mr. Thomason, the general manager, with his intention of coming. A horse would be sent to meet him at the Central Station in Birmingham; he would call at the depot in that town, and then ride out to Rowley Regis. Here there were lodgings kept always ready for him at the works, and he would sleep there, perhaps, two nights, returning on the third day by Smethwick, and, riding in to Birmingham, catch a last express for London. He would busy himself, on arriving at Rowley, by glancing through the order books, and then he would start on a rapid tour of personal inspection round the works. He preferred to go alone; he liked to come into direct communication with the workers in every grade. Until nearly the close of his life, he knew every man personally, his marvellous memory aiding him, and he would recollect from visit to visit any little domestic incident or imbroglio that happened to be interesting any particular individual. He was surprisingly polite, and this seems to have been occasionally intimidating, politeness not being much cultivated in the Staffordshire Potteries. His courtesy, and his almost miraculous clairvoyance, served not a little to preserve his prestige among the men.

He cared—I am told by all his managers—much less for the commercial than for the manufacturing part of the business. He took the former very quietly; as to the latter, he was of ceaseless keenness. He was always cheerful, always pleased, always lavish of deserved commendation, but never satisfied to abide in the *status quo*. Only one thing vexed him constantly; he could not contrive to do anything for the social life of his people at Rowley. He was anxious to ameliorate the roughness of these lives, into which so little of enjoyment or variety could possibly pass. He made various suggestions. He provided a vast eating-room for those (and they were the majority) who came from a great distance. He proposed clubrooms and an Institute. But none of these schemes received the least encouragement from the men. The fact was that conditions were highly unfavourable. Rowley Regis stood alone, quite in the country, and the people came to it from distant points about a wide circle. When work was over, they were anxious to get home. They were not like the Lambeth people, acquainted with one another's homes, interested in the same local problems. The consequence was that all Sir Henry's overtures were rejected, and he acquiesced after a while, though always with regret.

Such was the condition of Rowley when, in 1889, Sir Henry decided to enlarge the works, and provide a new industry for the district, by opening a terracotta factory to supply the Midland towns. This he carried out, and the Rowley Regis Works became devoted to architectural terracotta, as well as to stoneware pipes, chimney pots and blue bricks. They became the largest of their kind in the British Empire, and in conjunction with the clay-beds at Netherton, they covered by 1890 an area of thirty acres, giving employment to about 700 men. Through the whole establishment a canal was drawn, connecting the works with the railway.

Yet another great fire at Lambeth in December 1888 revolutionised the works. It was quite a metropolitan event; for extent of range and amount of damage it ranked as the biggest London fire of the year. It broke out at 9 p.m. The manager of the factory was immediately on the spot, and remained there superintending the relief all night. Sir Henry Doulton was in the country, and it was not until the morning that he could be communicated with; indeed, the news reached him only just before his arrival. The manager, who received him, and who had to break to him the enormous amount of injury which had been done, tells me that in the whole course of his daily intercourse with Sir Henry Doulton, he never, on any other occasion, saw his face express so much emotion. He seemed stunned, bewildered; and as he gazed on the charred ruins, the tears ran down his cheeks. But this condition lasted but for a few minutes. Presently he turned to speak to his companion and as he did so, his eye fell on the groups of dejected workmen who were standing round him, their occupation gone. He drew himself up, and a new expression came into his face and, with all his old vivacity, he said, 'Well, now what are we going to do? You must employ all these men, mind—all of them!'

When the management had time to look round they discovered that the smaller half of the vast establishment was left almost intact— the remainder being completely destroyed. Within twenty-four hours Sir Henry Doulton, who had by this time wholly regained his cheerfulness and resolution, had completed his arrangements. The works were to run continuously, in three shifts, night and day, so that nothing had to be stopped and nobody discharged. In a very short time, the rebuilding was in full swing, and it gave Sir Henry the opportunity entirely to remodel the general works. The clay-making sheds were the earliest to be restored, for this was the most serious and the most awkward loss. The workmen went into each section as the new parts were finished, and, so smoothly did the building proceed, that in ten months all was completely in its new convenient form. From 400 to 500 men had been kept constantly at work during the reconstruction. The fire, of course, destroyed much that was of value and of historic interest to the firm; in particular, a very large collection of the moulds of Mr. Tinworth's sculptures.

On the 28th November 1889 Sir Henry had the misfortune to lose his youngest brother Mr. James Duneau Doulton, who died at West Brighton at the age of fifty-four. He had been the business partner of the firm for many years, and he occupied himself more with the office than the factory, leaving Sir Henry free to devote himself to the practical and theoretical part of the work. Mr. J. D. Doulton was not only a very able business man, but highly esteemed and liked by the men. His loss was a very great affliction to Sir Henry, who had long leaned upon his younger brother, but at this moment Mr. Lewis Doulton was able to take a more definite share in the responsibilities of the firm, and in time to fill his uncle's place.[42]

At the close of 1890 the Doultons found themselves face to face with a critical labour difficulty. The men had got it into their heads that there were too many boy apprentices at the Lambeth Works. Accordingly, after a good deal of grumbling, a deputation representing the potters waited on Sir Henry Doulton, and objected to the employment of three youths lately apprenticed to the trade. The workmen declared that there was not enough prospect of demand to warrant the employment of these lads. They volunteered an expression of full confidence in the way in which Sir Henry had hitherto studied their interests, and admitted that they had never before suffered from any action of his, on this account. But they were alarmed that the number of apprentices should be increasing so fast. Sir Henry had no difficulty in proving to them that, in reality, it had been for several years declining, and as they were struck dumb by this, he smilingly advised them to go away and talk about it.

They talked, but they returned in talk to their old discomfort. No matter whether there were more apprentices or fewer in other times, there were certainly too many now, and they went doggedly back to Sir Henry. He asked them where, if apprentices were not to be trained, the workmen of the future were to come from? Were any potters out of employment in consequence of the abundance of

[42] A new partnership, which began with a capital of £290,192, had been formed in January 1881, the capital being divided thus: Henry Doulton, £158,037; James D. Doulton, £79,476; Henry Lewis Doulton, £52,679.

Two years after James D. Doulton's death in 1889 Sir Henry Doulton and his son, Henry Lewis, entered into a new partnership with a capital of £305,915 divided as follows: Sir Henry, £256,656; Henry Lewis Doulton, £49,259.

apprentices? On the contrary, at the moment he had some wheels vacant, and the immediate orders made it imperative that these vacancies should be filled. Moreover, no applications for work from journeymen had been received. Finally he gave them his word that none of them should suffer by his action in this matter. At the same time, he firmly declined to accede to their demand, because he considered that that would be to inflict a positive check on the future development of trade. The deputation seemed perfectly satisfied with these arguments, but unfortunately other counsels prevailed, and Sir Henry received, on the 3rd of December, a letter informing him that unless he removed the three lads from their wheels immediately, every piece-worker would cease work at once, and every day-worker on the following Thursday. Accordingly the throwers and stove-moulders, terracotta moulders and lathers to the number of 130, incontinently struck work.

The strike which began on so paltry a misunderstanding, led, unfortunately, to considerable bitterness of feeling. The men saw fit to make, on the 15th December, an appeal 'to the workmen of Great Britain' for subscriptions to enable them to carry on the struggle over Christmas. This appeal, however, was not responded to, for several of the leaders of the labour organisations were not convinced that the throwers were in the right, and had no inclination to encourage an imaginary grievance. The men began to parley with Sir Henry Doulton but he was obliged to point out to them that if they persevered in the strike, and ultimately gave way, they could not possibly expect to return on the same terms as before. He had been obliged to order new machines, by the use of which manual labour was largely reduced. At length, in March 1891, after the strike had lasted twelve weeks, it was brought to a close by the unconditional surrender of the men.

Through this painful affair, Sir Henry Doulton remained wonderfully calm. His firmness was absolute, and while some of those who served him well gave way to anticipations of trouble, he never allowed himself to be ruffled. At the same time, this strike made him indignant. He thought that of all wanton disturbances of business that in which workmen strike at their own class and band together to prevent the training of their young sons is the blindest and the most absurd. He was very much annoyed at the spirit which disorganised a great industry on such a paltry plea as that which the throwers had gone out upon. He was determined to resist the tyranny of the union to the full. At the same time, he was betrayed into no heat with individuals. The strikers came every now and then to discuss the situation with him; he always received them with the greatest courtesy, and was ready to listen to whatever they had to say. Although this strike at one time threatened to be formidable, and although it occupied the newspapers to a somewhat exaggerated degree, there were no serious disturbances in connection with it, and after its collapse, no permanent injury was found to have been done to the business.

A matter which greatly occupied the thoughts of Sir Henry Doulton at this time, and for the remainder of his life, was the best method of providing kind and reasonable relations between his workpeople and himself. He had long been aware that, in nine cases out of ten, the difficulties which arise between masters and men, capital and labour in all their social communications, are due to want of mutual understandings. He saw very plainly that the growth of limited companies, and the universal spreading of enterprises beyond the point at which one man's imagination can hold all the threads in hand, had led and was constantly further leading to estrangement. He saw, in his own works, the multiplication of labour, and its subdivision, fast producing among his men that indifference, that absence of a united sentiment, which above all other things he desired to see. In the old days, he had known every man, and every man's family and conditions. Now it was wholly out of the question for him to pretend to do so. And yet he was most unwilling to cease to regard his people as human beings, or to treat them as wheels in a vast machine. What was to be done?

In 1891 he took his manager into his confidence on this subject. Something must be done, he said, to keep in touch with the men outside business. This something—what was it to be? Nothing priggish, philanthropical, dictatorial, or else it would instantly defeat its own object. The two discussed the matter, and the manager was desired to make such discreet inquiries as would lead to finding out what would really give satisfaction to the men. Finally, it seemed that the formation in Lambeth, and close to the works although outside them, of some sort of Social Institute would be the best way of showing a regard for the workmen outside business, without seeming in any way to interfere with their personal tastes and habits.

Accordingly, in 1892, the Institute was started, and was the factor in Sir Henry Doulton's existence which for the remainder of his life, interested him more closely than perhaps any other. He bought a large empty house in High Street Lambeth; he cleared out partitions, strengthened and mended the walls and staircases, and restored the fine old rooms to their original character.

Early in 1893 it was felt wise to let the men have full self-management of the building, a veto only being held by Sir Henry Doulton. This suited the men; they could appreciate advantages which they themselves directed. At this moment he had the wisdom to appear to withdraw; he held himself apparently aloof from all the business of the Institute but all the while he was watching it with the keenest interest. Gradually the majority of the people at the works joined the Institute. An athletic club was formed, and this proved highly popular. By degrees, Sir Henry Doulton allowed himself to come more into evidence. He suggested that he might give the members a lecture, and this was so well attended that he was encouraged to deliver more. Ultimately, the Institute became self-supporting, and Sir Henry could not conceal his delight.

The great international exhibition at Chicago was the object of much speculation and excited widely different sentiments among the leading men in English commercial circles. It was the main topic of trade conversation at the close of 1892. England had occupied the largest area at Paris, at Philadelphia and at Vienna. Would she continue to do so at Chicago, and, if not, was it worth while to send? Sir Henry Doulton was always very firm about this. Whether for nations or for individuals, he was accustomed to say, 'Be first or not at all, for to be second is to be nowhere.' After a period of doubt, he made up his mind to concentrate his powers on a display at Chicago, which he thought would probably be, and as it turned out actually was, his last. All through 1892 he devoted his energies to the task of surpassing himself, and he secured the main part of the façade of the central avenue at Chicago in what was called the Manufactures Building, for the purpose of filling it with the finest exhibition of modern pottery ever brought together at a single show.

In the first week of May 1893 the Chicago Exhibition was opened. But Sir Henry Doulton did not cross the Atlantic, as he had half promised to himself to do. There were many reasons for staying

M

at home. In the first and most ostensible place, important changes were being made at the Lambeth terracotta works, and his presence was needful while these were being carried through. But, more privately, the condition of his health was now beginning to be threatening, and the physicians were anxious that he should refrain from a long and exhausting journey, and from the excitement of American hospitality. They urged him to stay in England, to take life quietly, and to ride on horseback as much as possible. None the less, the Chicago Exhibition holds an important place in the career of Sir Henry Doulton. It was his final and crowning triumph; he took in it far and away the best position in all the departments, and that in the face of such competition as had never been brought to bear upon him before.[43]

After the exhibition had ended Sir Henry Doulton presented to the city of Chicago the colossal 'America' group in terracotta, which the Doultons had erected in the roadway between Victoria House and the Canadian building. It was accepted, and placed in a small park on the west side of the city. It was a curious circumstance that the Mayor, Major Harrison, had just returned home from making the final arrangements for this transfer when he was murdered in his own house. This 'America' was the largest work of art ever turned out at Lambeth, and it had enjoyed some curious vicissitudes before it came to its rest in Jackson Park.

It had been originally designed, in 1851, by that talented, but little-known sculptor, the late John Bell, a man born into a transitional time, which never gave him a chance of developing his really remarkable powers of design. It was executed by him in marble, and may be admired to this day on its pedestal at the north-west angle of the Albert Memorial, Kensington Gardens. In 1874

---

[43] *The Art Journal* of April 1893, referring to the Doulton exhibits, wrote: 'Seldom has it happened in the experience of a single generation to see the birth and complete development of a new Art Industry. Yet in the short space of some twenty years there has been originated and perfected at the Lambeth Potteries, without the aid of previous tradition, a wealth of ceramic method that seems likely to become a conspicuous feature of that Renaissance of English Art which dates from the Victorian era. . . . At Burslem, on the contrary, the whole available skill and tradition of several generations has been brought successfully to bear. The most typical productions of these two Art Potteries form a striking and unique collection which, for range of material and versatility of design, cannot fail to help greatly the great reputation of this country for skill in ceramic decoration.'

John Bell called on Sir Henry Doulton in Lambeth, and suggested to him that the group might be reproduced for the coming exhibition at Philadelphia. He was even then an elderly man, but full of enthusiasm and eloquence. Henry Doulton was much struck with him and with his proposal. What Bell said was that no one had hitherto dared to produce terracotta on a really heroic scale. It could, however, he was convinced, be done; and he offered to make a complete and full-sized model for his 'America', from which a mould could be taken. Henry Doulton was not oblivious of the risks nor of the magnitude of the task, but he swept away the objections of his more cautious managers. 'This will be a grand opportunity,' he said, 'for showing the world, once for all, what can be done in terracotta.' The result proved his foresight; the cast was one of the finest ever turned out at Lambeth or anywhere else.

Without any other signals of decay than were comprised in a complete silvering of the hair and beard, Sir Henry Doulton had in 1895 reached the close of his third quarter of a century. He was still just as quick, just as stimulating and energetic as ever, still as much as ever devoted to poetry and pottery.

It is not to be believed, because he was so vigorous, so vivid and so alert, that he had never suffered in all the long struggle of his laborious years. Not without loss, not without partial defeat, is such a battle fought as his was. When the army returns to the sound of the drum, and all is laurel crowns and roses, the hours of depression are forgotten. Happy for them who can have, before their eyes close, some instant sense of having striven to good purpose and not in vain. I shall have written these pages foolishly if I have given the impression that Sir Henry Doulton had no sense of the frailty and futility which make the most fortunate existence something at last of a failure, even if, as Stevenson put it, the soldiers know it has been 'a faithful failure'. As Sir Henry Doulton's favourite among the moderns has put it:

> With aching hands and bleeding feet
> We dig and heap, lay stone on stone;
> We bear the burden and the heat
> Of the long day, and wish 'twere done.
> Not till the hours of light return,
> All we have built do we discern.

It was not until May 1896 that anything in the health of Sir Henry Doulton gave his family any real anxiety. Just, however, as the spring was breaking with peculiar loveliness upon all the sweeps and dingles of his Surrey home, he had a warning so serious that it took the sunshine out of his life. There were many rallyings, followed by relapses, and there was a gleam of hope again and again in the course of that dark year. However, looking back upon those months, it is impossible now not to recognise that Sir Henry was never himself in bodily health after May 1896. Nevertheless, it was wonderful how much enjoyment he succeeded in extracting from the Surrey landscape and from the society of those dear to him whenever he had a respite from pain. It is remembered that even when the company of a skilled nurse had become necessary, and he could scarcely creep about his garden, his enthusiasm was un-checked. One day in the summer of 1897, when his physical state was particularly distressing, but when the world seemed to have put on to an unusual degree the pomp of midsummer, the patient greatly surprised his nurse by telling her that she 'ought to go down upon her knees and thank God for the sight of so much beauty'.

His illness was accompanied by great pain. He bore his sufferings and his weakness, however, with an exemplary fortitude, and with a cheerfulness and thoughtfulness for others which never failed. Very happily, his brain was untouched; indeed, his lucidity was untroubled to the very latest hours of his existence, and those who loved him best were spared that most painful of all memories, a mind which has sunken below its own finer record. It is not necessary to dwell in any further detail on these last eighteen months of his life, the best hours of which were spent, where he best loved to be, at Woolpit.

To the last he preserved his love of the best literature, and his curiosity about its manifestations. He had all the new books on his favourite topics about him, and when it became fatiguing for him to hold a volume his daughters read aloud to him. He had been particularly anxious to see the second Lord Tennyson's life of his father, and by a pleasant coincidence this book was published just early enough in October to enable him to listen to the whole of its two volumes. 'It is a very unusual way of writing biography,' he said, 'and I don't think it would be well that it should be imitated. But I confess in this instance I like the way the son has done it.

What rich materials!' The two last books he enjoyed—the reading of the one being parallel to that of the other—were this *Life of Tennyson* and the *Essays* of Mr. Arthur Christopher Benson. Of the latter he said, 'A charming book! That is the sort of book I like.' These two works, both dealing with the lives and the art of poets, were finished but a few hours before he died. Sir Henry read *The Times,* holding it and turning it himself, to the last, only on the very morning of his death relinquishing it into his daughter's hands, and allowing the leaders, and an important article on 'The Engineering Dispute', to be read to him. 'I hope the masters will have the courage to be firm,' he said, when this latter reading was concluded.

This was on the morning of Wednesday the 17th of November 1897, and although Sir Henry Doulton's mind was so marvellously clear, it was evident to all about him that he was sinking. In the afternoon the symptoms of dissolution became more obvious still, and he took farewell of the members of his family. He sent messages of affection to one or two absent friends, in particular to Mr. Treherne and to myself. An hour or two before his death he saw the Rev. J. Andrews Reeve, the Rector of Lambeth. This gentleman writes:

> He told me on my coming to his bedside that he was in the Valley of the Shadow, which indeed was very evident. He was always courteous, and now he apologised for being able to say so little to me, and for speaking indistinctly. He asked after my Mother, whom he had lately seen; and then he called upon me to pray. All present knelt around the bed, while I said the *Nunc Dimittis,* our Lord's last words on the Cross, and a few other short prayers. I then took his hand, and gave him my blessing; and last of all I asked him to bless me and God's work in Lambeth. He at once responded, and said 'The Lord bless and keep thee, the Lord prosper and ennoble all thy work for Lambeth. Amen.'

After this he scarcely spoke, and he passed away very quietly on the evening of this day, the 17th of November 1897, being at that time in his seventy-eighth year.

Sir Henry Doulton was buried on Monday the 22nd of November in the cemetery of West Norwood, the funeral service being held in the church of St. Luke. It was a most impressive ceremony, an immense gathering of spectators, including more than 1,500 of his

town and country employees being present. The evidences of the
personal regard in which he was held were very affecting, and were
of a character to surprise as well as to gratify and touch the surviving
members of his family. All the oldest hands, some of whom had
been in the employment of the firm for more than sixty years, were
present. The scene in the church, which was crowded to overflowing, and almost entirely by men, was most impressive; only
two-thirds of those who attended could by any pressure find places
within, and the remainder, to the number of some 500, stayed
patiently outside in the churchyard or around the grave. The flag
on Lambeth church was half-mast high, and in every part of the
parish, especially along the line of the funeral, the testimonies to
respect and grief were abundant. The Rector of Lambeth conducted
the service. The day before, in his own church, he had borne an
eloquent testimony to his parishioner. He had said:

> We are mourning today the death of one of the most important
> of Lambeth men, the good friend and neighbour of us all, Sir
> Henry Doulton. He was a keen, active and prosperous man of
> business, an employer of thousands of men and women; he has
> served his generation by supplying human needs and by educating
> the taste for beautiful objects. In addition to these things, he has
> always been an honourable, an honest and a religious man. It is
> not for me to judge him or to praise him, least of all from this
> place. God rest him, and make him at last in heaven a useful and
> happy citizen of our New Jerusalem.

So departed Sir Henry Doulton, one of the most beloved of men,
leaving behind him a rare glow of love and regret, not only in the
group of devoted friends, but in a vast circle of those who only
touched him in the order of business, but who had long depended
upon his forethought and experience, and who were deeply convinced of his excellence. No employer of our time has been the
object of greater devotion among his workpeople than he, none has
striven more honestly to follow out the line of conduct which he
believed to be most beneficial to their interests. The time is long
distant when his name will be forgotten in Lambeth, or when the
mention of it will fail to call forth from all classes of men expressions
of respect and regret. He was a great potter, a great merchant, and
the Father of his People.

9

Recollections

The character of Sir Henry Doulton was drawn in clean and consistent lines. All the reminiscences, which those who met him under very various conditions have preserved of him, combine in a remarkable degree to fortify and to emphasise our conception of his individuality. There is, therefore, no element of confusion introduced in listening to the recollections of different friends and acquaintances, but a certain happy variety of approach, as of a head portrayed in a shadow or in light, against the sky, or in the penumbra of a room. It is always the same head, the portrait is in every case striking and consistent. I have endeavoured to collect such a series of portraits, believing that the impression which they give can only serve to build and give definition to the forms which I have sought to present in the foregoing pages.

From one of his managers I have received some very interesting impressions of Sir Henry Doulton's relation towards those whom he employed. As has been noted in its place in this biography, the firm of Doultons bought up a business at Burslem and gradually adapted it to their requirements.[44] My informant, Mr. John C. Bailey, at that time a very young man, whose years had been spent in Staffordshire, had perhaps scarcely seen Mr. Henry Doulton (as he then was) when he found himself summoned to Lambeth. After a day's business for the Burslem firm in London, he waited upon Mr. Doulton who struck him at once as very pleasant, but extremely forthright and direct. The fact is that his questions and method took the young man quite by surprise and left him not a little bewildered.

[44] See page 128.

After asking him a few questions about orders and so forth, Mr. Doulton abruptly said, 'Now, tell me how you spent yesterday.' 'I called,' was the reply, 'on Messrs. So-and-so, and on Messrs. So-and-so, and . . .' 'Yes, yes—but after business hours were over, I want to know what you did then?' The question seemed odd and inquisitorial. 'I dined at such a restaurant.' 'Ah! and then, after that, you didn't go straight to bed, I suppose?' The poor young fellow, without a notion how his confession might be received, admitted, 'Well, sir, I went to the opera.'

Upon this, Mr. Doulton beamed with benevolence and seemed to have dismissed all ideas of business from his mind, but Mr. Bailey's cross-examination was not at an end. He was astonished that the head of a gigantic business should relinquish himself in the middle of the morning to what seemed a perfectly idle curiosity. But although he did not understand, he dutifully responded, and Mr. Doulton continued his eager cross-examination. He discovered that Bailey was particularly fond of music, inquired what kind of music he liked best, elicited the fact that he had led the choir in his own town of Burslem; then came the sudden, apparently pointless question, delivered in a flash—'What did you get for doing that?' Bailey confessed that he got nothing. 'What? Nothing at all?' 'Well, nothing but a bound volume of Tennyson's works at Christmas.' 'Ah! Read them through?' 'No, sir. I am afraid I have never read them quite through, but I have read a good deal.' 'Do you know where this comes from: "Tears, idle tears, I know not what they mean"?'

'Yes, it is one of the songs put in between the cantos of "The Princess".' 'Quite right, and it is the most musical piece of blank verse in Tennyson, all of whose blank verse is music.'

So the conversation went on, and the mystified man, all unsuspecting, had no faintest idea that he was undergoing the strictest mental anatomy under the hands of a remarkably skilful practitioner, who was making not an inquiry at random, but who was carrying out a deep-laid scheme of his own. Everything was going badly at Burslem and Henry Doulton knew it. He had quite decided to make a radical change, and in looking about for a new manager his eye had lighted upon Bailey, and he had watched him, unsuspected, for several months. He had now sent for him, on a pretended errand of business, that he might form a personal opinion as to his tastes, his manners, his character. So, what seemed an outburst of the idlest curiosity, wasting a best part of the day, was really a calculated link in a chain of highly important tactics. Henry Doulton closed his first interview by inviting the young man to come and dine with him at the Round, Catch and Canon Club, where the conversation was of the easiest kind, on music, art and literature. Then, before he went back to Burslem, Bailey was struck dumb with surprise by being asked if he thought he could undertake the management of the Staffordshire branch of the business, which he has done ever since.

This anecdote is highly characteristic of Henry Doulton's methods. His boldness in choosing out for responsible positions young men, of whose capacity and character he had satisfied himself, was remarkable. To such a man, if he gave his confidence at all, he gave it fully. He made no suspicious reserves. His managers, if once he put his trust in them, were absolutely certain of his support. 'Whatever you do on the works,' he used to say, 'I shall support you in public no matter what words we may have about it in private.' The little point of Bailey's disinterested love of music is notable also. Henry Doulton said, not once, but over and over again, 'Always choose for a position of responsibility a young man who has a hobby that doesn't bring him any direct remuneration.' He replied on one occasion, to a question on this subject, 'I don't know *why* men who have hobbies make the best men of business, I can only tell you that it's my experience that they *do*!' That Bailey had been choirmaster at Burslem without remuneration showed that he had an active mind and a generous enthusiasm. These were golden qualities in Henry Doulton's estimation.

In connection with this may be taken the advice which he was in the habit of giving to his managers on the subject of their own appointments. 'In choosing a man,' he used to say, 'get a fellow out of your own place, if you possibly can, and the younger the better. Look round and select a man with a good character, rapid, intelligent, popular, *and always be careful to observe his ways with those below and above him,* for you will find it easier and quicker to teach a pleasant man the business than to graft tact and manners upon an ill-conditioned fellow who knows the work already. And, in business, whatever is necessary, politeness is.' Henry Doulton's own courtesy, as I have had occasion to say before, was rather daunting to the rough diamonds of Staffordshire. It was repeated with amazement that when he went into the enamelling room at Burslem, where the women were at work, he invariably took off his hat and kept it off. Such ceremony was absolutely unprecedented, and was gradually of no small effect in improving the manners of the place.

In the last years of Sir Henry Doulton's life, business had grown to such an extent in every one of the departments of his works, that detail gradually escaped him. It would not be true to say that his mental acumen lessened, but something of his marvellous memory declined. But in old days, to whichever of his country works he went down, his easy resumption of all parts of the industry was marvellous. He would bustle around, chatting with each foreman of departments, and managing as he moved to find a pleasant word for every workman. The rapidity of his eye was proverbial. The men were accustomed to say, before one of his visits, 'If there is a single bit of bad ware in the yard, Sir Henry will pounce upon it and bring it in!' Not infrequently he would have the workpeople suddenly gathered together in the showroom, and deliver them an improvised address on the practical part of the manufacture, passing from the mere criticism of the difference between good ware and bad to something higher, something about the art or the history of pottery. The consciousness that whatever they knew he knew, that he had passed through every branch of the practical manufacture himself, gave his workpeople a rare respect for the judgment of Sir Henry Doulton.

He was always very liberal to those who had gained his confidence, and of whose loyalty he was secure. He would say to one of his country managers, when he was making his customary round of inspection, 'Have you been up to town to see such or such a collection of pictures or designs?' The answer would be in the negative, and he would immediately be sent up to London, at Sir Henry's expense. It was quite a frequent practice of Sir Henry Doulton to send those in whom he put responsibility, whether as artists or managers, to foreign places, where they might be refreshed and stimulated with new ideas and forms.

One of the managers at Lambeth, Mr. H. Budden, gave me a very interesting account of the methods of Henry Doulton from 1886, when he first took an interest in this young man. The latter was then only twenty years of age, but Henry Doulton had kept his eye on him for some time, and believed him fitted to hold a post of responsibility above his years. One day he called him to speak with him and for some reason they were obliged to take refuge in a room very little used or visited. The interview over, as they left, Mr. Doulton, suddenly turning, caught his companion's arms in his hands and said in his quick way, 'Now, tell me everything that you saw in that room.' The young man, taken quite aback, stammered out what inventory of tables, chairs and pictures he could contrive. 'Pretty good!' said his employer, 'but now I will tell you what I noticed,' and the list seemed to his listener a prodigious one. This exemplifies one of Henry Doulton's great principles of self-education. If he saw that a young man had an eye, he cared not what pains he took to educate his visual sense. He would say, 'Whenever you experience anything, say immediately to yourself, "What is it I have seen?" Try to take a mental photograph in the act of observation.' He held this to be one of the essential forms of intelligent mental culture.

At Lambeth he was to the last the pervading spirit. Here he could exercise to the full his rare genius for application. Everything was used, every force put to its extreme account. His range of experience had become, by the passage of years, unique; the tradition of Lambeth was concentrated in him. If there was any question of procedure, he could give an answer, if no one else. His rapidity of mind and body, his untiring swiftness and vigilance, were remarkable to the end. One who worked with him for years has gone so far as to say to me, 'The secret of Sir Henry's success was his quickness.' It was unquestionably a great element in it. That it tempted him to some superficial errors, is possible. It appears that he was sometimes too much engrossed in detail; the most trifling episodes of the business would sometimes keep his mind engaged when it was required for larger uses. Yet, what others called trifles might be matters of importance to him, since he had the rare habit of referring everything back to principle.

His activity was sometimes a little vexatious. He was apt to pervade the works, as some of his managers thought, a little too restlessly. He was rushing here, gesticulating there, discussing great matters at a third place, all apparently in one instant of time. This was rather agitating to slow minds, and rather disturbing too. He would be heard, even after the age of seventy-five, coming down the staircase in a whirlwind, and flying up again two steps at a

time. If the whim seized him, he would rush into a kiln, attracted
perhaps by the sight of a beautiful piece of ware; take it out with his
own hands and carry it in an ecstasy of admiration to the showroom.
Nothing was safe from his ubiquity; no one could be sure of being
quiet. Yet, even if this omnipresence seemed a little annoying, it
often proved best in the end; his rapid step was a movement of
health and accuracy and life running through the whole establishment.

Professor William Knight, of St. Andrews, the biographer and
editor of Wordsworth, writes:

I wish I could be of real use to you in the preparation of the
Biography which you contemplate; but I am away from St.
Andrews, and have no access to MSS, and I fear I cannot do
much. What I can recall from the crypt of memory, apart from
letters, I write down with delight.

Sir Henry Doulton had a very unusual interest in Literature,
as well as in Art; and our correspondence was almost exclusively
on literary matters. I well remember the first evening I spent in
his home, when he lived at Tooting, and there was a large gathering of members of a Literary and Art Society, to which Sir Henry
belonged. I can recall the many effective things he said in criticism
of the paper which was read. . . .

He often talked of the poets of England, and of the poets'
office or function as supplemental to that of the scientific specialist.
His devotion to Art, and his appreciation of Science, did not make
him indifferent to—it rather intensified—his interest in the Poet's
work.

So many others will give you their recollections of Sir Henry,
as a worker in Art, and as an employer of labour, that it would be
superfluous for me to write down my reminiscences of his conversation when we were together in the great factory which he
created at Lambeth; but I say that it was *there,* and when he
accompanied his friends and guests through the works, that his
talk on all matters connected with Art was most instructive. He
was very modest in referring to the originality of his own work
in the department with which his name is now, and will be,
permanently associated; but it is doubtful if any of the great
potters of the world, from Egyptian times downward, have

designed and constructed anything better than that Doulton Ware which has carried the name of its inventor to the ends of the earth.

One of Sir Henry's oldest and most intimate friends, Mr. C. J. Todd, thus records his recollection of their holiday excursions:

Nearly thirty years have passed since Sir Henry Doulton joined the late James Anderson Rose and myself, in our usual continental visits at Easter. We generally devoted three weeks in each year to these tours, visiting in turn Belgium, Holland, Switzerland, Spain, Italy and France; our object being to see the various Art Galleries, and to make ourselves acquainted with the Chief Cathedrals and Churches of Europe.

Sir Henry was a delightful companion, and being gifted with a most retentive memory, he was always ready to draw on his rich store of knowledge for our information—his intimate acquaintance with the poetry of Wordsworth and Burns (both great favourites of his) enabled him to make a long journey seem short by repeating to us some of the choicest Works of these poets. His favourite pocket volumes were the *Golden Treasury* and a collection of Sonnets. He took very especial delight in Gothic Architecture, and would again and again desire to see his favourite Cathedrals—Chartes particularly attracted him, not alone for the beauty of its Gothic Works, but also for the richly coloured glass in its windows; but although he loved Art in all its phases, I am inclined to think that the beauties of Nature touched him most.

Our first journey to Italy was undertaken in 1872. We drove from Nice to Mentone, and that delightful drive gave him intense pleasure, as did that down to Spezzia, with its lemon trees laden with yellow fruit. I remember, too, with what deep delight he gazed from the terrace of Perugia on the valley beneath, filled as it then was with the blue haze that Titian delighted to paint; it was really difficult to get him away from it; indeed wherever we went, the charm of fine scenery always attracted him.

Dr. Steele was our guide in Rome (in 1881) his long residence there, and his intimate knowledge of its antiquities was an immense advantage to us. It was there that Sir Henry commissioned Mr. Albert Gilbert to execute in marble the beautiful group that now adorns the loggia of the house that he built on the Surrey Hills. I believe that this was the last work in marble from the chisel of that distinguished artist. Later Sir Henry obtained from Mr. Gilbert some of his charming works in metal, bronze or silver.[45]

In Spain we had for our courier a man who had accompanied Sir Charles Robinson through the land in search of art treasures, and his consequent knowledge greatly added to our enjoyment of the journey. At Toledo, under his guidance Sir Henry secured some good Moorish tiles.

We preferred Easter, in the solemn grandeur of the Seville Cathedral, to the pomp of St. Peter's at Rome at the same season. Later on we were at Mentone together for a month. He took with him to read Bryce's *History of the Constitution of the United States*; he was determined to get these volumes read in the evenings during our stay, and he succeeded. He thoroughly enjoyed the walks and drives in the neighbourhood.

On the death of our travelling companion John Anderson Rose, our delightful Easter trips came to an end, but the memory of them is to me, as it was to Sir Henry, a perpetual charm. . . .

Sir Henry Doulton's death was a severe loss to me, for during our long friendship we never had a word of difference, and, as indeed I have before said, he was, as companion and dear friend, most lovable—full of anecdote, and always enjoying a good story. He liked to discuss the topics of the day, and being thoroughly well informed on them, he fully held his own in conversation, and in the interchange of thought and opinion.

Mr. Thomas Raleigh, Registrar of the Privy Council and Fellow of All Souls' College, Oxford, writes as follows:

My acquaintance with Sir Henry Doulton began at a meeting of the Verulam Society where he presided and read a paper on the 'Intolerance of Scientific Men'. I am not sure that the thesis of the paper commanded my assent, but I was much impressed by the power of the speaker. If Sir Henry had entered politics and gone through the usual course of public meetings, he would, I think, have taken high rank as a debater. He spoke with ease and vigour; his enthusiastic interest in his subject communicated itself to his audience. His instinctive sense of form enabled him to avoid prolixity and dullness.

[45] See Chapter 7, page 112, for another version of this meeting with Gilbert.

By birth and early training Sir Henry Doulton was a Liberal, but the process of his own thoughts, and perhaps the influence of Burke, made him a Conservative. He told me that in his opinion the Liberals of our day think too much of abstract principles and too little of institutions. The principle of representative government, he said, is a sound one, but the Liberals are responsible for introducing the abstract idea that men had a *right* to vote. Following out this principle to its logical results, we admit great masses of inexperienced persons to the suffrage without attempting any discrimination. The result is that our imperial policy can never be consistent, because it is at the mercy of any of the currents of opinion which arise among a large miscellaneous mass of men.

So again, the principle of letting the Colonies manage their own affairs is a sound one; but the Liberals carried it so far that they were actually preparing to set the self-governing Colonies adrift when they were stopped by the movement in favour of imperial federation. I used to press Sir Henry to tell me exactly what was meant by 'federation', but he saw no necessity for precise definitions. There must be some kind of central Council, to organise imperial defence, and to improve the communications between different parts of empire; beyond this nothing need be regarded as a necessary part of the scheme. As an individual, he was in favour of an Imperial Customs Union, so framed as to benefit our trade with the Colonies at the expense of our trade with the foreigner. Free trade was another of the abstract principles which had been carried too far. Sir Henry entertained no doubt that foreign governments had done much to assist the trade of their subjects by measures of protection and encouragement, and he thought our government should profit by their example.

His training, if I mistake not, was Nonconformist, as well as Liberal. To the end of his life he was a believer in religious liberty, but he never accepted the formula of religious equality. For the Church of England as a national institution he had the greatest respect and affection; the dignity and beauty of her services appealed to his strongest feelings. To disestablish the Church would be to destroy a considerable power for good without any adequate motive. At the same time, he was always opposed to the assertion of anything like sacerdotal authority. The preachers whom he admired were those of what may be called the Broad

Church Evangelical School. I think he rather sympathised with
the Whig notion that the State should control the Church, and
if necessary, curtail her liberation, for the sake of peace and
comprehension.

In matters industrial and economical Sir Henry Doulton's
opinions were formed by observation and experience. He admitted
the advance in material prosperity which was brought about by
free trade and limited liability, but he was keenly sensible of the
dangers by which that advance was attended. He admired the
old-fashioned business virtues of the men under whom he had
himself been trained, and he disliked any change which might
have the effect of relaxing the tie of personal confidence between
trader and customer, employer and workman. It would have
been contrary to his political sentiments to prevent workmen from
combining, but he disapproved of the methods and policy of the
Unions with which he had been brought into contact. For him
Socialism had naturally no attractions. He thought that in the
conduct of a great business everything must depend on the energy
and foresight of its chiefs; he thought also that the legitimate
reward of superior energy consisted mainly in that kind of power
which trade-unionists and socialists are endeavouring to destroy.
Human nature being as it is, he thought, there must be some
reward, some prize in view, to induce able men to put forth all
their powers.

In this connection I ought perhaps to record an opinion which
Sir Henry more than once expressed in conversation with me. He
was an enemy of socialism, but he was not exactly an individua-
list; he was, I think, substantially in agreement with those who say
that economic questions should be considered from a family, not
from an individual, point of view. And it seemed to him that the
freedom of movement given by modern travelling facilities was
in some respects not favourable to family life. The modern young
woman is so keen to assert her independence that he was disposed
to doubt whether she would exercise the same influence in
keeping the family together as was exercised in former generations
by women of a more 'old-fashioned' type. It need hardly be said
that Sir Henry was a consistent adversary of 'women's rights' in
every form.

I have more than once heard persons who knew Sir Henry and

his work express surprise that a man so successful in business should have been distinguished by a sincere and ardent love of the beautiful. But is there anything surprising in the combination? I am disposed to say that the qualities which made a great administration are to a great extent the same as those which go to the making of a great artist. If Sir Henry Doulton had been a painter, he would have worked steadily and heartily in his vocation; he would have brought a keen intelligence to bear on it; he would have displayed patient ingenuity in adapting his means to his end. He was born to take an important place in the industrial world; business was his vocation; and he brought an artistic sense to bear on it. And even in those departments of his work with which art has little or nothing to do, he could always discover sources of intellectual interest. He knew by experience that the management of a great concern is a branch of the art of governing men.

Sir Henry Doulton was one of the earliest and the most intelligent of those who welcomed, some twenty years ago, the revival of English sculpture in the hands of Mr. Hamo Thornycroft and Mr. Alfred Gilbert. Of the pleasure which his first introduction to Mr. Gilbert and his work gave him at Rome in 1882, I have already spoken. He continued to observe with enthusiasm the beautiful creations of that artist. Nor did he less enjoy those of his great rival, and a special interest attaches to the following reminiscences which Mr. Thornycroft has been kind enough to contribute to this memoir:

What always struck me most in my intercourse with Sir Henry Doulton was his enthusiasm for the matter in hand. It was on this object—whatever it might be—that he concentrated his vivacity, always sensitively eager, always brightly optimistic.

One occasion recurs vividly to my memory. About the year 1884, he was taking me over his great pottery works at Lambeth, and explaining in detail the various processes and manufactures of his famous ware. It struck me, as he did so, that his manner in so conducting a visitor was unique. Never was there such an enthusiasm, such a concentrated eager pride, shown by a manufacturer before. One came to recognise that this intensity was habitual in him, that he could not contemplate what he thought admirable more coolly. His pride seemed to reach a burning point when we

N

came to the Art Department, where he was employing a great number of women, all of whom had received under his auspices a certain amount of art training. They were decorating the pottery and giving it its typical character as 'art ware'. Here Sir Henry moved through the excellently fitted studios with an extraordinary air of joyousness. But the very climax of his enthusiasm was reached when we neared the modelling room of his great *protégé*, Tinworth. Here, it was intimated, there must be no reserve, and a sort of pledge of good behaviour was taken before you might be presented to the genius. The ceremony then took place, and, for the first time, Sir Henry would be silent for a moment, while the artist, in his direct way, was expounding his somewhat quaint rendering of Biblical subjects in the great clay panels. Meanwhile, with his luminous and eloquent eyes, Sir Henry would turn from his *protégé* to the visitor and back again, as if the process of initiation was almost too ecstatic to be borne.

Sir Henry Doulton's genial and courteous manner to all his workmen as we passed together through the busy workshop, and his evident recognition of the qualities of each individual was extremely striking. He had himself gone through all the stages of the potter's training when a boy. He told me that he could sympathise with all of them much better from understanding in detail what it was upon which each one was engaged. He could recollect what it had been to sit before the wheel all day long, and he took care to have a kind word for those who did so still. My impression, from repeated observation, is that his men were much attached to him. I remember that on occasion of a great strike at the Works many of them came quietly to him and explained that they felt the utmost regret in being obliged, in obedience to the Union, to strike against a friend whom they so highly respected.

His country house at Ewhurst was beautiful in itself, and beautifully situated. Here he was revealed as the same ardent appreciator of whatever lay close around him, and of whatever owed (in part at least) its authorship to himself. Here it was that I had special occasion to note his delight in the society of his friends, and his hospitable kindness to them. I have never known a man so actively engaged in business life who gave evidence of having been so constant a reader. His acquaintance with the poets was extraordinary, and he was ready to quote them in a manner and with a fulness which scarcely seemed to belong to the present century. In his attitude to art, he was still less modern. Indeed, his tastes in painting lay entirely in the pre-Victorian epoch—as it seemed, at least, to me—in Turner and Stanfield and their immediate contemporaries, almost to the exclusion of the more recent schools. In this, as in so much else, he was peculiarly British. The exotic, or at all events, the modern exotic, scarcely seemed to appeal to him at all.

Miss Hannah B. Barlow, the interesting artist whose connection with the Doultons has been dwelt upon in earlier pages of this work, writes:

When first I came to the Potteries, few people knew what reverses I had had in my home, and what a dreadful undertaking it was to me to meet strangers. I shall never forget the first time I encountered Sir Henry Doulton, how great my alarm was, and how kindly and considerately he received me. He was always encouraging. He made it impossible for me not to enjoy my work, and his great love of animals made his visits to my studio most helpful. He would rarely come without telling me of some trait of the life of horses or cattle which he had observed, or some grouping of them in the fields which he believed would aid my imagination.

I always noticed that Sir Henry Doulton never forgot a promise. Once he told me, in the course of conversation, that he would give me a long-haired kitten. Weeks passed, and I began to tell myself that he had certainly forgotten. But, no! One day, in he came with the most charming little fluffy white kitten I ever remember to have seen, my friend and companion for more than ten years. Sir Henry presented me with the grandest model that it has ever been my fortune to work from—the splendid deerhound 'Rob Roy'. In all the years I have worked at Lambeth, I never once had the sensation that money was the ultimate object of my art. Sir Henry and his family have always shown an extraordinary tact in preventing such a feeling. I hold this to have been one of the great charms of my work at Lambeth. Sir Henry always seemed to urge me to do my best, without respect to its commercial value to him, and his enthusiastic interest in my designs had the effect of constantly rousing me to try to do still better things.

Of late years, it was not possible for him to be such a constant visitor to the Studios. Since he has ceased to come, we have missed him very much. My sister Florence agrees with me that some of the pleasantest memories of our life are of the days when we began the decoration-work upon the stoneware, and with them the eager and generous sympathy of Sir Henry Doulton is indissolubly connected.

A very particular interest attends the reminiscences which Professor A. H. Church, F.R.S., has been kind enough to write for me. One of the most eminent chemists of the age, and Professor of Chemistry to the Royal Academy since 1879, Mr. Church possessed exactly the qualities of science and connoisseurship in combination which were serviceable to Sir Henry Doulton. A very warm friendship existed between these distinguished men, and Doulton delighted in the conversation of Professor Church. I remember with what extreme warmth he spoke to me of the Professor's monograph on *English Earthenware,* and again of his work on *Colour.* The marvellous collections of metal-work, pottery and precious stones which Professor Church has brought together at Kew were Doulton's endless delight, and as the Professor speaks here, with great modesty, of the advantage which accrued to him from intercourse with the potter, it is but scant honesty on the part of a biographer to point out that the latter received in this delightful friendship at least as much as he gave.

Professor Church writes:

I think it was on the occasion when Henry Doulton's decorative stoneware was first publicly shown about 1868 that I made the acquaintance of the great English potter of the 19th century. There was a decided *furore* on the subject amongst connoisseurs; every piece exhibited had been eagerly bought. H. D. already knew me by name as a student and collector of old English pots, who had brought into prominence the merits of the white salt-glazed stoneware of 18th century Burslem—the refined precursor of Henry Doulton's own productions. I had also examined and even owned specimens of the much earlier stoneware of John Dwight of Fulham. So while I, on the one hand, was eager to learn all I could about these new products of the Lambeth kiln, Henry Doulton, on the other hand, was anxious to extend his knowledge of the history of the early phases of this branch of ceramic art.

We met, and I soon became a frequent caller at Lambeth, often bringing with me bits of old English wares, remarkable for body, texture of surface, design or colour. We discussed the differences between old and modern wares brought about by differences in fuel (coal versus wood) and by the disuse of saggers. At first, Henry Doulton would not believe that the 18th century stoneware was fired at or would stand the high temperature of his own sanitary-ware kilns. But he was convinced by the result of his re-firing of one of my old Burslem plates made about the year 1760; it stood the test, suffering in no wise save by a slight embrowning of the glaze—a change easily explained by the modern method of heating etc.

Then we argued the question of colouring, the first test being a richly coloured octagonal plate of tortoiseshell ware, the second a marvellous teapot in my collection, where the lapis-blue glaze covering the exterior was obviously a salt-glaze produced *au grand feu*. On this ground were floral designs in opaque enamel white with black outlines and details, all in pigments subsequently added and fixed at the lesser heat of the enamelling kiln. Now Henry Doulton desired to secure similar results with one firing only, so as to attain complete homogeneity of effect with a softness and richness impossible by the old method. Here the study of German and Flemish stonewares came in to help. For in them the puce of manganese appeared by the side of the blues of cobalt and the browns due to iron. By associating washes of china-clay with the incised work of the old English 'scratched blue' and with limiting ridges or cloisons of the body itself, complex yet harmonious effects, in which the drawing of the design was preserved, were reached at Lambeth. The gamut of colours, too, was slowly augmented by taking hints from the *flambé* porcelains of China, and by adding oxide of tin, purple of Cassius, and, I think, oxide of chromium, to the palette of the stoneware potter. There was no servile copying here. Henry Doulton had no wish to suggest it and no occasion to permit it. Indeed no one will venture to suggest that one painter plagiarises the works of another because both employ the same pigments.

Henry Doulton doubtless discussed with other friends also the directions in which his ornamental stoneware might be best developed on the technical side, and he was able to make many of his ideas assume concrete form through the practical experience of his lieutenants in the potworks. Henry Doulton possessed indeed that kind of mental alertness which could appreciate artistic and scientific suggestion, along with that will-power and that sympathetic persuasiveness which sufficed to effect its translation into technical practice. I cannot but think that the surface full of interest, the fortuitously happy colour-effects, and the imperishable nature of his ordinary sanitary and chemical stoneware appealed strongly to the imagination of Henry Doulton. So, when the first attempts were made at Lambeth to treat this material decoratively, he was glad to favour the production of objects for which indeed a public appetite had to be created, but which would challenge the admiration of connoisseurs.

It was a source of satisfaction to Henry Doulton that some at least of his ware would be visible and admired, though most of it would of necessity be buried in the earth or hidden in the dingy recesses of chemical works and laboratories. Henry Doulton's well-known sympathy with the craftsmen and the artists in his employ was marked by that individual character which helped to impart a personal accent to the choicer productions of modern Lambeth.

Henry Doulton wisely restricted the forms and destinations of his stoneware, for he realised at the outset that it was not and could not be made suitable for ordinary table services. Even the old fine white stoneware of Burslem, fired with wood and in saggers, is not agreeable in use. The hard papillose glaze causes noise and attrition with silver spoons and forks.

I do not know how far Henry Doulton grasped the explanations which I offered him of the chemical reactions occurring in the process of glazing with common salt—the central and characteristic operation in the manufacture of stoneware. But that he propounded questions on this subject and on the influence of sulphur and of iron on the results, and was much interested in the physical structure, as revealed under the microscope, of thin sections of various porcelains and earthenwares, may be taken as proof that he was not content with outward appearances, but wanted to penetrate beneath the surface of things.

Henry Doulton gathered some choice specimens of Oriental and other pottery not merely for his educational museum at Lambeth but for enjoyment at home. I recall his pleased expression when I gave him the choice Whieldon plate before mentioned—one of the most deliciously coloured specimens of tortoiseshell described more minutely in my *English Earthenware* (p. 33)—and he thoroughly appreciated a fine piece of Böttger red ware, partly polished on the lapidary's wheel, partly left matt, which on my own responsibility I had bought for him at Christie's, where to our amusement it had been catalogued as a specimen of natural porphyry.

Henry Doulton's appreciation of the peculiar merits in colour, texture, form, employment and association of decorative methods and motives, in the work of other and of older potteries, impressed me as generous and sound.

Few additional touches can be needed to complete the portrait of Sir Henry Doulton. His nature will, however, not have been completely presented if I do not dwell a little further on his personal idiosyncrasies. He was a man of spare and light figure, agile, restless, hypersensitive. In every glance, in every gesture, he betrayed the fact that he was one of those elect spirits who would be governed by their nerves, if they had not early and resolutely determined to be the governors. In a brilliant passage, Feuillet, that close observer of humanity, has divided the men who succeed into three classes; '*les bilieux,*' he says, '*sont démagogues, les sanguins sont démocrates, et les nerveux sont aristocrates.*' Henry Doulton was sanguine and nervous at the same time, and this fine combination of constitutions permitted him to choose. His career, indeed, was an incessant choice. Alternately, the nervous and the sanguine temperaments asserted the upper hand, and the curious oscillations in his interests must be attributed to their successive and recurrent action.

It was a natural result of this condition that his physical endurance was not equal to his mental eagerness. It was aided, however, or supplemented, by an extraordinary power of recuperation, so that although the fire within him often seemed to burn very low, it, as often, after a brief rest, sprang up again as lively as before. He was very easily tired, very seldom exhausted, and the ability to recover was perennial. He had great command over himself, and he held his nerves in hand, as if he were carefully and yet boldly driving tandem. No picture of Henry Doulton would be complete without a tribute to his splendid command of his temper. Sometimes, a whole set of valuable and delicate pots would be entirely spoilt in the kiln, for such accidents are inherent to the potter's art, and are one of its sorest trials. In such cases, Doulton's serenity was never known to be upset; rather an excessively brilliant smile would show the careful observer that he was feeling the loss keenly, but not by a word or gesture of irritation would he permit himself to be betrayed. An intense feeling of consideration for others had not a little to do with this self-control. If he was to relieve his feelings by an outburst, somebody would be greatly grieved and embarrassed, and it was a religion with Doulton to spare others from discomfort. This never-failing consideration was one of his most pleasing characteristics.

In conversation, he had the curious habit of seeming to fix his interlocutor with his large, lustrous eyes, but—as it were—without really seeing him. His look was not focussed on the person with whom he spoke, but seemed to go past him. If it be not thought too ingenious, I would say that this was the result of his having practically found the impact of his personality a little trying to those with whom he spoke. He was more ardent, more eager, more enthusiastic than ninety-nine hundredths of the people with whom he came into contact, and he looked away that he might put them at their ease. He was always anxious to impress the minds of those with him, to draw them rapidly along the same road on which he was travelling, and a species of unexpressed generosity obliged him to refrain from taking them by storm by his purely physical ardour. He was rather Socratic, too, sometimes, in the way in which he helped the hesitating to an unembarrassed expression of opinion by means of a series of questions.

Two external pleasures never failed to calm the fervour of the spirit, and to take Henry Doulton away from the throng of his thoughts. Those were music and horse exercise. I have spoken on several occasions in this volume of the prominent place which riding took in the life of a man indifferent to every kind of sport and game. In later years, his greatest physical indulgence was a mail-phaeton. When he ceased to be able to go abroad for his holiday this amusement took the place of travel. For several summers in succession, from 1891 onwards, with Mr. Todd or another friend, he would start from his house, like a schoolboy, in the wildest of spirits, and wreathed in smiles. What matter if, while oblivious of everything, he was spouting poetry, the reins on the backs of the horses, something awkward should suddenly happen in the slippery Ewhurst lanes? If anybody remonstrated, 'Where's your nerve?' would reply the enthusiastic driver, who is said to have returned, long past the age of seventy, from one of these delightful excursions, shouting, 'We have been nearly smashed up a dozen times, but—here we are!'

In music he was less of an executant, nor do I understand that it was the more complicated and classical art which appealed to him. In the old days, when he sang bass in the club with his friends William Blades and Joseph Pewtress, it was the simple part-music which he was accustomed to. His highest flights were in the motets of the Antiquarian Society. This was the kind of melody in which he always delighted, and towards the end of his life he was a constant attendant at the dinners of the Round, Catch and Canon Club, where some of the most gifted and highly trained vocal talent in England could be heard joining in the delicious old madrigals and glees. Henry Doulton always had the book open before him; his hand was moving with a rhythmic motion, and those who sat quite near might overhear him chanting in a faint appreciative murmur.

In public matters, as in private, he was an enthusiast. Of his political convictions, something has already been said. To my mind, the most interesting and original of his traits in this respect was his attitude towards colonial questions. Early and late he was in this matter perfectly consistent. In 1863, I find him exclaiming, 'May the day never come when England will be neglected and despised by those children whom, from selfish motives, she has abandoned to their fate!' The spread of the sentiments of the Manchester School left him isolated and indignant. 'I scorn,' he says, June 11th, 1872, 'the statesmen who look on separation with indifference, and say it does not matter whether the connection of the colonies with the Empire is maintained or not.' It was difficult for him to break entirely with that Radical Party in whose principles he had been brought up, but the Little Englandism of Bright and Gladstone drove him to the other camp. About 1880 I find him forming an anthology of utterances about the colonies by the Liberal statesmen of the hour, and punctuating these quotations with his scorn and anger. He lived, one may rejoice to think, just long enough to see the sentiments which he had nourished in isolation through so many dark years of indifferentism, accepted at last by the awakened conscience of the nation.

This study of a loyal and ardent nature, of a man eminently illuminative in his generation, must now be brought to a close. I have endeavoured to paint the portrait of a successful merchant, who was an impassioned lover of beauty; of a man of business who conducted his labours under the guidance of his imagination; of a manufacturer, severely practical, who was yet an enthusiast and an idealist. Such figures are rare in our crowded society of today, and they grow rarer. Praise, then, to the few

> Who, though so noble, share in the world's toil,
> And, though so tasked, keep free from dust and soil.

APPENDIX I

The Culture of the Imagination

An address given by Sir Henry Doulton to the
Smethwick Institute, 8th October, 1891

When your committee did me the honour to ask me to be the president of your society for the year, and assured me that my duties would be light, and probably confined to the proceedings of this evening, I felt I could not decline such a request, associated as I have been in a very humble degree with Smethwick for nearly forty years. On thinking of what I should say to you, my mind reverted to some of the earliest recollections of my childhood in connection with this district; when my father stimulated my curiosity and wonder by assuring me that if one early summer morning he left London by coach for Birmingham, he should take supper there the same evening; and of another visit when the noble Town Hall was opened, my father told me that he had seen an organ up some of the pipes of which a man might crawl; and that he had heard the gifted Malibran sing.

I thought, too, later on, of my own journeys to Dudley by the only conveyance of the time, the canal boat; or by omnibus through Smethwick; of the frequent refreshers of the driver at the wayside inns, which made the journey so tedious; of the notices on some land on the road between Birmingham and Smethwick, warning any traveller who might be tempted to leave the dusty road that man-traps and spring-guns were set on the grounds. I contrasted with all this your present railroad conveniences, and your parks for recreation and amusement and realised in some poor degree the marvellous changes of the past forty years.

The great metropolis of the Midlands has, since the time referred to, enlarged its Town Hall, even adding to its original beauty, and clustered around it are now art galleries, museums, libraries, and last of all, and crowning all, as all civilisation and property is based on the security of law, the beautiful law courts, recently opened by the Prince of Wales.

Smethwick, while sharing in the advantages of the growing progress and fame of the metropolis of the Midlands, has also its own special interests and associations. I remember when Smethwick was busy with preparations for the exhibition of 1851, and call to mind that it is due to the enterprise of Smethwick manufacturers, Fox & Henderson, and Messrs. Chance, that at a critical time the exhibition of 1851, the parent of all other exhibitions, took a practicable shape. It is happily not only material growth—represented as it is in your great manufacturing establishments, in your halls of commerce and municipal buildings—in connection with which this district has made such remarkable progress. You have also not been unmindful of the higher claims of science, art, and literature, of which such institutions as this are the outcome. We are learning that, *pari-passu* with material progress, there should be advance in art and science; and that there must be this union in a healthy commercial community. We are now taking means to promote this; and may I say that our efforts are the more likely to be ultimately successful if, while energetic, they still are tentative, and based on individual energy and municipal enterprise.

It may not be out of place to remind you that the lesson has been taught us in the past by some eminent examples whose sphere of action has been in the Midland district; and I might say in the county in which we now are. Perhaps the two most distinguished men connected with our modern industrial progress are James Watt and Josiah Wedgwood.

That young giant, the steam engine, which has changed the globe and almost annihilated time and space, though not actually born in your neighbourhood, was here rocked in its cradle and, nurtured by the genius and perseverance of Watt, grew in efficiency, strength and beauty. The struggles of James Watt, not only his wrestling with the elements of nature till he made them subservient to his will, but his trying fight with those who were on the watch to pilfer the labour of his brains, and appropriate his discoveries as soon as they were perfected (for every one of his patents had to be defended) gives additional interest to the career of this remarkable man. But Watt was no one-idea-man. His tastes and pursuits were liberal and diversified. Botany, chemistry and geology were the favourite studies of his leisure hours and in conversation his mind is said to have shown the diversified information of an encyclopaedia. While he had a predominant object in view, the perfection of the steam engine, he was interested in most of the arts and sciences and despite the worries and vexations of continued litigation, he died calmly at the age of eighty-three, thanking God for his useful life and its serene and quiet close. Sentiment grew around the great discoverer as it does so naturally around the homes of distinguished soldiers, statesmen, and poets; pilgrims from all parts of the globe would often visit Handsworth Church and gaze on the monument of James Watt by Chantrey and linger around the scenes of his early struggles. I may remind you that it was at Smethwick that Murdoch, the associate of Boulton and Watt, first publicly showed the practical application of gas by lighting the works at Soho in 1807–8. Subsequently in 1811, he read a paper before the Royal Society on the 'Economical use of coal gas as an illuminating power'.

And as a potter, may I not congratulate you that your county was the birthplace and the scene of the life and labours of one of England's most illustrious sons, Josiah Wedgwood; who, eminently successful as a manufacturer, combined scientific skill and artistic taste in such a remarkable degree. In industrial skill and activity in combination with virtues of mind and heart, his is perhaps our greatest name in the honoured roll of English discoverers and manufacturers. A man who, though absorbing as were the claims of business, found time and made opportunities to originate many enterprises and promote all that in his admirable judgment were practicable; while his heart responded to every call of patriotism and to all wise social schemes having for their object the moral and physical improvement of the masses. Compared with the far reaching results of Watt's discoveries in their immense influence upon the world, Wedgwood's discoveries and influence are relatively small. But in true dignity and worth of character, high aims and successful blending of the beautiful with the scientific and practical and in a wise philanthropy—in short in the rounded and complete life—Wedgwood's was almost the ideal life of a man of business. What alike distinguished Watt and Wedgwood was that both sought knowledge for its own sake as well as for its pecuniary reward, a spirit most desirable to encourage at all times, but specially in our day when trade strives to be not the handmaid, but the mistress of science.

The advantages of our modern Polytechnics and Schools of Art and Science, with their studios and laboratories, in saving the preliminary struggles of such men as Wedgwood to obtain elementary knowledge, and to enable students to avail themselves of the accumulated experience of those who were pioneers in the special work in which they are interested, cannot be overrated. They enable him to start from vantage ground and lighten his early work. The student, however, should always bear in mind that nothing can compensate for individual experience and that discipline which is obtained from the struggle with difficulties. For what is really ours is of our own making, and 'what cost us nothing is nothing to us'.

The large pecuniary rewards of commerce will I think always go to the few, to those who have ability combined with practical sagacity; but there are other and higher rewards open to all. The pursuit of knowledge for its own sake, the enchantment which lies in its acquisition, and in the manifold pleasures derivable from increasing interest in what lies around us in a world so rich in beauty and design, and in the accumulated knowledge of past generations, who have left such a precious heritage of beautiful works and noble thoughts; these are delights open to all, pleasures which time will not exhaust or change of fortune lessen, which can give healthful pleasure to vigorous youth, and solace to weakened age.

I am not sure that it is always desirable that the studies of our leisure should be connected with our business. I have great sympathy with three shoemakers of whom my friend Mr. Sparkes told me. In a town where one of the most important industries is the making of shoes, the master of the Art School was cheered by the application of three shoemakers who wished to join his art class. He had waited long for pupils connected with the staple trade of the town, and welcomed the three recruits with pleasure. He had prepared for their reception and placed before them the cast of a human foot, which he supposed it would be their ambition to draw. 'Oh no,' they said, 'we do not want this, we have enough of this all day long, we want to learn to paint pictures.'

I am pleased to see that your programme indicates a variety of instruction and recreation. The advantage of such an institution as this is in teaching not only the variety but the harmony of all knowledge. It is important that in an age of specialism we should grasp this idea.

Science and art, and especially the highest art, poetry, are often represented as antagonistic. Now it is only imperfect science that is inartistic. Modern science is in its infancy, certainly its applications are, and naturally they are crude; like childish drawings, they are wanting in perspective. Almost all great scientific discoveries have been flashes of inspiration, before they became truths verified by experience, they were intuitions of genius. Abstract science is the fruitful parent of material good, and the imaginative speculations of the poets of science anticipate discoveries which experiments confirm.

'All true science,' says Sir J. Crichton Browne, 'rests on imaginings, and is, strictly speaking, a body of established truth which imagination has built up.' In the discoveries of Columbus, Newton, Faraday, we see

> How intuition breaks thro' time and space
> And mocks experiments' successive race.

Their discoveries were first seen in the light of the imagination. Newton's imagination conceived the law of gravitation, and when by a series of calculations he drew near to its demonstration it is said he was quite overpowered by his emotion. 'Without imagination,' says Tyndall,

'Newton would never have invented fluxions, or Davy have decomposed the earths and alkalies.' And Faraday, the great discoverer of magneto-electricity, was always guessing by hypothesis, making theoretic divination the stepping stones to experimental results.

We often hear that this is a scientific age, and so it cannot be a poetic or artistic age. The progress of science is undoubted. The inventions and discoveries of this generation, marvellous as they are, are yet but the prelude to what lies before in the probably not distant future, for keen intellects are engrossed with problems which time and perseverance will probably solve.

It is not in human nature, certainly not in nineteenth-century human nature, to rest contented to count the pebbles on the shore while the whole ocean lies outstretched before us. Neither is it in human nature to dispense with the poetic elements in man. But poetry and science are not incompatible. If they are, and one or the other is to go, it will not be poetry. There is an unfathomable store of it in human nature. It is born anew with every child that comes into this world of mystery and beauty 'Poetry is the first and last of all knowledge, it is immortal as the heart of man.'

In Shelley's exquisite essay on the 'Defence of Poetry' he says, 'Poetry is the record of the best and happiest moments of the best and happiest minds.' And he, the most unearthly of poets, whose poetry seems to be removed from the plane of human associations, though full of aerial music and exuberance of fancy, even he recognises the ultimate harmony of poetry and science. 'Poetry is the breath and finer spirit of all knowledge, it is the impassioned expression which is the countenance of all science. Poetry is at once the centre and circumference of knowledge; it is that which comprehends all science.' In truth there is no reason why these permanent elements of our nature should not be brought into ever new combinations of delight. Campbell, wishing to retain his infantine impression of the rainbow wrote:

> Still seem as to my childhood's sight
> A midway station given,
> For happy spirits to alight
> Betwixt the earth and heaven.
>
> Can all that optics teach unfold
> Thy form to please me so,
> As when I dreamt of gems and gold
> Hid in they radiant bow?

But the return of the childlike faith is impossible to the man of science, and undesirable. Does the scientist who knows what the rainbow is, cease to delight in its glory as he sees the triumphal arch span the heavens? The laws that govern the clouds, rain, dew, frost and snow are pretty well understood now; yet who, with any imagination, feels them on that account to be less subtle combinations of beauty and less fruitful incentives to the imagination, which plays about and illumines the seen as well as the unseen? Does the knowledge of the fact that lightning is electricity destroy the grandeur of one of those flashes which, 'Ere a man hath power to say "Behold!" the jaws of darkness do devour it up.'

The beautiful in the external forms of matter, in the harmonies of light and colour, and in the modulation of sweet sounds, are the themes of the poet; and the laws which they obey are the studies of the man of science. Poetry connects common forms, colours and sounds with exalted ideas. Science rightly rejoices in ministering to the requirements of civilisation, it increases the comforts of life and adds to its enjoyments. But art is a lifting power, helping us to a higher communion with influences which give to all things life and beauty. The search of the scientist is for truth, and the true is the beautiful. *'Le beau est la splendeur du vrai.'* Every discovery in natural phenomena is the revelation of a new truth to the mind, of new beauties in creation.

It is true that the spiritualising of nature, peopling the earth with fairies, genii, and mysterious forms, which gives a noble tone to the early literature, has in later times been lost by minds delighting only in the accumulation of minor facts, regardless of the laws by which they are regulated and the harmony which unites them. But in science we may find the elements of the most exalted poetry; analogies connecting the illimitable world with the world of thought, on which the greatest minds may expatiate. Poetry which is quickened by the contemplation of those vast and mysterious powers which science shows us are ever working in the universe, is at least as high and ennobling as science when it gives us some luxury, the result of new chemical combinations.

But in fact there is no antagonism. The phenomena of reality are as wonderful as any ideal conception, and beauty and truth and truth and beauty are interchangeable. The revelation of truth is the poetry of science. To study science then for purely utilitarian ends is to narrow its sphere. Its useful applications are not to be undervalued, but utility is not the motive that ever has inspired the greatest discoverers. It was the search for truth, the desire to know, which inspired a Galileo and a Herschell, though the result of their discoveries in astronomy has been to perfect navigation, and to give man a control over nature conducive in the highest degree to his safety and happiness. To draw from science great principles, masterly deductions, and elevating ideas, is a mental exercise of the highest kind tending to the elevation of thought and feeling; and this is the poetry of science.

Of course a man of science may never get beyond analysing and comparing. His interest may not travel beyond the microscope, the crucible or the dissecting room, or he may see in the grandest scenes of nature only subjects for scientific observation, but if he be not only a man of accurate knowledge, but of large soul and keen susceptibility, his admiration will be fuller and more instructive, more complete than that of the mere scientist, his imagination will take in all that the physicist does and much more. Investigation need not be a bar to wonder and reverence; on the contrary to the highest minds it is a stimulus; the larger minded men of science have had their imaginations quickened and their reverence deepened by their discoveries.

Kepler, after he had discovered the laws of planetary motion, said all that he had been able to do was to read a few thoughts of God. And Faraday, that true knight of God, says Tyndall, 'worked in the temper of a poet; and like the poet he continually reached that point of emotion which produces poetic creation'.

Science is the pursuit of order, the search for law, the search for the thought of the Creator and Designer; and order and design are characteristics of beauty. Not till man and nature and human life lie in the last light of science, that is, of knowledge and of truth, will poetry reach the fulness of its triumph.

But wisdom is ever justified of her children. Some seventy years ago, Wordsworth, the most potent force in the poetry of the nineteenth century, wrote: 'If the labours of men of science should ever create any material revolution, direct or indirect, in our condition, and in the impressions which we habitually receive, the poet will sleep then no more than at present, he will be ready to follow the steps of the man of science . . . the remotest discovery of the chemist, the botanist, or mineralogist will be as proper objects of the poet's art as any upon which it can be employed. If the time should ever come when what is now called science thus familiarised to men, shall be ready to put on as it were a form of flesh and blood, the poet will lend his divine spirit to aid the transfiguration, and will welcome the being thus produced as a dear and genuine inmate of the household of man.' This was written over seventy years ago.

Wordsworth has been unjustly charged as narrow and unsympathetic with modern progress. In 1844 he brought on himself a storm of abuse for venturing to protest against a projected railway through a beautiful part of the Lake District. At that time the utilitarian spirit was in the ascendant, and no spot was so beautiful, no ruin so venerable, as to secure them from the inroads of the engineer and contractor. If fifty years ago

O

science had been allied with artistic feeling, our beautiful country would have been spared some of the scars which needlessly disfigure her surface. It is the bounden duty of our modern engineers, a duty they owe to posterity, to avoid as far as possible hiding or obscuring the beauties of the country; and to make our stations, viaducts and bridges more beautiful, I was going to say, less hideous, than they often are.

One might then say that as the results of science are perfect so are they beautiful. In that outburst of genius at the beginning of the fifteenth century the union was complete. For example Michelangelo and Leonardo da Vinci were great artists as well as great engineers. One of the most beautiful works in the world, Giotto's tower at Florence, was built for use as a bell tower; and the fortifications of Nuremburg, designed by Albert Dürer for defence, are religiously preserved for their beauty.

To return to Wordsworth. The importance of maintaining our commons and open spaces for health and recreation was not understood or appreciated, as by experience I well know, even thirty years ago. Nearly fifty years ago Wordsworth proved himself a true poet, a seer, by protesting against sacrificing everything to mere utility. The sonnet which brought about the shower of ridicule was not only an outburst of indignation, it was a prophetic glance into the needs of the future:

> Is there no nook of English ground secure
> From rash assault? Schemes of retirement sown
> In youth, and 'mid the world kept pure
> As when the earliest flowers of hope were blowing,
> Must perish.

But the natural indignation at the wanton destruction of the beautiful did not blind Wordsworth to the advantages of science, or to the anticipation of its harmony with all that is highest in man's art. A few years afterwards he wrote: 'Steam-boats, Viaducts, and Railways':

> Motions and means, by land and sea, at war
> With old poetic feeling, not for this
> Shall ye, by poets even, be judged amiss!
> Nor shall your presence, howsoe'er it mar
> The loveliness of nature, prove a bar
> To the mind's gaining that prophetic sense
> Of future change, that point of vision, whence
> May be discovered what in soul ye are.

You may not be uninterested if I give you in a few words an account of an interview I had with Wordsworth in 1849, six months before his death.

On expressing the pleasure I felt at seeing one to whom I owed so much enjoyment and instruction, he said that it was a poor thing in a poet to write merely to please and amuse; that at the outset of life he had set before himself a higher aim, and that the frequent testimony he received in his old age that his efforts had not been fruitless was a great comfort. There were then no signs of speedy decay, his courteous dignity and affability were most impressive. He introduced me to his wife and sister, to whom he owed so much. He took me round his garden and pointed out the most beautiful views, and I read on a stone the following inscription:

> In these fair vales hath many a tree
> At Wordsworth's suit been spared;
> And from the builder's hand this stone
> For some rude beauty of its own
> Was rescued by the Bard.

Little thinking that the concluding lines would so soon be read with such pathetic interest.

> So let it rest; and time will come
> When here the tender hearted
> May heave a gentle sigh for him,
> As one of the departed.

A few weeks ago I read an account of an interesting practical application of the most fruitful scientific discovery of this century, on Lake Windermere; a most remarkable confirmation of what I have been urging that science and beauty are not antagonistic, but that as science becomes more perfect, her applications will become more and more beautiful.

On Lake Windermere—the scene of so much of Wordsworth's exquisite description of scenery, and associated with Coleridge, Southey, Professor Wilson, and other great names in the literature of the nineteenth century—an electric boat is propelled by electric power generated from a waterfall which rushes into Windermere. Coal, smoke and oil are all dispensed with, and one of the most beautiful objects in nature, falling water, is transformed into its equivalent of electrical energy, and what Dr. Wendell Holmes calls the 'electric witch' has displaced the 'steam fiend'.

I would then urge on all, especially on my young friends, the importance of cultivating the imagination. In doing so I am in no wise asking you to neglect the study of abstract science or its practical applications. But I would beseech you not to allow to wither by neglect those higher and more spiritual powers which are cultured by the exercise of the imagination, and fed by the study of the works of our great poets. The cultivation of poetry is never more to be desired than when, from an excess of the selfish and calculating principle, the accumulations of the materials of external life exceed the quantity of the power of assimilating them to the internal laws of human nature. The body has become too unwieldy for that which animates it.

Poetry aims at truth as really as science, but it is not only with the object itself, but with its moral and spiritual analogies. It is the object itself, plus the soul of man. The scientific explanation is not the whole, and poetry does its work when it superadds to the mechanism of nature glimpses of beauty and spiritual analogies. The best poetry is distinguished by truthfulness, accuracy and faithfulness to the aspects of nature, as also to human passions and human experience. Fidelity and sincerity are the marked characteristics of the great poets of all time. Homer, Chaucer, Spencer, Milton, Cowper, Burns, Wordsworth and our own Laureate, are examples of this truth.

'The end of the poet is to see and express the loveliness that is in the flower, not only the beauty of colour and of form, but the sentiment which, so to speak, looks out from it, and which is meant to awaken in us an answering emotion. For this end he must observe accurately, since the form and hues of the flower discerned by the eye are a large part of what gives it relation and meaning to the soul. The outward facts of the wild flowers he must not distort, but reverently observe them; but when observed he must not rest in them, but see them as they stand related to the earth out of which they grow, to the wood which surrounds them, to the sky above them, which waits on them with its ministries of dew, rain, and sunshine, indeed to the whole world, of which they are a part, and to the human heart, to which they tenderly appeal.'

How poetical do the common objects of nature appear when described by a great poet. I need only remind you of 'The Mountain Daisy' of Burns

> Wee modest crimson tipped flower,

which he has glorified for all time. One discovers at once by their open-air writings those poets who have looked direct on the face alike of nature and of men. In Milton, especially in the earlier poems, we have the pure outer air of the country, the fragrance of the fields, and aspects of English scenery, which he was one of the first to note, but which he has enshrined in immortal verse, 'L'Allegro', 'Il Penseroso', written in very early life. And again, after so many years given to other pursuits; when to his outward sight appeared:

> Nor sun or moon or stars throughout the year
> Or man or woman

nature still lived in his heart and mind. How vividly he describes the daily ever new aspects of nature.

> Sweet is the breath of morn, her rising sweet,
> With charm of earliest birds; pleasant the sun,
> When first on this delightful land he spreads
> His orient beams, on herb, trees, fruit, and flower,
> Glistering with dew: fragrant the fertile earth
> After soft showers; and sweet the coming on
> Of grateful evening mild; then silent night,
> With this her solemn bird, and this fair moon,
> And these the gems of heaven, her starry train.

Now observe the perfect alliteration, and how, beautiful as is nature, it is human fellowship and love which glorifies all

> But neither breath of morn, when she ascends
> With charm of earliest birds; nor rising sun
> On this delightful land; nor herb, fruit, flower,
> Glistering with dew; nor fragrance after showers;
> Nor grateful evening mild; nor silent night,
> With this her solemn bird; nor walk by moon,
> Or glittering starlight, without thee is sweet.

Who can see a skylark rise from the earth, pouring forth a very rain of melody, without thinking of Shelley's exquisite lyric on the 'Ethereal Minstrel', or as, with added moral and spiritual significance, it is described by Wordsworth as

> Type of the wise, who soar, but never roam;
> True to the kindred points of Heaven and home!

making earth more joyous and Heaven more sublime. I cannot but think in this age of high pressure and of examination, when knowledge is so often mistaken for wisdom, and when all that belongs to material comfort is so sedulously sought for; when the wisdom of the heart and what concerns our higher and purer nature is too often neglected; we need more than ever to refresh and invigorate our imagination with the well springs of poetry in which our English literature is so rich.

Such studies will teach us to form truer ideals of life, and open out to us sources of the highest and purest pleasures. None of us can afford to neglect the poetic element in life. Happy are those 'whose hearts the holy forms of young Imagination have kept pure', and who life long have kept freshness of vision for the seen, and have glimpses of the unseen amidst the absorbing cares of modern life. To those who have a round of daily toil and of absorbing and responsible duties, I know no such freshening, healing, ennobling influence as that to be derived from converse with our great poets.

To take down from our library shelves, 'Where the lords of thought await our call', one's Spencer, or Milton, or Shakespeare, or Shelley, or Wordsworth, in those leisure minutes which come to all, is to forget for the time all mundane cares, and to be lifted above the mists of this lower life.

> Olympian bards who sing
> Divine ideas below
> Which always find us young
> And always keep us so.

Poetry may be to us an angel ladder by which we may attain

> An ampler ether, a diviner air.

Great poets stand on the steps to show us the way upward, and though we must descend again to common earth, we shall bring with us some illumination from above which will brighten our countenances, and cheer us on the way.

It is the poet's vocation to open our eyes to the beautiful.

> He from thick films shall purge the visual ray,
> And on the sightless eyeballs pour the day.

It is, says Ruskin, the 'great imaginative faculty which gives us inheritance of the past, grasp of the present, and authority over the future'. Its practical advantages too are not to be slighted. In daily life we want the imaginative faculty to see for others as well as for ourselves; to enable us to look beyond our immediate circle of minute interests and selfish pleasures.

Most of the friction of life, its misunderstandings and antagonisms, arise from our not having imagination enough to conceive the view taken from a standpoint different to that we occupy, or to conceive of the thoughts quite natural to another mind. Imagination is the air of the mind—the freshening vitalising power; and to be possessed of it is to have the best form of health. The imagination is not—as even a Bishop Butler described it—'a restless and mischievous faculty'. It is essentially a healthy one. One of the most distinguished physicians of the day, and perhaps the highest English authority on subjects connected with the brain as the organ of the mind, Sir James Crichton Browne, gave an address at the Medical Congress in 1889, on 'The Hygienic Uses of the Imagination'. He said its exercise and development was essential to a healthy nature, and he gives this beautiful illustration, 'Imagination might be spoken of as a pioneer opening up new pathways in the brain, or as mode of transit between its territories. The man that is without imagination is like a country without road or railways, in which locomotion is laborious and slow. And the brain richly gifted with it like one in which steam and electricity have established easy and rapid communication.' The notion that the cultivation of the imagination is incompatible with practical sagacity in the affairs of life will not bear examination.

In conclusion may I say that in poetry as in all art we should cultivate catholicity. In poetry there are many mansions, and although we shall naturally have our favourites, let us exercise some imagination in entering into the thoughts and tastes of others. Though Pope had, I think, a false idea of poetry (he certainly was not one of nature's open-air poets), yet we may still admire his sparkling epigrams and couplets, as well as the organ notes of Milton, the wild ethereal music of Shelley, the homely pathos of Cowper, and the profound philosophy, yet exquisite simplicity of Wordsworth.

The appreciation of the higher poetry, however, will grow with the years, with experience and cultivation. We take some poets as we do infantile ailments, but no man I venture to say ever survived his admiration of Shakespeare, Milton, or Wordsworth. While there should be no sectarianism in art or poetry, one thing only would I urge, especially on my young hearers; guard your hearts against the influence of those writers who would sap your moral vigour and taint your purity.

There is a department of imaginative literature, if it is not desecrating the word to use it in this connection, I mean prose fiction, which is not always pure and healthy. And cosmopolitan and catholic as we should be, I sometimes think that a nation which has such masters of pure, delightful and instructive fiction as Goldsmith, Scott, Thackeray, Dickens, and George Eliot (to say nothing of living writers) have a healthy stream of pure imaginative literature, compared with which much Parisian, Russian, and even some Norwegian fiction is turbid and unclean. The great instrument of moral good is the imagination and poetry administers to the effect by acting on the cause. While I think it is one of the best features of our age that closer study and minuter investigation is daily bringing us to recognise that all knowledge tends to harmony; yet I would respectfully submit to this Society, and especially to its younger members, that our pressing need now is the culture of the imagination, and to this end I counsel a wider study of our imaginative poets, tending as it would to lift us out of the mechanical routine of our daily lives, and to enlarge and strengthen our higher and more spiritual powers.

The debt of gratitude we owe to our great poets in the enrichment of literature and life cannot be over estimated. Let us then show our gratitude by a closer study of their works.

> Blessings be with them and eternal praise
> Who gave us nobler loves and nobler cares,
> The poets, who on earth have made us heirs
> Of truth and pure delight by heavenly lays.

Extracts from other lectures and addresses by Sir Henry Doulton

Pottery, Art and Design

The central principle animating all our efforts [in the Doulton Wares] is the cultivation of what I may term the individuality of the individual. The tendency of the present age is to deal with people in masses, to make them all go in one direction.

The potter of today must cultivate both science and art. It is important for potters to acquire a knowledge of the scientific principles underlying their trade—mineralogy, chemistry, the laws of heat and mechanics. It is to excellence and certainty of results and economy, due to intelligent control of the circumstances of its production, as well as to artistic treatment, that we must look for the chief triumph in pottery.

The scientific range is large, yet after all more is left to the eye and hand, to individual taste and skill, than in most industries, and so an artistic training is also all important to the potter.

The potter is fortunate in his work; his art is undoubtedly one of the most attractive and seductive. I will not say it is one of the most profitable —certainly not in its highest developments—but it is and always has been one of the most interesting. It is, through the long ages, the best evidence of the artistic skill of man.

Manufacturers may do much to lead public taste in the appreciation of good art but they must to some extent be guided by the diversity of tastes that prevails and ever will prevail. . . . There is a great deal of dogmatism on what is and what is not fine art. In art there are many mansions and we should cultivate catholicity of taste. There are no abstract canons of

P

taste, no ideal standards of beauty, the unchangeable reflex of eternal and divine prototypes, on which are modelled all outward realities.

The personal is the true vivifying element in art, for the determining and essential constituent of art is the personality of the artist. However clear the limitations of any special department of art may seem to be, there are few boundaries over which the imagination of the original artist may not overleap. Any theory that does not leave the opportunity for the development of character must be faulty.

To distinguish between eccentricity and genius may be difficult but it is surely better to bear with singularity than to crush originality.

Judging from my own experience and observation, the one test of a true artist is that he is rarely satisfied with his own work. There is always an ideal in his mind which he never attains.

Art for art's sake, which has nowadays its teachers and its votaries, is a pernicious principle. As artists you can no more dispense with the moral element than we can in life or literature. The good alone is the real, the permanent. The vicious is the false, the decaying. In a nation, or a poem, or a work of art, it may be temporarily attractive but it is the measure of weakness, the element of decay.

The progress of the art of pottery affords many striking instances of the laws of growth, perfection and decay. As schools of philosophy, poetry and painting are subject to rise, culmination, decay and fall, so is the potter's art. Except in the East, where tradition operates so powerfully, and where tribes, castes and families carry on their trade for ages, these industries rarely maintain their highest development through more than two or three generations.

In our own country we have several examples of schools of pottery which have existed but are now extinct. Chelsea, Bow, Lowestoft, Liverpool, Bristol and Swansea have all become names of the past, notwithstanding their high excellence and the extensive patronage which they once received. Most of these have succumbed before the introduction of cheaper methods of decoration and more economical modes of manu-facture. Indeed, it is a striking fact that, with scarcely an exception, only those potteries have been able to maintain a long-lived career which have relied for their staple manufacture on utilitarian rather than decorative wares. This principle is true even of artistic pottery. A proportion of the useful seems to be an essential condition of any degree of permanence. A school of decorative pottery only is short-lived—firstly, because it is dependent on individual taste and culture and, secondly, because it is not by itself remunerative.

Wedgwood, Worcester and Minton have, undoubtedly, maintained their continuous production through so long a period by careful attention to domestic requirements as well as original art wares.

There is with the public of the present time a morbid craving after novelties, irrespective of their intrinsic excellence, which leaves neither designer nor manufacturer time to develop full capabilities of his productions before the passing day of their public appreciation has gone by.

Of course, public taste cannot altogether be disregarded; and if a master is to provide for the dependent army of workers the demand must to some extent regulate the supply—although the intelligent and enterprising manufacturer will always endeavour to lead the public taste; certainly, if he leaves it at too great a distance it is at a great cost.

It is needful that beauty of design should go hand in hand with economy of technique; it is still more necessary that those who have this matter in hand should realise that their true mission is not accomplished until they have rendered art 'a language understanded of the people'.

Then, and then only, will designers find ready outlet for their conceptions; then, and then only, will manufacturers realise that their interest is to produce good art rather than bad, and strive after excellence rather than novelty, after grace rather than cheapness.

The artists of England cannot all be Royal Academicians of the great luminary in Piccadilly! Some may even be altogether outside the planetary system which it can weigh or measure. Yet it is possible that these neglected lights may be radiances of another and even larger system only discoverable by powers more catholic, comprehensive and accurate than Burlington House commands.

Industry and industrial relations

The stratification, as I may call it, of our modern life, inevitable as it may be, is none the less regrettable. Time was when the manufacturer lived with his workmen, the banker with his clerks. It is isolation that leads to misunderstanding, and misrepresentation to antagonism.

In the industrial struggle which lies before us—I was going to say the industrial warfare—when nations, backed by the whole force of their governments, are competing for that industrial supremacy in the world which has so long been held by England, we must brace every nerve for the contest.

This is no time for standing still. Stagnation follows apathy, and stagnation is the precursor of decay and dissolution. It is useless to moan over the irrecoverable past, as some do, and ask for conditions of production impossible in our present social state.

The world will not stand still for us to gather the scanty harvest of an exhausted soil. The soil is ours and in England, though it needs constant cultivation, it is rich in the stored-up wealth of our mines; in the capabilities of our much-abused climate; in accumulated capital, the fruit of the enterprise and energy of those who have gone before us; but beyond all in the faculty of progress which has hitherto distinguished Englishmen, in their quickness of perception; in their capacity for work; in their real delight in active labours of body and mind. The pre-eminence in applied Art and Science may yet be ours. It is worth struggling for. It would be the culminating glory of a race whose language, laws and literature are spread over the globe.

As Lord Bacon puts it: 'Time is a great innovator, and if as times alter for the worse, wisdom and counsel do not change for the better, what will be the end?'

Had *we* not changed for the better, it is more than probable that our business would have come to grief. The starch works which once stood on the site of our present Albert Embankment buildings were probably the largest of the kind in England, but the proprietors did not keep pace with the times, and allowed more energetic rivals to attract the business elsewhere.

When shoe-laces took the place of buckles, the makers of the latter foolishly petitioned Parliament to protect their interests, instead of at once recognising that other times have other manners.

There are three steps in the law of Nature which it is well to remember. If there is stagnation, decay soon follows, and finally dissolution. Such a calamity can only be avoided by introducing new methods and manufactures as the old become obsolete. In our own early days, our chief business was in blacking and oil bottles. Although we still [1896] make the former, the latter have been entirely superseded by metal drums. New lines had, therefore, to be introduced to keep our wheels going. There is still the same urgent call for new departures and adjustments . . . and unless we are ever on the alert to keep pace with public requirements, stagnation and decay must inevitably overtake us.

Education

No great teacher can submit to be gagged and trammelled. To fetter him is to denude him of half his power.

I feel that there is a danger nowadays of the suppression of individuality—a kind of modern invalidism which threatens the manlier elements of life. . . . Speaking for myself I feel there is a dangerous tendency on the part of the Government to annex education. While Government may aid education, we should be jealous of its attempt to control.

[Our public schools] cultivate courage, discipline and obedience; they have strengthened our colonising aptitude and have done much to foster and encourage our imperial qualities. I have mentioned obedience, for those rule best who have first learned to obey.

I have great faith in the wider diffusion of education so long as it is not emasculated in accordance with the views of some of our modern sages who would have religion, philosophy and even modern history excluded from its curriculum. If it is an education cultivating *the whole nature of man* it will vindicate the wisdom of our ancestors as well as proclaim the march of intellect, and will recognise reverence as the herald of all true progress.

If man were a mere thinking machine such a system of education as John Stuart Mill was subjected to and approves would be perfect. But there is a wisdom of the heart as well as of the head. The school or college training which takes no account of the affections is miserably deficient but what of the *home* training from which it is absent? . . . No greater blessing can be given to a man than to have a wise and devoted mother. He learns lessons at her knee that no time or sorrow can efface.

Religion

It is possible, even I think very probable, that the forms of religious belief may be so altered that in some years hence we should hardly know them. But the sense of dependence on Divine influence and the need of communion with the unseen and external will be then just what they are now. Neither is the spirit of enquiry to be deprecated. Doubt is not sin. One qualification one does make, namely that enquiring scepticism should be reverential.

The Irish question

The failure of England to conciliate Ireland would seem to be the opprobrium of English statesmanship as it is an undoubted element of national weakness. . . . We have failed to unite in bonds of amity, as an integral part of a great Empire, a race with many virtues and endowments admirably adapted to supplement English deficiencies. A brave, imaginative, religious and sensitive people, quick to resent slight and injustice, but affectionate and enthusiastically loyal when they repose confidence— a people, too, occupying an advanced post towards the continent of America whom, looking to the future, it daily becomes more and more important to conciliate and attach to the Empire.

The estrangement of Ireland is due in large measure to the persecution to which she has been subjected by the dominant country, mainly on account of her tenacious Catholicism. A wise and statesmanlike recognition of the claims of the Catholic Church in Ireland, and some assured and moderate aid towards the education and sustenance of her clergy, would have mitigated, and probably removed, the deplorable alienation from which both countries suffer. . . . In connection with Protestant ascendancy in Ireland there have been deeds of intolerance and inhumanity the remembrance or recital of which should make Englishmen blush for very shame.

Women's rights

I am not one of those who are disposed to join in the agitation for what are called 'women's rights', but I have a strong love and admiration for women, and I believe that their power and influence are far above those of our own sex. It is a trite observation that most good and great men

have had remarkable mothers; and although we are not great, yet doubtless we can all say of a mother, a wife, or a sister:

> If aught of goodness or of grace be
> mine, hers be the glory,
> She led me on in Wisdom's path,
> and set the light before me.

The true sphere of woman is the family and household, and I believe
that the contact of women with the strifes and rivalries in which public
men are involved would weaken that beneficent influence which they
exert over our sex.

The great problem as to female employment presents many difficulties,
but I am exceedingly happy in the knowledge that the faltering steps I
took some ten years ago have led to so complete and satisfactory a solution of this question.

Probably I had some prejudices in regard to women's work. My first
visit to the Continent many years ago gave me unfavourable impressions
as to women's employment. I found that women not only made, but
sold the goods, and kept the books, while their husbands were to be
found lounging in the neighbouring cafés; and in my experience I have
often observed that when women did men's work, the men were inclined
to be indolent.

In Staffordshire I have seen women and young girls employed in the
most coarse and degrading labour, such as turning the wheels, wedging
the clay, etc. I always declined to employ female labour in the ordinary
work of the factory, and it was not until Mr. Rix had placed before me a
well-organised scheme that I agreed to employ girls and women in our
art department.

I still feel that women's work should be as far as possible restricted to
occupations not involving severe labour, and as much as practicable to
the Arts that beautify and adorn life.

The effort, like most good ones, had a small beginning. It was tentative.
But the admirable organisation triumphed, and it has given me from that
time to this, the most absolute and perfect satisfaction.

Politics

Each party [Liberal and Conservative, 1885] claims for itself exclusive
wisdom and to have conferred the greatest benefits on the community.
Neither party can justly make such claims. In England some of our best
legislation has been a matter of compromise, and this is one of the reasons

we have not had so many revolutions as France, where the struggles of parties are carried to the bitter end.

Excess of Party Spirit I deprecate as being dangerous to the community. It engenders envy, hatred, malice and all uncharitableness. It warps the judgment, inflames the passions, and is fatal to fairness and candour.

A nation is never so really noble as when under the pressure of some great calamity or when, after some national deliverance, party feeling is forgotten and the nation's heart beats as the heart of one man. I do not deprecate a *reasonable* attachment to party. We are governed by party and this form of Government is, at present, the only form that is practicable. Attachment to one freely leads to criticism of the other—and wholesome criticism is better than cynicism or apathy.

In walking through the London streets, or travelling through any part of England, I often feel a justifiable pride in being an Englishman. Our Constitution is the growth of centuries, the treasured wisdom and experience of generations. Those who do not realise this are not true guides. It is the opinion of unprejudiced foreigners that there is more individual freedom in England than in any other country in the world.

No doubt the House of Lords wants reforming, as does everything else that has lasted so long a time. I may remind you that we have many eloquent and wise statesmen in the House of Lords, whose speeches compare most favourably with any in the House of Commons for eloquence and statesmanlike grasp.

Destruction is always easier than construction. Every potter knows how easy it is to impair a beautiful vase, and he also knows the knowledge, experience and care that are necessary to produce one.

What is this immutable principle of *Free Trade* that its working is never to be enquired into? Who are these popes of a day whose dogmas are to be considered infallible? We are told we have no more right to question the doctrine of *Free Trade* than we have to question the law of gravitation or the Ten Commandments. This new gospel has been set aside by its advocates when it suited their purpose to do so, and the principles of political economy have been relegated to Jupiter or Saturn when they have stood in the way of party interests. When *Free Trade* was proposed it was contended that every nation would follow our example, but not a single nation has done so. All have protected themselves by high tariffs.

What were the prognostications, or rather promises, of Messrs. Cobden and Bright when we adopted the principles of *Free Trade*? First, we were to have universal peace. Commerce was to raise her wand and strike a universal peace through sea and land. You will remember the Exhibition of 1851, where not a single war-like instrument was allowed to be shown. *Free Trade* was to bring the millennium. 'No war or battle sound the world around.' It was thought the dream of the poet was realised, 'The idle spear and shield were high uphung.'

This time was followed by some of the most bloody and costly wars which have ever devastated the world, and the lamentable outcome may be remarked in the Inventions Exhibition of 1885, where the most perfect machine exhibited is the Maxim gun, guaranteed to fire 500 shots a minute. If we survey our position in the world, we are the sole Free Traders in a world of Protectionists. The whole world has armed itself with hostile tariffs.

The proposal that the State should make purchase of land would give rise to jobbery. . . . What we want now [1885] is *to restore confidence, not to frighten capital away*. If one class of property is to be appropriated compulsorily why not another? Why not factories, shops, ships? Individual freedom and the rights of property, believe me, lie at the basis of modern society, and are the true foundation of laws and morals. And, I might add, of the family too, with all its hallowing associations and benign influences.

The welfare of the nation is best served by individual enterprise. State Socialism has been tried and has failed, and will ever fail. It would be the industrious providing for the thriftless, the idle, and the debased.

Let us be a united people—patriots rather than partisans—Englishmen first, then Conservatives or Radicals. Let us hope that the present depression [1885] may be removed and the prosperity and welfare of all classes promoted, as far as may be, by wise and just legislation, and secured by our energy and enterprise, and by the exercise of national virtue.

Index